INDIGENOUS DIALECTICS

A volume in the series

Cornell Modern Indonesia Project

Edited by Eric Tagliacozzo and Thomas B. Pepinsky

A list of titles in this series is available at cornellpress.cornell.edu.

INDIGENOUS DIALECTICS

The Relationship Between the State and
Indigeneity in Indonesia

Timo Duile

SOUTHEAST ASIA PROGRAM PUBLICATIONS
AN IMPRINT OF CORNELL UNIVERSITY PRESS   ITHACA AND LONDON

The research for this book was funded by the German Research Foundation
(DFG, Deutsche Forschungsgemeinschaft, Project No. 400134948).

First published 2025 by Cornell University Press

Librarians: A CIP catalog record for this book is available from the Library
of Congress.

ISBN 9781501784897 (hardcover)
ISBN 9781501784903 (paperback)
ISBN 9781501784927 (pdf)
ISBN 9781501784910 (epub)

GPSR EU contact: Sam Thornton, Mare Nostrum Group B.V., Mauritskade 21D,
1091 GC, Amsterdam, NL, gpsr@mare-nostrum.co.uk.

I dedicate this book to my wife, Nadya Karima Melati, and
to my friends in South Sulawesi who helped me during my research.
Without their help and hospitality, this book would not have been possible.

Contents

Abbreviations and Non-English Terms

All non-English terms are italicized and are Indonesian, unless otherwise indicated in the text or in the translations provided in parentheses.

adat: custom, customary

akidah (**Arabic**): realm of belief

aluk tojolo (**Duri**): traditional religion

AMAN: *Aliansi Masyarakat Adat Nusantara*, Indigenous Alliance of the Archipelago

Berdaulat Secara Politik, Mandiri Secara Ekonomi, Bermartabat Secara Budaya: economically independent, sovereign in political matters, culturally dignified (AMAN's motto)

beschikkingsrecht (**Dutch**): right of allocation

BUMMA: *Badan Usaha Milik Masyarakat Adat*, enterprise owned by indigenous community

bupati: regent

bumiputera: sons of the soil

BTI: *Barisan Tani Indonesia*, Indonesian Peasant Front

Darul Islam: House of Islam (armed Islamist group in the 1950s and 1960s)

desa: village

dusun: hamlet

fiqh (**Arabic**): realm of Islamic jurisprudence

Golkar: *Golongan Karya*, Party of the Functional Groups

gotong royong: mutual help/assistance

hak ulayat: right of avail

Islam Nusantara: Islam of the archipelago (concept of an Indonesianized Islam)

kedaulatan: sovereignty

kekeluargaan: family principle

kelompok ekonomi: economic or business group

kelompok ekonomi perempuan adat: business groups of indigenous women

kepala desa: village head

kepercayaan: traditional believes/religions

keswadaan kedayaan: self-sufficiency/self-reliance

Ketuhanan yang Maha Esa: principle of an almighty divine entity (first pillar of the *Pancasila*) *lembaga adat*: customary body/institution

lembang (**Toraja**): traditional political unit in Toraja

masyarakat hukum adat: customary law society

masyarakat adat: customary society

Muhammadiyah: followers of Muhammed (modernist Islamic mass organization)

MUI: *Majelis Ulama Indonesia*, Indonesian Ulama Council

mufakat: unanimous agreement

musholla: Islamic prayer's room

muswil: *musyawarah wilayah*, regional council

musyawarah: deliberation

MPR: *Majelis Permusyawaratan Rakyat*, People's Consultative Assembly

Nawacita: program of Nine National Priorities during the presidency of Joko Widodo

NU: *Nahdlatul Ulama*, Revival of the Ulama (traditionalist Islamic mass organization)

PAN: *Partai Amanat Nasional*, National Mandate Party

Pancasila: five pillars (Indonesia's national ideology)

panguntura (**Duri**): supernatural being in Duri mythology

pantangan (**Duri**): taboo

PDI-P: *Partai Demokrasi Indonesia–Perjuangan*, Indonesian Democratic Party of Struggle

pemali (**Duri**): prohibition

pemangku adat: indigenous leader

pembangunan: development

pendalaman: interior

perda: *peraturan daerah*, local regulation

pesisir: coastal realm

PKI: *Partai Komunis Indonesia*, the Communist Party of Indonesia

PKS: *Partai Keadilan Sejahtera*, Justice and Prosperity Party

PNI: *Partai Nasional Indonesia*, Indonesian National Party

pribumi: sons of the soil

puang (**Duri, Toraja**): nobility, traditional leader

reformasi: reform era

RUU: *Rencana Undang-Undang*, proposed law

shirik: idolatry, superstition, polytheism

SK: *Surat Keputusa* (Decision Letter)

somboyya (**Makassar**): king

Taman Siswa: Garden of Pupils (educational movement)

tongkonan (**Toraja**): ancestor houses of noble families, also a term for larger social units in Toraja society

UU: *Undang-Undang*, law

UU Cipta Kerja: Job Creation Law

WALHI: *Wahana Lingkungan Hidup Indonesia*, Indonesian Forum of the Environment

YLBHI: *Yayasan Lembarga Bantuan Hukum Indonesia*, Indonesian Legal Aid Help Foundation

INDIGENOUS
DIALECTICS

INTRODUCTION
The Ideology of Being Indigenous and Its Critique

At the dawn of the authoritarian Suharto regime, indigeneity as a new political force emerged in Indonesia. In 1993, human rights and environmental activists gathered for an informal meeting in Tanah Toraja, South Sulawesi, and formed the Indigenous Peoples' Rights Advocacy Network (*Jaringan Pembelaan Hak-Hak Masyarakat Adat*, JAPHAMA) which later, in 1999, helped to establish the Indigenous Alliance of the Archipelago (*Aliansi Masyarakat Adat Nusantara*, AMAN). AMAN not only calls for recognition of Indigenous culture, but also demands sovereignty and, especially, the acknowledgment of Indigenous land rights, which has often caused conflicts with state authorities and agricultural corporations. The initial meeting in 1993 was originally to be held in the city of Makassar but had to be relocated to Toraja as the activists were subject to intimidation from the local state apparatus in Makassar. On that day, the acknowledged authority of a progressive Torajan village chief, Sombolinggi, kept the local police and military at bay. Twenty-four years after the initial meeting in Toraja, Sombolinggi's daughter, Rukka Sombolinggi, had become the general secretary of AMAN, and she came back to South Sulawesi to join the South Sulawesi AMAN congress held in Sinjai. Twenty years after AMAN had announced that it would not recognize the state if the state did not recognize Indigenous peoples, the police were omnipresent at the Sinjai meeting. This time, however, the police were not a threat. Rukka even thanked them for coming, and Indonesian red-and-white flags hung together with AMAN flags from bamboo poles. Representatives from local governments in South Sulawesi were present and talked to the audience while other politicians greeted them on banners, wishing ANAN a successful congress. Indeed, some Indigenous communities had been acknowledged by local governments and had successfully applied for land titles.

It appeared that a significant shift had occurred in state–Indigenous relations in Indonesia from confrontation to cooperation; Indigenous activists even conducted their struggles from within the state apparatus. What does this tell us about the relation between indigeneity and the state? Are Indigenous communities entities of their own, distinct from the Indonesian state, which have to establish ties to gain autonomy? Or is the relation between Indigenous peoples and the nation-state better grasped in other terms?

Cooperation and a notion of compliance with the Indonesian nation and the state have always been part of the Indigenous struggle, just as confrontation remains present in recent Indigenous peoples–state relations. To understand these relations, one must take into account that Indigenous peoples and the Indonesian nation-state are not simply two distinct entities. Instead, I argue that the notion of indigeneity has always been an integral part of what it means to be Indonesian: On the one hand, indigeneity, in various forms, has emerged as an internal contradiction and a constituent part of Indonesian identity and the state; on the other hand, indigeneity came into existence through and in the state and the nation. This is true not for recognition by postauthoritarian state institutions alone. Rather, throughout the history of Indonesia, the notion of *adat* (custom, or customary law), which now serves as the Indonesian concept of indigeneity, has been conceptualized by the state and its ideological apparatuses: first, by the colonial state as an abstract umbrella term for local customs and especially customary laws; and, second, as both a foundation of Indonesianness and as ancient traditions that had to be overcome. *Adat*, as the internal contradictions of Indonesian identity and the political economies in various periods in Indonesian history, has proven to be persistent and now serves as an ideological base for a rural movement. Indigeneity is always a flawed identity in the sense that it relies on the state. It comes into existence when it passes into and through its other, namely the state and the nation—a process I call *Indigenous dialectics*. In this book, I demonstrate that it is precisely these seemingly impure or flawed characteristics of indigeneity as an ideology—which always have to claim to be original and actual in the first place—that enable political agency and provide the potential for rural change.

Since 2012, I have met Indigenous activists on countless occasions. I have long discussed Indigenous notions of nature with Indigenous activists in Kalimantan in their air-conditioned offices and have been on fieldtrips with grassroots activists to Indigenous communities surrounded and threatened by palm oil plantations. I have been the guest of Indigenous communities in the jungle discussing strategies for political struggles. At international conferences, I have met AMAN activists, have listened to their talks, and have discussed issues with them afterward in cafés. Some I have met in their offices in Jakarta not only to talk about political theory and the research published about them by scholars but also to listen to their stories about how they experience indigeneity. The approaches in this book are developed from my interactions with Indigenous activists over the years. I attempt to analyze their struggle, aspirations, and contradictions. For the main part of this book, I conducted fieldwork in Enrekang, South Sulawesi, which I visited for the first time in 2015 when a local regulation (*peraturan daerah*) for the acknowledgment of Indigenous communities was under debate in the Enrekang parliament. Most of the fieldwork was carried out between January and December 2019. I also interviewed and engaged with AMAN activists at other levels, namely in Makassar (i.e., on the provincial level) and in their offices in Jakarta and Bogor (representing the national level) and joined Indigenous activists on their fieldtrips. In addition to ethnographic notes and interviews, legal documents as well as documents from the legislative process of Indigenous recognition provide the main data source for my analysis. The historical part analyzes laws and discourses to outline the dialectical relation between the state and indigeneity/indigenism on a national level. Thus, in this book, I focus on South Sulawesi and shed light, in particular, on the case study of Indigenous recognition of Duri communities in the regency of Enrekang. The case study represents an ethnography of a legal text as I not only analyze the document but also trace the political processes and social consequences, relying on participant observation and interviews.

Indigeneity: Its Critique and Dialectics

By shedding light on indigeneity in Indonesia and especially in South Sulawesi, I also contribute to general debates on what indigeneity is, how it relates to the state, and whether it is a reactionary or progressive political force. I briefly outline some crucial features of indigeneity and the scholarly debates on it and explain how I approach the questions of indigeneity theoretically. The theoretical approach offers a new form of critique that differs from the form of critique provided in the field of critical Indigenous studies. Critical Indigenous studies, as a field of Indigenous studies that was established in the last decade by Indigenous scholars, mostly concerns Indigenous issues in first-world locations. Critical Indigenous studies can be defined as a domain of power and knowledge wherein scholars rely on, use, and operationalize Indigenous knowledge. It aims to develop theories as well as to build academic infrastructure for Indigenous scholars. Often, its critique is concerned with Western taxonomy that is criticized to achieve Indigenous academic and, in a wider sense, epistemic autonomy (e.g., see Moreton-Robinson 2013; Hokowhitu 2021). Inspired by standpoint theory, critical Indigenous studies often conceptualizes indigeneity and Indigenous knowledge as radically different from Western knowledge. In contrast, the critique that the dialectical approach followed in this book can offer conceptualizes indigeneity as relative difference, that is, as always already embedded into the opposite that it criticizes. It is based on the assumption that indigeneity has no absolute autonomy from what is conceptualized as its other (e.g., the state, capitalist economies, or modernity). Thus, the aim of a dialectical critique of indigeneity is not to provide a space in which indigeneity can assert itself (in society, academia, or in academic theories) but rather to understand and criticize the mechanisms and processes from which indigeneity can emerge as the other.

What, in that case, is indigeneity? Originally a term used in biology to denote plants and animals native to a particular environment or region, the term has been adopted by human rights movements and introduced into various international legal regimes, most prominently by the International Labor Organization (ILO) and the United Nations (UN). Indigeneity is commonly used as an umbrella term for categories such as *native* and *aboriginal* and was originally applied in the context of settler colonies and the postcolonial states originating from them (Bens 2020, 3). A general discussion of the various definitions of indigeneity would certainly be beyond the scope of this book. I do outline, however, the most influential definition in the international context: the ILO Convention 169, which has been a major instrument for Indigenous activists all over the world. Even though many countries have not signed the convention, it sets a default stance for the definition of indigeneity as a political identity maneuvering in national and international law regimes. In the ILO handbook *Understanding the Indigenous and Tribal Peoples Convention, 1989 (No. 169)* (ILO 2013), Indigenous peoples are defined as "[descended] from populations, who inhabited the country or geographical region at the time of conquest, colonization, or establishment of present state boundaries. They retain some or all of their own social, economic, cultural and political institutions, irrespective of their legal status" (ILO 2013, 2).

Crucial in this definition are the criteria of place (a place of inhabitance in a country or geographic region) and time (populations who inhabited those places first and are therefore the original inhabitants). Moreover, a distinction from other parts of society in the respective states is crucial when stressing the identity of the original through the social, economic, cultural, and political institutions they have, as the ILO definition puts it, retained (this might invoke the somewhat-problematic idea that Indigenous people as a solid group stand outside history). Although the ILO Convention has been criticized for incorporating Indigenous peoples into capitalist state machineries (Goodale 2016, 443–444), it without doubt opens a discursive space for a new, emerging political subjectivity. Place and time serve as markers of difference, just as culture does. To emerge as a formation of political subjectivity, however, another aspect is important, namely power or power relations. This aspect is stressed in the definition by Jose Martìnez Cobo, then UN special rapporteur of the Sub-Commission on Prevention of Discrimination and Protection of Minorities. According to this definition, Indigenous peoples form nondominant sectors of the societies in their respective countries (Martìnez Cobo 1986, § 379).

Jonas Bens (2020, 4–5) suggests that three established ways to approach indigeneity in academia all refer to these definitions. The first approach, the "straightforward theory" (Bens 2020, 4), simply outlines that indigeneity is an identity of descendants of communities that inhabited territories in colonial and postcolonial states in times before these territories were occupied by either a foreign force or the dominant modern state. Indigeneity is then only a matter of kinship. In a second approach, indigeneity is discussed as a phenomenon unfolding within colonial and postcolonial power relations. Indigeneity is, in this view, not something that exists from the very beginning but something that emerges within the structure of colonialism and indigeneity is thus a structural position within power relations. This approach has mostly been stressed in research in settler colonies by both academic researchers (e.g., Veracini 2010; Bateman and Pilkington 2011; Mikdashi 2013) and by Indigenous scholar-activists (Alfred 1999; Simpson 2017; Corntassel 2018). It can also be applied, however, in postcolonial states in Africa and Asia that have no history as settler colonies. Applied to that context, indigeneity is an identity formation that has developed in relation to the postcolonial state and its hegemonic society as well as the state's dominant ideology and economic regimes. With regard to Indonesia, indigeneity as *adat* has also been analyzed within its relation to colonialism and as a political identity emerging within a relation to the postcolonial state (e.g., Moniaga 2007; Acciaioli 2007; Benda-Beckmann 2019). These analyses are often supportive of the idea of Indigenous movements and suggest that they have some progressive potential. The third approach also suggests that indigeneity can emerge only within (post-)colonial or state-power relations but is in general more critical of indigeneity as a political force. Indigeneity in this case is analyzed as a variant of collective identity formations based on reactionary Western concepts of ethnic communities. Indigeneity, according to this approach, is by no means something original but is imported along with colonialism and holds the dangerous potential of categorizing people by ethnic identity (e.g., Eriksen 2002; Kuper 2003a, 2003b). The problematic or even reactionary potential of indigenism, indigeneity, and *adat* movements in Indonesia is also discussed by some scholars (e.g., Bourchier 1998; Davidson 2007; van Klinken 2007; Bedner and Arizona 2019).

In other words, indigeneity does not serve only as a form of critique against dispossession and cultural marginalization, but is itself often an object of critique. Is it realistic to assume that Indigenous communities are egalitarian despite the fact that internal power struggles occur in these communities? Can Indigenous communities be independent in economic and political terms, yet be integral and even constitutive parts of the national state, its identity, and its political economy? Is it not naïve of Indigenous activists to engage in neoliberal regimes and to claim to provide alternatives beyond capitalism? Is indigenism, even in its seemingly harmless form, not just a part of dangerous identity politics? In the general critical literature on Indigenous peoples and indigeneity, one can usually find several foci of critique. One concerns reactionary politics coupling indigeneity with special rights for people of certain ancestry (Niezen 2003, 13; most prominently, Kuper 2003a, 2003b). This critique stimulated a large debate among anthropologists in the early and mid-2000s (e.g., see Kenrick and Lewis 2004). Another critique is the image of the "ecologically noble savage," often applied by Indigenous movements to legitimize their land claims. This has also provoked debate in cultural anthropology (Tsing 2007, 55–57; for an overview, see Hames 2007) and until the 2020s the question of whether Indigenous peoples are guardians of nature or potentially dangerous for their natural environments remains a hot topic in the context of climate change, predatory extractivism, and Indigenous land claims. Another focus of critique deals with the question of whether the recognition of Indigenous rights is just another form of neoliberal politics, as Indigenous communities are, precisely through recognition, embedded into the very frames they reject, that is, the capitalist economy and the state (Goodale 2016).

Merlan (2009) has argued that scholarly debates on indigeneity developed around criterial and relational approaches: "By 'criterial,' I mean definitions that propose some set of criteria, or conditions, that enable identification of the 'indigenous' as a global 'kind.' By 'relational,' I mean definitions that emphasize grounding in relations between the 'indigenous' and their 'others' rather than in properties inherent only to those we call 'indigenous' themselves" (Merlan 2009, 305).

One could argue that a criterial definition tends to be essentialist—the criteria always say something about how Indigenous people are Indigenous—whereas relational definitions deconstruct notions of indigeneity by explaining that there is no pregiven definition of indigeneity but that its meaning depends on the actual historic and social relations on the local level. In contrast, the criterial approach aims at the global level, where it is used, for instance, in international legal debates. In regard to the Indonesian context, it has been argued that the application of the notion of indigeneity to describe *adat* and the *adat* movement is problematic, and that the notion of *masyarakat adat* was meant as a "strategic equivalent" (*padanan strategis*) for the notion of indigeneity (Zakaria 2024, 34). As Chua and Idrus (2022, 19) put it, however, "there is no doubt that indigeneity is 'out there' and circulating throughout the region [of Southeast Asia] in various forms and articulations."

How can we make sense of this global concept in the context of Indonesia? Studying the *adat* movement requires studying it as a phenomenon in its own right that developed from different contexts than those of the former settler colonies in the Americas or in Australia, from where the first Indigenous movements derived. In this case as well, we see a distinction between global, grand narratives of what indigeneity is and the local notion of indigeneity as *adat*. In times in which academic debates are heavily influenced by postmodernism, it is not surprising that many scholars argue in favor of local or relational definitions and approaches. This is for good reason, as an application of criteria from other places universalizes definitions that are inherently particular. This has also caused some serious problems in regard to the normative question of whether we need a universal concept of Indigenous peoples and their rights (Bowen 2000). It is also clear, however, that activists and marginalized people around the world have applied the notion of indigeneity, and they seem to share at least some minimal definitions of what it means to be Indigenous—that is, some notion of culture that predates modern or invasive forms of culture and economy and the notion of being marginalized, or at least not dominant, in a wider society or nation-state. When I refer to the *adat* movement as an Indigenous movement and *adat* as indigeneity in this book, I mean indigeneity in a localized form. However, from this localized indigeneity, the very notion of indigeneity in a global or criterial sense is influenced. In fact, no criterial definition of indigeneity is independent from concrete, relational definitions, and no relational or local definition of indigeneity can emerge as indigeneity without a global or criterial definition. Indigenous movements and practices from around the world constantly contribute to and shift our understanding of what indigeneity is—and their struggle is shaped by concepts and criteria that circulate globally and thus make certain forms of marginalization and exploitation comprehensible in a new manner, namely, as a matter of marginalization and exploitation of Indigenous people by their other. In other words, I suggest understanding the criterial (or global) definition and approaches as being in a dialectical relation with relational (or local) approaches.

To exist, indigeneity has to "fall" from a global, criterial definition (i.e., from the realm of the abstract-universal) into concrete, relational practices that then retroactively rely on global or criterial concepts of indigeneity. It does so as a traveling concept: When crossing cultural boundaries, traveling concepts undergo changes. These changes should not be regarded as impediments or as contradictions that make these concepts of no use in different contexts. Rather, the changes are driving factors enabling dialogues that place concepts and cultural formations within new pertinent contexts (Neumann and Nünning 2012, 4). In this sense, indigeneity has traveled from former settler-colonial contexts to Indonesia in the 1990s where it occupied a position within discourses of *adat*. *Adat* was, of course, never conceptualized as indigeneity in the first place. In the particular political and economic context of the late-Suharto era, *adat* as indigeneity became a lens through which people conceptualized their social and political situations. Thus, the *adat* movement is about indigeneity as an transnational phenomenon and its Indonesian interpretation (Merlan 2013, 187–189).

As in other parts of the world, the desire to claim special rights (and sometimes superiority) because of ancestry has serious political implications in Indonesia. In 2016, when hundreds of thousands of Muslims rallied in Jakarta against the governor of the city—a Christian and ethnic Chinese who was accused of blasphemy—anti-Chinese resentments rose again and reminded some of the atmosphere of the violent attacks on Chinese citizens in 1998. The notion of *pribumi* (sons of the soil) once again became an ideology of identification. This concept refers to the native majority, especially in urban contexts and is used in contrast to Indonesian citizens of Chinese descent (Tsing 2007, 54–55). To my knowledge, however, AMAN has never applied this notion. Their concept of *masyarakat adat*, meaning people or societies who live in accordance with custom/customary law, is potentially more inclusive. It can refer to indigeneity as the identity of those who originally occupied a certain territory, but it can also refer to a group of people who live in a certain place and are therefore subject to *adat* law as customary law—regardless of their ethnic background (Bowen 2000, 15; Warren 2007; Erb 2007). I have observed similar processes in Kalimantan and South Sulawesi. In rural communities in these places, ethnic categories are often less important, as long as members of a community know the others in person. Rituals, marriage, or simply residence can make one Indigenous if *adat* rules are obeyed. In this sense, *adat* can be an inclusive identity. Indigeneity as *adat*, however, can also easily become an exclusive category in Indonesia. For instance, in the conflict-laden setting of the Moluccas, ethic identities are the predominant defining factor for indigeneity, which excludes people from other parts of the archipelago, for instance,

Bugis from Sulawesi as well as transmigrants (Palmer 2004; Kadir 2019). Religious difference often plays a crucial role in defining indigeneity (Bräuchler 2010a) and *adat* thus serves as a tool for violent conflict. *Adat*, in these cases, emerges in the form of examples of the collective cultural rights of a group of people, which can also mean a return to feudal hereditary leaders and the non-equal treatment of outsiders. This contradicts individuals' human rights to egalitarianism (Bräuchler 2010b, 3).

Another question is whether *adat* is useful for political processes and whether it can achieve progressive outcomes. Some scholars have stressed that the concept of *adat*, even though it was developed in late colonialism, is still useful as a political category when one is aware of the potential pitfalls and reassesses the changing context in which *adat* is applied (e.g., Moniaga 2007; Acciaioli 2007; Benda-Beckmann 2019). Some research has found that Indigenous movements in Indonesia are potentially dangerous, sometimes because they apply identity politics, or because Indigenous communities at the grassroots level hardly fit into the ideal of egalitarian communities, or because *adat* is a deeply problematic term, namely a colonial invention hardly useful for progressive struggles. These rather skeptical interventions (e.g., Burns 2004; Davidson 2007; Fisher and van der Muur 2019) point out the problems the Indigenous movement has to deal with when it subscribes to progressive ideals. Another crucial critique comes from Tania Li. She has investigated Indigenous communities and movements in Indonesia over the past twenty years, especially in regard to governmentality and assemblages into which they are embedded. Departing from the insight that Indigenous identities are in many cases resource politics applying a tribal slot (Li 2000) she has criticized rural practices associated with Indigenous communities as projects fitting comfortably into the neoliberal governmentality prevalent in rural Indonesia (Li 2005, 2007, 2016). This critique is especially insightful for scholars interested in the political economy of indigeneity politics in Indonesia and beyond. Tania Li wrote in 2001 when the Indigenous movement was about to start its struggle:

> Indonesia has a history of popular struggles that were phrased in the early days of independence under Sukarno, and later under the influence of the Indonesian communist party, not as the claims of distinctive, culture bound communities (*masyarakat adat*), but as struggles of "the people" (*rakyat*). Is the shift of focus from people to culture, which coincides with a shift of the site of struggle from agricultural land to forests and nature, the best approach to justice? (Li 2001, 649)

Many of us would certainly answer "no," me included. But we have to keep in mind that class struggles do not always emerge in the form of a class-conscious subject. In many cases, class struggles are framed through other identities, for instance, in Islamic terms. Most prominently, the Banten rebellion of 1888 and other Islamic movements in colonial Java have shown how the masses, estranged from traditional leaders and exposed to economic contradictions, may articulate their protests in Islamic terms (as explained by Kartodirdjo 1984; see also Ali 1994). But the phenomenon of expressing economic contradictions by means of religious or Indigenous anger prevails throughout Indonesian history. Class struggles and economic contradictions assert themselves through many means and, in some cases, these means have been quite successful in material terms, although they are always in danger of falling into reactionary identity politics. The question remains whether egalitarian concepts of land tenure, cooperative production, and collective ownership of the means of production, (land but also machines for agriculture and added value) can be carried out under the banner of indigeneity without falling into the pitfalls of identity politics.

In this book, I discuss and analyze the relation between these regressive aspects of indigeneity and its progressive potentials. This is already an issue when analyzing the history of indigeneity and *adat* but also in contemporary and local contexts where different notions of *adat* are applied. Although *adat* and indigeneity clearly have the potential to turn into reactionary and regressive political ideologies, they also can serve as tools to express cultural and economic demands from marginalized rural classes. As I will argue, however, the progressive potential of indigeneity usually comes into existence when it emerges as an ideology of radical change against hierarchic traditions. In the case study of the Duri, it is explained how the progressive potential of indigeneity relies on the anti-Indigenous efforts of the Darul-Islam movement.

When talking about indigeneity, noneconomic factors have to be taken into account as well. Although I often draw on political economy and its relations with indigeneity, factors such as Indigenous ways of life or worldviews and traditional religions that are often regarded as backward are important for understanding the notion of indigeneity. To accommodate these dimensions of indigeneity, I address these issues, especially with the issue of religion. Maybe surprisingly, the Indigenous moment in Indonesia does not deploy traditional beliefs and worldviews in its political struggle. The question of noneconomic factors and their relevance is a serious one. On the one hand, a strong focus on political economy tends to neglect other forces and can lead to class reductionism; in such an economic account, indigeneity would simply be dismissed as false consciousness. On the other hand, an analysis that does not consider the economic preconditions in which indigeneity develops tends to culturalize the ideology of indigeneity and neglect the fact that indigeneity serves a crucial function in production and rural class struggles over the means of production and access to resources.

I often mention the political economy and its relevance for the ideology of indigeneity. Therefore, it is important to shortly outline the notions of political economy and the ideology of being Indigenous. In regard to political economy and to avoid a reductionist approach, I draw on dialectical notions between the material and the nonmaterial (a dichotomy that can also take the form of body and language, nature and culture, and so on) as developed by the Ljubljana school (for a general account on this issue, see Dolar 2020). Crucial for this account is that it is not an issue of whether the cultural/discursive or the material dimension (of which political economy is a part) is the true substance that the anthropologist should be concerned with. Rather, political economy can be explained only through the lens of identity and discourses, just as cultural and identity issues can be explained only through the lens of political economy. In terms of theoretical analysis, I treat these dimensions as simultaneously constitutive for each other. They are different dimensions in the sense that they address different realms of social reality, but they are two sides of the same coin.

In the dialectical approach I suggest, the notion of social totality is crucial. By social totality, I do not simply mean the process of production, but social totality's inherent contradiction between materialism and nonmaterial issues, such as identity. Therefore, the notion of totality is neither an argument for materialism nor for idealism; it is rather an argument for overcoming that dualism as well as for taking into account that the totality is necessarily "flawed" in the sense that entities such as political economy (i.e., the material dimension) or identity, religion, and so on (i.e., the discursive dimension) emerge only in a dialectical relation to their respective others. We are able to see both dimensions only from the very field of their tensions and overlaps. This means that this field of tensions and overlaps between the material and discursive dimensions preexists these two dimensions, which retrospectively emerge as seemingly separate categories. This field of tensions and overlaps is what I call the *social totality* as, from there, all categories for social analysis, be they material or discursive, emerge.

This has concrete consequences for the way I approach the notion of indigeneity as an ideology. Neither discourse nor political economy are the true substantiality of indigeneity, but indigeneity is the political subjectivity that comes into existence through the material dimension of discourses as well as the discursive framing of struggles over resources. This is how I approach the notion of political economy in this book: The political economy of Indigenous peoples is what comes into existence when it interferes with the discursive dimension.

The term *ideology* evokes notions of discourse and representation. When addressing indigeneity as an ideology, however, this book uses the notion of ideology as a representation of people's relations to their material conditions (Althusser 2014, 183; for a more detailed theoretical account in ideology and indigeneity in Indonesia, see Duile 2021). As an ideological concept, the notions of *adat*, tradition, or indigeneity serve a crucial function within different political economies because these concepts represent how different actors such as, for instance, anthropologists of the colonial era, Indonesian independence fighters, representatives of the Suharto regime, or Indigenous activists make sense of social-economic conditions. Again, however, this is no simple economic reductionism: Indigeneity is no simple effect of the relations of production. Rather, what appears to be ideology has a relative autonomy from the material base. The economic conditions may be determined in the last instance, but, as Althusser argues "from the first moment to the last, the lonely hour of the 'last instance' never comes" (2005, 113). With such an approach, I contribute to the scholarship of political economy of indigeneity without falling into economic reductionism.

The main theoretical contribution of this book is the development and analysis of what I call Indigenous dialectics. A starting point in theoretical terms is what Jonas Bens (2020) has called the Indigenous paradox, namely the idea that indigeneity comes into being only through its paradoxical relation with the state. Indigenous peoples, Bens argues in his account on court cases in the Americas, must claim sovereignty and, in their most extreme form, a position outside the very state that they want to acknowledge their rights. In other words, they reject state sovereignty but simultaneously require it for their rights. In Indonesia, the conditions are somewhat different from those in the Americas as the modern state of Indonesia is not the result of a settler colony. Indigenous peoples therefore do not need to stress their independence in the way that their counterparts in the United States, Australia, or Canada do. The question of sovereignty is of importance for Indigenous movements in Indonesia as well (Acciaioli 2007, 303–307). The approach I develop starts from this paradoxical notion of indigeneity but analyzes it as a contradictive one in a dialectical sense. I draw on a Hegelian concept as interpreted by the Ljubljana school. In a dialectical approach, it is emphasized that a "substance" or entity (e.g., a society or a political identity) cannot be identical with itself. To become a subject, to become anything at all, it has to become different from itself. Object and subject are thus two sides of the same substance. In other words, disparity with itself is the constitutive nature of every substance. In terms of social reality, this means that there is a social totality, but this is never a harmonious field. On the contrary, the notion of social totality means nothing but the field of contradictions of the totality itself. Contradictions are a necessary condition of its existence. Slavoj Žižek (2012, 378) writes: "The Hegelian totality is not the ideal of an organic Whole, but a critical notion—to locate a phenomenon in its totality does not mean to see the hidden harmony of the Whole, but to include in a system all its 'symptoms,' antagonisms, and inconsistencies as integral parts."

Particular social and political identities can emerge only because social totality is never identical to itself. Economic and cultural contradictions give rise to social formations which challenge society, no matter how supposedly harmonious it is. To emerge as a whole, for instance, as a nation or a national society, any social entity has to contain its contradictions such as social movements. I outline how indigeneity emerges as a contradiction to the state and its ideological and economic foundations, and yet both the state/nation and indigeneity are mutually dependent to a point that they even contain each other. In a dialectical approach, one looks for self-difference within the social entities and identities in question. This, however, is never a static situation: The state and indigeneity approach themselves through their respective others, and they sublate each other only to create new contradictions. This dialectical relation of indigeneity and the state between their negation and affirmation, sublation and the formation of new contradictions represents a continuity throughout Indonesian history. In particular, at least three attempts have been made at reconciliation between the state and *adat* in Indonesian history, which I will explain in more detail: (1) In colonial times, the Leiden school argued for a separate realm of *adat* within the colonial state whereby the colonial state should respect and protect *adat* from the potentially devastating forces of the capitalist market; (2) in independent Indonesia, the new state aimed to rely on *adat* as an originally Indonesian notion that should inspire the new nation; and (3) in recent years, Indigenous activists have been trying to gain recognition from the state, arguing that *masyarakat adat* is an integral part of the nation. The Hegelian notion of recognition is crucial; it is not a positive gesture in which conflicts are resolved, but "retroactive insight(s) into how there never really was a serious conflict, (on) how two opponents were always on the same side" (Žižek 2012, 204).

By shedding light on the issue of indigeneity, I analyze a concept—which is in itself not dialectical—in a dialectical manner. Occasionally, I write about thesis, antithesis, and synthesis, but I do not attempt to apply dialectics as a system or method of a totalizing system. Rather, my aim is to talk about "local dialectics" in the sense of Fredric Jameson, and "it is this plurality [of local dialectics] which cancels the claim of the dialectic to articulate the laws of a universe governed by some unified field theory or 'theory of everything.'" (Jameson 2009, 15). Hence, the title of this book is *Indigenous Dialectics.*

The notion of a (social) totality is nonetheless a "dialectical requirement," but "not something one ends with, but something one begins with" (Jameson 2009, 15) in an analysis. The dialectics is not a method or a system to determine what is to come but rather is a mode of thought that enables us to see social totality as the totality of contradictions. I use dialectics as a mode of thought that enables us to think beyond dichotomies presenting themselves as given entities and to see the unity in opposites such as the state and Indigenous peoples.

Another insight deriving from such a dialectical approach is that indigeneity can appear only as original and seemingly self-identical through its initial conflict with a hegemonic social force such as the state. This transition of the antithesis is aimed at becoming identical to itself after it has to emerge as an antithesis in the first place. Indigeneity relates to itself through its other, and it can do so only in retrospect. Without the colonial endeavor, postcolonial state formation, and the economic processes of original accumulation in Indonesia's margins, the notion of an Indigenous realm would be impossible. Any attempt to become self-identical, that is, to fully become authentically and autonomously Indigenous, has to fail. To exist as a political subjectivity, the Indigenous subject always has to rely on the social totality and the state in which it is embedded. In other words, the necessary flaws in this identity ensure its existence, political subjectivity, and agency.

The Content of This Book

In the first chapter, I outline how the notions of *adat*, indigenism, and indigeneity developed from the late colonial era until postauthoritarian Indonesia. The history of *adat* and indigeneity and their recent implications for the political process have been well documented in a range of insightful research (e.g., Bourchier 1998; Li 2001; Burns 2004; 2007; Acciaioli 2007; Fasseur 2007; Moniaga 2007; Bedner and van Huis 2008; Arizona and Cahyadi 2013; Bedner and Arizona 2019). In chapter 1, I evaluate the historical processes in terms of a critical assessment of indigeneity embedded into shifting economic contexts and political processes. I demonstrate how indigeneity has been applied in Indonesian history with different meanings and political aims. In the late colonial period, the concept of *adat*, as developed by the Leiden school, pointed toward economic contradictions but framed these in merely cultural terms. In the struggle for independence and in the early years of independent Indonesia, *adat* became more than just a means to identify Indonesian identity. Economic issues also played a crucial role as the state acknowledged *adat* territory and simultaneously subordinated *adat* to the state. I argue in this chapter that *adat* occupied a contradictive position: *Adat* became, on the one hand, a symbol of outdated feudalism and tradition (as such, it was to be abolished). On the other hand, *adat* was maintained as a symbol of the cultural characteristics of the Indonesian people. The deployment of *adat* in the Basic Forestry Law of 1960 represents a synthesis of these contradictions but indeed a synthesis producing new contradictions, especially in the so-called New Order era between 1967 and 1998. This explains how "national interests" (or, more precisely, what the government declared as such) became the only game in town and *adat* eventually emerged as an oppositional force, rooted in both transnational discourses on Indigenous peoples and the Indonesian history of *adat*.

In chapter 2, I argue that in post-Suharto-Indonesia, the *adat* movement, once a force in opposition to the state, engaged with state institutions and began to apply hegemonic discourses of the predominant political economy. As with Indigenous peoples elsewhere, AMAN has to maintain a position against the state while it is, at the same time, dependent on the state and derives most of its agency from its engagement and even entanglement with the state. I show that AMAN has intensified, especially in recent years, its engagement with state institutions, which has opened new opportunities but also may come at the expense of the organization's critical and radical potential.

The first two chapters have two important functions for the main part on indigeneity in South Sulawesi and the Duri highlands. First, they outline the national framework in which indigeneity has emerged. Discourses and laws on the national scale have influenced the circumstances in South Sulawesi and the local struggles for Indigenous recognition as local actors often rely on national laws and discourses. Second, I develop the approach of Indigenous dialectics in the first two chapters by demonstrating how indigeneity passed dialectically through its other—the state and the nation—and points toward both internal contradictions of the state that allowed for the emergence of indigeneity as a concept and a political force, and to the fact that indigeneity is an integral part of the state and Indonesian nation. The concept of indigeneity as a dialectical identity is thus applied later on. In other words, my account in chapters 1 and 2 is not just a genealogy of *adat* and the *masyarakat adat* movement but also an investigation of how *adat* as indigeneity and a set of political identities developed in dialectical relations with the state and its political economy.

In chapters 3 and 4, I focus on the province of South Sulawesi. These chapters contribute to the scholarship of *adat* movements in the province (e.g., Tyson 2010; Klenke 2013; Fisher and van der Muur 2019). They review some of the literature and analyze more recent processes of Indigenous peoples–state relations. After shedding some light on the history of the province and the ways that ethnic identity is applied, I examine how Indigenous activists struggle for recognition in different parts of the province. I show that *adat* is deployed in South Sulawesi in various political ways that are sometimes at odds with AMAN's understanding of the term. Although local politicians and traditional nobility claim the notion of *adat*, AMAN has developed other, rather egalitarian approaches. Indigeneity expresses struggles in the political economy, and it develops both against and with the state. I draw on different cases, for instance those of Toraja and Gowa, and analyze some legal documents to show how *adat* is deployed politically in the context of South Sulawesi and to which contradictions it points. Chapters 3 and 4 also illuminate the provincial frame of the case study on local processes of Indigenous recognition outlined in the following.

In chapters 5 and 6, I lay on the regency of Enrekang and especially on the Duri, an ethic group living in the uplands in the northern part of the regency of Enrekang. The Duri consist of about 130,000 people, almost all of Islamic faith. They are, because of their religious beliefs, often considered to be Bugis, which is the dominant ethnic group of the nearby lowlands, but the Duri language is closely related to neighboring Toraja, a mostly Christian highland group. Although there is a reasonable number of insightful and classical ethnographic accounts on the larger ethnic groups in South Sulawesi, namely the Bugis, Makassar, and Toraja (on the Toraja, see Volkman 1985; Nooy-Palm 1986; Hollan and Wellenkamp 1996; on the Makassarese, see Koentjaraningrat 1980; Rössler 1990; on the Bugis, see Pelras 1996, 2000; Acciaioli 2004), the smaller ethic groups such as the Maiwa, Enrekang or Duri have received far less attention. My account is an attempt to fill at least part of this gap. In regard to history, I show how indigeneity came into being among the Duri. The antitraditional Darul Islam movement, which occupied remote parts of the province from the mid-1950s until the 1960s, had an enormous impact on this process. On the one hand, the destruction of traditional hierarchies and beliefs (in Duri known as *aluk tojolo*) and the rapid introduction of a kind of Islamic socialism might have destroyed much that could be considered Indigenous, for instance, traditional belief systems and political institutions. On the other hand, the new societies became more equal (e.g., compared with the neighboring Toraja where traditional stratification still prevails in politics and society today), which makes the Duri communities fit better into AMAN's image of rather egalitarian social entities.

Numerous contributions in academia deal with the struggle of Indigenous populations in environmental conflicts in Indonesia (e.g., Peluso 1995; Anderson 2012; van der Muur 2018; Haug 2014; Bräuchler 2018; Großmann 2019). The expansion of the palm oil industry, mining, and land reclamation have had tremendous impacts on these peoples' lives. In many cases, *adat* has become a powerful tool in the struggle against corporations or state institutions. *Adat* as a political force often unfolds in settings that are highly conflictual, and this fact has been stressed by both Indigenous activists and scholars. Despite the fact that numerous violent conflicts have broken out over land in Indonesia, many cases in which *adat* develops as an ideology are less conflictual. Rural communities demand resources from land that has been declared state forest for both subsistence and small businesses, but only occasionally face small-scale repression, if any. These cases do not receive much attention as they are far less spectacular than conflicts involving the armed forces, the state apparatus, hired thugs, courts, and angry protests or even armed Indigenous peoples. In chapters 5 and 6 on Enrekang and the Duri communities, I shed some light on cases of Indigenous recognition in which conflicts have, for the most part, been absent or of low intensity. I believe that we can learn as much from such cases as we can learn from more conflict-laden struggles.

Despite the rapid recognition of Indigenous communities in the Duri highlands, there is a large underlying conflict, namely the contradiction between producers and the ownership structure, originating from original accumulation when the state declared *adat* territories state forest. But as original accumulation had rather little economic effect in Enrekang (and elsewhere outside the conflictual setting described by many anthropologists), the relations of ownership and labor have come to be expressed in an Indigenous critique in Enrekang. I explain how recognition of Indigenous communities among the Duri started with considerable support from the local state administration as all actors agreed on the aim of improving the local economy through Indigenous recognition. The implications of that, I argue, are twofold. On the one hand, a clearly neoliberal paradigm is at work, suggesting that Indigenous communities can become entrepreneurs when given access to *adat* forest: They are potentially more successful in extracting value from the forest than the Forestry Department or companies ever were in Enrekang's highlands. On the other hand, Indigenous communities gain control over land as the main means of production and thus become able to establish a solidarity economy in which decisions are not made top down and revenues are quite equally distributed to fit the (imaginary) ideal of Indigenous communities as less hierarchical social entities, as AMAN promotes them.

In November 2019, I was able to join AMAN activists at the regional assembly in Karampuang, Sinjai regency, where AMAN activists from Jakarta, Makassar, Enrekang, and other parts of South Sulawesi, as well as politicians and common villagers from the Indigenous community of Karampuang, met. The assembly provided a great opportunity to observe how these actors interact and how they apply and discuss Indigenous issues. In chapter 7, I shed light on how Indigenous activists from different levels interact and negotiate indigeneity. In this chapter, I bring together insight from the other chapters that discuss the notion of indigeneity at different scales (national, provincial, and local). Moreover, I argue that different types of activists apply different notions of indigeneity and state–Indigenous peoples relations. They point toward the internal contradictions of indigeneity that make indigeneity as a political ideology possible in the first place.

In the conclusion, I not only summarize the main findings but also discuss them in the context of general debates on indigeneity. I summarize how indigeneity came into existence dialectically and how it developed dialectically in relation to the state and the political economy. The conclusion provides a discussion concerning the question of whether the ideology of indigeneity in Indonesia is a progressive or reactionary force. What critique does the ideology of indigeneity offer and how should it be criticized? Indigeneity is a challenging subject for critical scholars because it expresses economic contradictions, but it does so in terms of cultural identity. The question is thus whether these expressions can nonetheless lead to economic change that is progressive in nature. The Indigenous movement's focus on engagement with the state has not alienated it from grassroots activism, but the fight for exclusively Indigenous legislation has made wider alliances potentially difficult. Also, some activists on all scales have embraced neoliberal concepts of entrepreneurship and the ideological notions of economic growth and development. In contrast, I outline that indigeneity on occasion criticizes fundamental mechanisms of the political economy, for instance during protests against the so-called omnibus law (*UU Cipta Kerja*, Job Creation Law) in 2020. Moreover, through seemingly uncritical compliance with state institutions and the adaptation of mainstream economic discourses, new possibilities emerge for local economies in which the means of production are owned collectively and surplus value is distributed rather equally. Therefore, a critique of the ideology of indigeneity must preserve the very critique that indigeneity offers and must also take into account the ideology's blind spots. To put it dialectically, a critique of the ideology of indigeneity has the task of sublating indigeneity—that is, the task of simultaneously preserving, abolishing, and transcending it.

INDIGENEITY AND THE INDONESIAN NATION I

From Colonialism to the New Order

The concept of indigeneity as a modern political-cultural force emerged in the 1960s in former settler colonies, mostly throughout the Americas, and it was not before the late 1980s that people in Asia adopted this concept for their purposes (Barnes 1995, 1–2). In Indonesia, the concept was first adopted in the mid-1990s as *masyarakat adat* (societies of custom/customary law). It drew on a long history of the conceptualization of *adat* societies. To understand the application of indigeneity in local Indonesian contexts, it is crucial to understand this history and the national framework in which this concept has developed from the colonial era until the post-*reformasi* (post-reform era) context after the mid-2000s. In this chapter, which deals with indigeneity and the Indonesian nation, I provide an overview of this national framework. My second purpose is to develop a dialectical approach on state–Indigenous peoples relations, which I also apply to the local context in South Sulawesi. By shedding light on the scholarly literature on *adat* and Indigenous peoples in Indonesia, I suggest understanding indigeneity as, on the one hand, an integral part of the Indonesian nation, because it stresses the original, precolonial features of Indonesian identity. On the other hand, indigeneity as *adat* has simultaneously emerged as the other of the nation, for instance as traditional backwardness that has to be overcome, either in a populist-egalitarian attempt like during the struggle for independence or as an obstacle to Suharto's authoritarian developmentalism. Indigeneity, conceptualized as *masyarakat adat*, also maintains this contradictive relationship to the state: On the one hand, it portrays itself as the core of Indonesian identity and a plural state, and on the other hand, it demands sovereignty in cultural, economic, and even some political issues. Instead of seeing these contradictions as flaws and obstacles to a supposedly original and self-sustaining political force, however, these contradictions lay at the very core of Indigenous agency and are even the crucial condition for the existence of the notion of indigeneity.

Adat and Late Colonialism: Recognition of Difference, Colonial Invention, and Economic Strategy

Scholarly debates over the origins of the concept of *adat* are not new but have become especially virulent since *adat* became a political term in the wake of the Indigenous movement in the late New Order era and *reformasi* Indonesia. In 1993, activists chose the term *masyarakat adat* as the Indonesian translation for "Indigenous peoples" (Moniaga 2007, 291–282). To understand that concept as it is applied by activists and has been adopted in state discourses and legislation, however, it is crucial to shed light on the origins of the concept.

I demonstrate that the roots of indigeneity lay, among others, in political-economic processes in the late colonial era, namely in the question of how the state should conceptualize and organize society to balance capitalist demands, on the one hand, and socioeconomic cohesion, on the other hand (the latter is indeed also a capitalist demand because it ensures the function of a specific mode of production). The notion of *adat* as it emerged in the late colonial period has to be seen within the context of what Peter Boomgard (2007, 250–252) had called "political forests": As colonial states in Southeast Asia introduced scientific concepts of forestry (which often were not sustainable in practice because they obtained their knowledge from European ecological contexts and failed to acknowledge the importance of local forms of land tenure), the colonial state claimed control over large parts of the forests, arguing that local communities were not able to use the forests in an appropriate—that is, scientific and capitalist—manner.

Much research has examined particular cases throughout Indonesia in the late colonial era (e.g., for West Sumatra, see von Benda-Beckmann and von Benda-Beckmann 2013, 61–99; for Java, see Breman 1983; for Central Sulawesi, see Li 2007, 61–78). I focus, however, on general developments in the Netherlands Indies since the time of the so-called ethical period when Indigenous land was partially acknowledged under a wider frame of liberal market regimes. The conceptualization of *adat* as so-called nativeness played a crucial role. *Adat* was already at the core of scholarly and political debates in the late colonial era when researchers and politicians argued about whether Indigenous populations should be treated as distinct peoples with their own cultural and customary legacies or be incorporated into the modern state, law, and economy. As I argue alongside Tania Li (2007, 2010), the rationale of the colonial endeavor was not simply to appropriate land from Indigenous populations and hand it over to the market as a commodity and a means of production. Instead, a rationality was at work that had to balance and negotiate different aims and objectives, which often were contradictive and embedded in both divergent discourses and economic practices. Consequently, this contradictive approach is mirrored in scholarly discourses about how the colonial government should treat native populations, which law (European or *adat* law) they should apply, and whether they should be exposed to capitalist markets or should be protected from market integration.

Adat signifies customary law as well as wider customs, including institutions and rituals ensuring the social cohesion and function of local communities. The term is of Arabic origin and has been used not only in the Netherlands Indies but also in various places in Asia to capture the notion of traditional and original (i.e., distinct from colonial/Western) ways of regulating social disputes and laws (Pichler 2014, 123; von Benda-Beckmann 2019). In its widest sense, *adat* represents a cosmological order that makes the world intelligible (Acciaioli 1985, 182). This also includes, of course, regulations that many scholars refer to as law, and in its most prominent account, *adat* was conceptualized as customary law by the Dutch scholar van Vollenhoven and his Leiden school.

The conceptualization and systematization of customary law was an effect of the Dutch effort to rule and economically exploit the colony effectively. As the Dutch had limited resources of people, they governed large parts of the Dutch East Indies through indirect rule. Local sultans and other nobility were incorporated into colonial rule, especially into economic regimes, and were allowed to internally maintain their customs and laws, that is, *adat*. This law was applied to *inlanders* (Dutch: natives) or, in Malay, *pribumi* (sons of the soil), whereas Europeans were subject to Dutch law. This legal dualism— particularly as it was introduced in 1854—had diverse functions and implications. As Moniaga (2007, 277) outlines, some Indonesian scholars view this legal dualism as a tool to maintain the racial superiority of the Dutch over the *inlanders* (Hartono 1979). In contrast, scholars have argued that the recognition of *adat* (and thus the legal dualism inevitably emerging from it) was sign of respect for the native population (Wingyosoebroto 1994). Peter Burns (2007) has argued that *adat* as law was mainly a Dutch invention and that *adat* could not be actual law given that law requires a third, superior party that "functions to resolve conflicts in that society and, acting in that role, to make plain, to its members, the obligations to be observed, and the opportunities to be enjoyed" (Burns 2007, 69). Other scholars have argued against the account that *adat* law was a Dutch invention (von Benda-Beckmann 2019). This critique, however, does not deny that colonialism had a significant impact on *adat* in the way it was applied and conceptualized.

The fact that *adat* was conceptualized as law points to the question of how Indigenous populations have been seen by scholars at the center of the colonial project. Van Vollenhoven and his students in Leiden were ahead of their time, as they applied the anthropological gesture of describing the natives according to their own concepts and they argued against applying Western concepts to non-Western societies. But why did they do this? Was it merely because of their concern with Indigenous peoples and the distinct culture they wanted to preserve? This may appear to be the case at first glance; if, however, we think of the Leiden school as part of the colonial state apparatus, the Leiden school also expressed a certain ideology in the sense of their relation to the colonial economy and the colonial state. Analyzing the Leiden school in terms of ideology does not mean denying its progressive potential. It is precisely through the othering of the Leiden school—which I argue is clearly a conservative gesture— that the basis for potentially progressive constellations is provided. Perceiving social practices of *adat* as law points toward a concept of otherness that is nevertheless based on the very same concept as Western societies: The idea is that distinct spaces of law—a Western one and an Indigenous one—must be separated through clear borders to maintain the exotic object as distinct and to ensure the other's survival. It is just through the relation to European/Dutch society and its law, however, that *adat* emerges as a category for many distinct local societies. Although the abstract concept of law is the base for sameness, it is also the condition of otherness, because van Vollenhoven argued against the dominant evolutionist thinking of his time and stressed that using legal terminology from Europe to capture Indigenous legal systems would distort the inherent logic and meaning of those Indigenous legal systems (Benda-Beckmann 2019, 38).

To understand the origins of the debate between the Leiden *adat* law school and its competitor, the Utrecht school, which argued in favor of a single, European law for both Europeans and natives in the colony, it is crucial to consider the legal dualism introduced in the government regulation (Dutch: *regerings-reglement*) of 1854. By that time, the Dutch government had gained control of the interior of Java and large parts of the coastal areas of the outer islands of the Netherlands East Indies. Therefore, the jurisdiction of distinct parts of the population in the colony had become an important issue. According to Article 75 of the government regulation, Europeans were subject to jurisdiction, legislation, and legal procedures based on regulations conforming as much as possible to laws in the Netherlands. Natives and citizens of Chinese descent were legal subjects of their respective laws (Fasseur 2007, 50).

The late nineteenth century, however, saw an increasing mobilization of the distinct ethnic groups, most of all on Java, and the question emerged whether in such a society a unifying law would be more appropriate than the legal dualism between the Dutch and the hundreds of distinct native law systems. In the early twentieth century, both liberal and conservative governments in the Netherlands East Indies seemed to agree that a unification of law would be appropriate, and they aimed to radically modify Article 75. It was the era of the so-called ethical policy in the colony, when the colonial administration claimed to promote welfare and modernization for natives. For instance, Conrad Theodor van Deventer, a liberal politician and an initiator of the ethical policy, strongly argued for the unification of law as he saw legal dualism as an obstacle to economic development. Other lawyers and politicians, such as Dirk Fock and Timon Henricus Fokker, argued for unification as well, often using economic arguments. Western law rather than fragmented native law could lead to juridical certainty for the Indigenous part of the population, and they valued juridical certainty as an inevitable condition for economic development (Fasseur 2007, 58–59). Academic support for these political ideas came from scholars at Utrecht University. Their foremost concern was economic growth because it was seen as a necessary condition for a prosperous society in the colony. Rather than debating the redistribution of wealth, economic growth became the dominant narrative. This narrative relied on the impression that natives could determine their economic destiny on their own once they were treated equally in terms of law. Unequal legal conditions were identified as the main obstacle to the economic growth necessary to develop the Indigenous population (Burns 2004; von Benda-Beckmann 2019, 403). The proposed modification of Article 75, which aimed to introduce a unifying European law, was never put into force as it was met with a dissident majority in the second chamber of the Dutch parliament. It was also the result of van Vollenhoven's struggle against a unifying European law that many in the second chamber changed sides. In the new regulation, issued in 1919, *adat* law became the standard law for most natives, making European law the exception to the rule when the needs of the native society required it (Fasseur 2007, 59–60).

How did van Vollenhoven and the Leiden school conceptualize *adat* as law and as a legal entity distinct from European law? Van Vollenhoven's concept was rather conservative as he referred to the approach of the *Rechtsgeschichteschule* (German: law history school) of German Romantic legal historians, which assumed that each people had a specific system of law. Burns (1989, 98–101) has showed that van Vollenhoven was inspired by the concept of *volksgeist* (German: people spirit or nation spirit), an assumed essence of a people, mediated through the French writer Ernest Renan. David Bourchier (1998, 205) additionally mentions Savigny's conservative-organicist historical school of law as an important influence on the Leiden school. Li (2007, 48) concludes that the *adat* school at Leiden was "guided by a nostalgic and humanist desire for the other to remain other."

Van Vollenhoven collected data from government commissions, officials, missionaries, and scholars in the colony, and then looked for common patterns in *adat* laws. He concluded that the Dutch East Indies formed a legal-cultural area. Crucial for *adat* law throughout the colony, he argued, was a concept he labeled *beschikkingsrecht* (Dutch: right of allocation) (Burns 2007, 73–74). In his publication *Miskenningen van het adatrecht* (Misevaluations of *Adat* Law), he argued that *beschikkingsrecht* consists of six features common throughout the archipelago. These features became the benchmarks for the term *adat* (van Vollenhoven 1909, 19–20, as quoted in Burns 2007, 74): The first feature is community competence over undeveloped land, because the community can make free use of virgin land for any purpose the community wants. The second feature refers to use of community land by outsiders who can make similar use of the land when they receive permission from the jural community. The third feature concerns payment for use of community land, which for outsiders is mandatory. The fourth feature is community competence over land under cultivation as the community retains a residual right to intervene in the disposal of lands that are already under use. According to the fifth feature, the community has a collective responsibility with respect to outsiders, meaning that it makes good any loss, damage, or harm suffered by outsiders on its territory. The sixth feature is the perpetuity of communal rights, meaning that the jural community is not required to surrender these rights entirely.

Because jural communities were usually small and relatively autonomous villages, van Vollenhoven sometimes called them *zelfstandige inlandsche rechtsgemeenschappen* (Dutch: autonomous native jural communities). In addition to the noted features, the jural communities also shared institutions of community service, communal budgets, and dispute management. The features outlined can be summarized by the term *hak ulayat* (right of avail), a term originally from the Minangkabau language of West Sumatra but now a generic term in Indonesian. *Hak ulayat* denoted the communal property over which the *adat* law community should maintain and exercise its original social and political control. In van Vollenhoven's argumentation, *hak ulayat* demonstrated that the autonomous native communities had an Indigenous concept of authority over common land, including land not under permanent cultivation (von Benda-Beckmann 2019, 404–405).

Another feature that became a legacy was the juxtaposition of *adat*, on the one hand, and religion and Islamic law, on the other. The influential orientalist and the adviser on native affairs to the Dutch colonial government Snouck Hurgronje and van Vollenhoven argued that a weakening of *adat* would inevitably strengthen political Islam, a lesson they probably learned from the Padri War in the early nineteenth century in West Sumatra in which Islamic modernizers organized uprisings against both the Dutch colonizers and traditional *adat* elites. Snouck Hurgronje helped the Dutch government to crush resistance against Dutch rule in Aceh, known as the Aceh War (1873–1914), and to establish Dutch colonial rule in Aceh to gain access to resources such as black pepper and oil. His analysis of Acehnese society concluded that traditional leaders could be coopted into colonial rule, whereas Islamic authorities (*ulama*) should not be considered trustworthy partners. Hence, he drew a strict separation between *adat* and religion. Van Vollenhoven was rather careful in this respect (von Benda-Beckmann 2019, 400). The idea that *adat* represented political-jural competition for Islam, however, was likely a reason for the Dutch to strengthen the former over the latter. *Adat* elites were, in many places in the East Indies, much better incorporated into indirect colonial rule than Islamic authorities. The ambivalent function of *adat* is clear. Although it was conceptualized as the original and traditional essence of the Dutch East Indies and was valued and recognized in the influential orientalist discourses in the Netherlands, it was nevertheless an instrument for political rule and the maintenance of colonial power structures potentially challenged by other political forces, such as modernist Islam.

In penal law, the recognition of *adat* law led to a dualistic system (Fasseur 2007, 55–60). In terms of land tenure, however, the acknowledgment of *adat* in the legal realm was only of limited impact. Although *adat* acknowledged both individual and collective forms of possession, it was nonetheless unified as a concept and thus juxtaposed against Western, individual landownership. In 1870, the government of the East Indies issued a new agricultural law (Dutch: *agrarische wet*) declaring all land not under European ownership as state land. Within the category of state land, *adat* had a certain significance but was always at the mercy of the colonial state. The law was a compromise in the sense that it formally recognized native rights of *hak ulayat* but ensured that the state was in control of the forests and other land not in permanent cultivation (Li 2007, 39). *Adat* land was categorized as *free* or *non-free land*. Free land was land not in permanent use, for instance, forests, including forests from which the native population extensively extracted resources, such as fruits, timber, or rattan. This land was regarded as natural, uncultivated land. It included all untitled land not in constant use (Fitzpatrick 2007, 133). Non-free land, in contrast, meant land in permanent cultivation, for instance rice paddies (Pichler 2014, 125). Collective *adat* ownership was applied only to land falling under this category.

Although the law claimed to acknowledge *adat* and *adat* ownership, how it was influenced by liberal, Lockean notions of property is striking: Land becomes a possession if labor is invested. In the case of the agrarian law, even permanent work is required, and instead of individual property, an *adat* community establishes only a right to use. In this regard, the new agricultural law of 1870 was an interesting chimera of liberal notions applied to Indigenous communities and the dominance of individual landownership (only individually owned land was not under the domain of the state). Moreover, this law gave natives in villages no room for expansion because their collective landownership could not be expanded into state-owned free land. The law also allowed for land allocation for European-owned plantations (Burns 1989; Peluso and Vandergeest 2001; Li 2010, 392). In many cases, an *adat* community claimed *hak ulayat* for what the state considered free land. As a sign of recognition, the colonial state granted recognition money for that land, but this money was often far from fair compensation (Harsono 2003, 46).

The initial motivation for the 1870 law was the government's aim to attract private capital to develop new plantations. In the view of market liberalism, *adat* was an obstacle because its acknowledgment made it potentially more difficult and expensive to open up land for market production. Besides the acknowledgment of *adat* by the Dutch government in the government regulation of 1911 there was still a drive toward a more capital-friendly approach. The Dutch colonial-capitalist lobby spent huge sums on the new Faculty of Indology at Utrecht University, which was established in 1925. Like its competitor in Leiden, the faculty was established to educate colonial officials, but unlike van Vollenhoven's faculty, they put a strong emphasis on the concerns of private capital. It was therefore not surprising that they promoted legal theories arguing against what van Vollenhoven and his students had suggested (Bedner and Arizona 2019, 417–418).

In addition to colonial legal dualism, there was also a colonial economic dualism labeled a "communal fix" (Li 2010, 386). Li has argued that it was a common approach in colonies during late colonialism to create distinct groups within the population: one group designated to become individual market subjects with individual possessions, and another group protected from the very real risk of dispossession by conceptualizing their attachment to land on a collective, non-Western basis. As such, the concept of the communal fix and the corresponding rationality, which sought to balance the interests of the free market and its potentially impoverishing effects, corresponded to economic contradictions within the capitalist colonial market. As an abstract idea, supported individual ownership rights were progressive insofar as they were based upon an equal treatment of both Europeans and natives under a unified law. Under actual economic conditions, however, such a liberal approach would have resulted in the colonized soon dispossessing themselves through land sale or mortgage (Li 2010, 387). Also, van Vollenhoven and the Leiden scholars were concerned with potential social upheaval or even civil war (Burns 1989, 15; Li 2010, 393–394). In other words, they clearly saw what was at stake in terms of the political economy, even though they saw it through the lens of culture.

Especially outside Java, that is, in the periphery of the Dutch East Indies, *adat* became the principal way of constructing difference between the colonizers and the colonized during the late colonial period (Li 2007, 48). I agree with Keebet von Benda-Beckmann (2019, 405–406) when she argues that *adat* was not a mere invention of the colonial government. The Leiden school indeed went to great lengths to gather empirical material and stressed that *adat* was far from static. I also suggest, however, that Burns (2007, 69) is right in a certain sense when he argues that "*adatrecht* was a Dutch invention," an argument also made by Lev (1985, 63–64), who says that before the Dutch made it a category of law, *adat* was of importance only in contexts of local political and economic interests. *Adat* was a Dutch invention insofar as it was an ideological formation taken into political debates by the ideological state apparatuses, namely in the form of the Leiden school. By establishing scientific discourses in Leiden and Utrecht, it became politically and economically relevant as an abstract concept and was applied as a wide concept both politically and economically.

As the Utrecht school argued against the recognition of *adat* and for a unifying law, this liberal approach represented directly the cause of capital. The Leiden school seemingly represented the cause of the natives, but within the wider economic context, it served the colonial endeavor insofar as it provided scientific support for social cohesion when Leiden scholars warned about potential disastrous economic (and thus sociopolitical) consequences if Indigenous communities were fully exposed to the market. In this context, it is important to remember that van Vollenhoven and his Leiden school never challenged the legitimacy of colonial rule and, consequently, colonial capitalism. Li (2007, 49) concludes that van Vollenhoven did not see the protection of *adat* and native land tenure as a contradiction to capitalist development. Van Vollenhoven believed that natives would more likely comply with colonialists' requirements for land concession precisely when they were recognized. Moreover, Li stresses that he did not regard *adat* law as a sacred cow. As a wholesome alternative to European law and land tenure, *adat* law could and should not be above European law, which always set the conditions for legal processes of expropriation of the natives.

We can see how *adat* has developed dialectically. As liberal capitalism was introduced with a supposedly ethical policy, impoverishment would have been an unintended but inevitable consequence of liberal capitalism, namely its internal contradiction. The ideology of *adat* as outlined by the Leiden school represented a synthesis as it maintained capitalism and suggested realms out- side the free market. *Adat*, in this regard, was also contradictive: It not only was the other of the Dutch colonial state but also was incorporated into its very political framework, as the *adat* realm had been acknowledged in the legal dualism and land tenure laws. This contradiction was inherent in the way it was incorporated, namely through simultaneous recognition and subordina- tion. In other words, from its very beginning *adat* (as an umbrella term for local customs and laws) was part of the state as well as its other. It is true that local customs existed before the Dutch came and, in this way, *adat* is not an invention of the Dutch. However, *adat* as an abstraction, as an umbrella term for customary law in a defined area, only came into existence through the colo- nial project of which the Leiden school was an integral part. *Adat* as an abstrac- tion transcended local contexts and became a term of importance for colonial governance. *Adat* became the self-difference of the colonial state, and it has thus maintained this role of the state's self-difference after independence in various ways.

Negotiating Indigeneity in the Indonesian Revolution and the Early Years of Independent Indonesia

Ki Hadjar Dewantara is one of the famous figures in the Indonesian struggle for independence. He is known especially for his journalistic article "If I Were a Dutchman" in which he criticized colonialism as early as 1913. Later, he estab- lished the *Taman Siswa* school for natives to extend education beyond a tiny elite among the natives and to ordinary people. As a man of noble descent, he rejected his royal title in exchange for Ki Hadjar Dewantara, literally denoting well-respected teacher and mediator between earth and the higher realm (Xin 2018). This rejection of traditional hierarchies on the one hand *and* positive references to tradition on the other—in this case, to traditional ways of concep- tualizing education—was common within Indonesia's movement against colonial rule and points to the very frame within which Indonesians had to conceptualize their Indonesian-ness during the late colonial order and in the early years of the independent republic. Ki Hadjar Dewantara is also known as the first translator of the *Internationale* into Indonesian. In his Indonesian translation, *adat* appears in the second part of the first verse: *Lenjapkan adat dan paham tua / kita rakyat sadar-sadar / Dunia sudah berganti rupa / untuk kemenangan kita.* My literal translation is: "get rid of *adat* and old thoughts / we, the people, become conscious / the world changes its appearance / for our victory." This rejection of the old tradition was indeed a leitmotif among the youth struggling for independence. National struggle therefore meant anticolonial and antifeudal struggle, and this included the struggle against *adat*. It was not only communists who fostered these ideas; socialist and nationalist forces also agreed (Elson 2008, 55–56).

Pembangunan, a notion later translated as development in technocratic terms under Suharto and a keyword of the authoritarian Suharto era, has its roots in the era of the struggle for independence. Sutan Takdir Alisjahbana, an influential cultural critic and nationalist intellectual, used the notion of the *bangun* in the double sense the word offered: as "building," because an entirely new nation was to be built from scratch, which relied on a new society against old traditions, and in the sense of "awakening," by which he meant the awakening of a popular consciousness (Heryanto 1988, 10). Tradition, however, was not just the negation of the new nation but also its internal contradiction. Some of Indonesia's independence fighters subscribed to concepts of tradition as long as they were compatible with egalitarian ideals. As that holds true for a great part of the independence movement, David Bourchier (1998) stresses that conservative Indonesians also were arguing for an independent Indonesia based on a hierarchical, traditional society. These people of the conservative intelligentsia appropriated their ideas from the Leiden school. Just as van Vollenhoven conceptualized a realm of *adat* law, conservative Indonesian intellectuals did so in regard to a broader concept of culture. Indonesian culture, to them, was essentially harmonious, communalistic, hierarchical, and organically integrated through arche-politics (Duile and Bens 2017, 144-146). In other words, the concept of the *adat* community as outlined by van Vollenhoven and his students was taken as a blueprint for the larger entity of the new Indonesian state. *Adat* was even perceived as a code word for "original Indonesian culture" (Koesnoe 1996, 15–16).

The Indonesian Constitution, which was weak on individual liberal civil rights but strong in terms of Indigenous principles of communal deliberation (*musyawarah*) and unanimous agreement (*mufakat*), was drafted in 1945 by Leiden-trained Soepomo. Soepomo also juxtaposed Indonesian integralism against liberalism and communism. Even though Soepomo borrowed traditional concepts, such as *musyawarah* and *mufakat* for the process of nation-building, he was convinced that particular *adat* law was something that would disappear. Applying an evolutionist argument to the issue, he thought of Indonesia as a new political entity replacing all particular *adat* law communities but nevertheless relying on their legacy in abstract terms (Soepomo 1947; Bedner and Arizona 2019, 418–419). In addition to the idea of elevating *adat* as a blueprint for state law or expecting the disappearance of particular *adat* societies as they integrated into state law as a successor of *adat* ideals, a third approach suggested that *adat* should not and could not be incorporated into the state. Following the Leiden school, adherents of this third approach argued that tensions between *adat* and state law should not be resolved by making *adat* an abstract state law or by letting *adat* vanish. Rather, *adat* should be acknowledged as the law and cultural properties of particular groups, and empirical approaches should inform policy choices in particular cases (Bedner and Arizona 2019, 419).

As in the thinking of Soepomo and Koensoe, *adat* played a role in nation-building as it at least contributed through its legacy to Indonesian identity and a unifying national law, that is, the overcoming of the legal pluralism introduced by the Dutch. This conservative indigenism, with its notion of harmony and social hierarchy, was revitalized later during the so-called New Order era under Suharto (1967–1998). In the struggle for independence and in the early years of independent Indonesia, however, populist indigenism stole the show from conservative indigenism. Populist indigenism, as stressed by Indonesia's first president Sukarno, referred to the native principle of *gotong royong* (mutual help/assistance) and stressed the egalitarian features of indigeneity. It became the dominant discourse in the so-called Guided Democracy era (1957–1965) when Sukarno deployed populist indigenism to abolish institutions and practices associated with liberal Western democracy. As indigenism as the source of Indonesian identity was prevailing in political discourses, army leadership made use of the imaginary harmonious *adat* village as a blueprint for the state and suggested that the state should be modeled according to *kekeluargaan* (family principle) as a native concept (Bourchier 1998, 205–206).

The populist and the conservative forms of indigenism shared, however, the notion of indigenism as a unifying force for the process of nation-building. Particular *adat* communities were one source from which Indonesia's founding fathers took their ideas of what it meant to be Indonesian. The Indonesian Constitution of 1945 even acknowledged the existence of particular *adat* groups. Recognition of indigeneity as a foundation of the state was declared in Article 18, which acknowledged that Indonesia should be formed of the existing sociopolitical units, both large and small, with their customary rights. An explanatory note to Article 18 even used Dutch terminology:

> In Indonesian territory, there are ± 254 *Zelfbesturende Landschappen* [Dutch for "self-governing territories"; my translation] and *Volksgemeenschappen* [Dutch for "people's communities"; my translation] such as villages in Java and Bali, Nagari in Minangkabau, Kampung and Marga in Palembang and so forth. These regions retain their original institutions and are thereby considered as special regions. The National Republic of Indonesia respects the existence of these regions and all these regions' regulations that relate to their original rights. (quoted from Colchester et al. 2007, 46)

This did not mean, however, a general recognition of *adat* land rights (Pichler 2014, 126). On the contrary, *adat* as a category of particular groups was, in terms of political economy, subordinated under state interests. Because Indigenous communities no longer needed to be protected against the dangerous effects of the colonial capitalist market, their resources became the domain of the state and its project of national development (Bedner and Arizona 2019, 418).

The concept of customary law communities also played a role in the Basic Agrarian Law (*Undang-Undang Pokok Agraria*) put into force in 1960. In the government's view, the law aimed to combine aspects of modern law—that is, rule-based and nationwide applicability and the overcoming of colonial legal dualism—as well as traditional, Indonesian aspects of mutual cooperation and social function they believed to be inherent in traditional tenure systems (Bakker and Moniaga 2010, 188). As Bedner and Arizona (2019, 419) argue, this concept reflected both the idea that *adat* could be appliedas an inspiration for national law (as suggested by Koesnoe) and that *adat* eventually would disappear as national law became the prime legal entity (as argued by Soepomo). Article 5 recognizes customary law (*hukum adat*) as the general agrarian law in Indonesia, but only as long as it does not contradict national interests and the interests of the state. Customary law societies (*masyarakat hukum adat*) are mentioned and recognized in Article 2(4) and Article 3. They are only a matter of concern, however, as far as their existence can be proven, and, again, *adat* can always be overridden by what are labeled national interests. Most important, Article 2(1) refers to the Indonesian Constitution of 1945 and states that "the lands . . . including its natural resources are on the highest level controlled by the state." Although some Indonesian commentators have stressed that the *adat*-based features of the Basic Agrarian Law outline a specific Indonesian character for the law, it is, in fact, a law that clearly subordinates *adat* law to the state (Fitzpatrick 2007, 137).

To capture the spirit and the thrust of the law, it is worth looking into a juridical commentary from 1962. As was common during that time, the Basic Agrarian Law was labeled a revolutionary law as it ended the dualism in Indonesian agrarian law, and the commentary states that *adat* law became the unified law, "as the original Indonesian law" (Harsono 1962, 2; my translation). As the opposite of the genuine Indonesian agrarian law based on *adat* and socialist Indonesian society, the commentary refers to Western agrarian law, which has a liberal-individualistic spirit (Harsono 1962, 40–42). The commentary also stresses that Indonesia would have to get rid of feudalistic elements in agrarian law (Harsono 1962, 55–61), but only sultanates (Surakarta and Yogyakarta) are mentioned. This critique of feudalism thus does not apply to small *adat* communities. When it comes directly to *adat*, the commentary reads: "That customary law is used as the basis for the national agrarian law and it is in accordance with the personality of our people because customary law is our original law. Meanwhile, . . . customary law must still be cleaned of its non-original flaws (Harsono 1962, 105; my translation)." These nonoriginal flaws include anything that contradicts the interests of the nation and the state as well as the egalitarian ideals of Indonesian socialism (Harsono 1962, 139–143). In the argument outlined by Harsono, the ideas of the nation and Indonesian socialism appear to be concepts within the original features of *adat*.

On the one hand, *adat* was designed in a way that fit with the values of Indonesian socialism. On the other hand, leftist movements at that time had other political identities to rely on, namely the Indonesian concept of the peasantry, as it was outlined in Sukarno's concept of the *marhaen* as the foundation of his political philosophy of *marhenisme*. Rather than thinking of traditional customs as essential to Indonesian identity, Sukarno conceptualized the Indonesian peasant as one owning his own plot of land and a simple means of production. Sukarno's concept of the *marhaen* as the socioeconomic foundation of the Indonesian nation was, because of his Marxist influence, explicitly modern and came without any notion of *adat* (Aminuddin et al. 2019). This discursive formation is the main reason why the Basic Agrarian Law restricted the recognition of *adat* communities. The interests of peasants and plantation laborers could be addressed through land reforms aiming for more equal land distribution (Bedner and Arizona 2019, 419). The Basic Agrarian Law was designed to redistribute land from foreign companies to the state (and, theoretically, to peasants). Even though these regulations were never put into force, the Basic Agrarian Law, as well as Law 2/1960 on Share Tenancy, aimed to facilitate peasant's interests, when addressing regionally different maximal limits on individual landownership, by regulating the share of costs and benefits between tenants and landowners and by abolishing landlordism (Ambarwati et al. 2016, 266). The incidents of 1965–1966, when the Communist Party and its affiliated organizations were brutally eradicated, put a harsh end to all efforts to achieve more equal land distribution, but the main discourses before 1965 centered on equality, social justice, modernization, and anticolonialism. Generally speaking, the spirit of the law and of the times during these early years reflected the popular struggles of the Indonesian people rather than of particular ethnic communities of customary law (Li 2001, 649).

Against Indigeneity as the Particular: Suharto's Developmentalism and the Ideology of Hierarchy

Thus far, I have argued that indigeneity emerged in and against the state. In Indonesia, like in many other postcolonial states that were not settler colonies, the national struggle for liberation has created a state that already claimed to be Indigenous in the sense that it was established and governed by natives. However, Indigenous peoples nonetheless need to rely on their difference from this state, and in many conversations I had with Indigenous activists in Jakarta, they referred to colonialism as the benchmark of difference to their Indigenous identity. With the terms colonialism and colonization they did not only refer to the Dutch and the Japanese. In many cases, Indigenous activists referred to the authoritarian so-called New Order (1967–1998) as a regime that applied a colonialist approach toward Indigenous communities.

The incidents of September 30, 1965, marked the beginning of the biggest change of direction in Indonesia in terms of its political economy. In the following months, one of the largest mass killings since World War II took place in the country. Hundreds of thousands actual and alleged communists were killed and Indonesia, previously a leading member of the nonaligned movement with a government notorious in the West for its anticapitalist and anti-imperialist rhetoric and policies, was incorporated into the US-dominated capitalist sphere. This violent and fundamental change had massive consequences for the way indigeneity was applied because it tremendously affected property regimes in general and land tenure specifically.

Between October 1965 and March 1967, Suharto and right-wing factions within the armed forces managed to outmaneuver Sukarno and establish a new, anticommunist rule in Indonesia. The so-called New Order had to bring multiple goals together. It had to address political instability as well as far-reaching economic problems. Anticommunism became a central tool for addressing these issues and strengthening political power. As a consequence, antipolitics prevailed, meaning that political issues were translated into technical problems executed by officials. The old style of politics in which politicians sought support though mobilization was not in line with the new political culture. Technocratic neoliberal economists trained at the University of California in Berkeley, a group later known as the "Berkeley mafia," suggested opening the country to foreign capital (Thee 2012, 69–89).

The military took a strong role in ensuring that resource extraction and dispossession were conducted smoothly. Critics were labeled as communists and through this means not only were expelled from political discourse but also were criminalized. Anticommunism was indeed a new feature of the New Order, but numerous continuities persisted as well. One main continuity was the legacy of the idea of Indonesian unity as a people not concerned with controversial political debate and liberal democracy but with consensus (Duile and Bens 2017, 144–146). This consensus was said to be an Indigenous Indonesian way of dealing with politics. Under Suharto, this conservative indigenism "with the spirit of *kekeluargaan* [the nation as family] of organic wholeness, harmony, stillness" (Bourchier 1998, 207) was applied to underpin strategies of demobilization and depoliticization. *Kekeluargaan* and the quest for harmonious consensus through deliberation (*musyawarah dan mufakat*) came to represent indigeneity applied to the whole nation. Although indigeneity had been deployed during the Sukarno era to develop an Indonesian way of overcoming legal dualism and organizing redistribution of land, it was deployed for political demobilization and stability in New Order Indonesia. Suharto's conservative indigenism emphasized order and hierarchy, claiming that they were intrinsic, traditional Indonesian features and values precisely because traditional societies all over the archipelago relied in many cases on social stratification, especially those that were more complex and powerful. In this regard, ideological ways of making history emerged in which the larger (and highly hierarchical) kingdoms of, for instance, Sri Wijaya and Majapahit were said to be the predecessors of modern Indonesia (Lukito 2016, 138–139).

In both populist and conservative indigenism, however, indigeneity was not addressed in the sense of identities of particular marginal groups but as a feature of the Indonesian people as a whole. It was not *adat* as the custom of communities but domesticated ethnicity and regional cultural expressions that became the focus of the cultural politics of the new era, and this had impacts beyond the New Order. Specific cultural characteristics such as architecture, dresses, dances, or weapons were defined for each province. Cultural artifacts, such as textbooks or, most prominently, in the Taman Mini theme park, did not represent the cultural characteristics of a specific ethnic group, although they often embodied the notion of ethnicity. Instead, they represented the culture of a province. People did speak about ethnicity and their ethnic origins but kept it as apolitical as possible. Ethnic symbols were often present within public spaces, but the regime's fear that particular ethnicity would lead to social tensions or even secession led to the removal of ethnicity from official discourses. In other cases, the New Order regime associated traditional communal ways of life with communism. In West Kalimantan, for instance, traditional long houses, a symbol of Dayak ethnicity, were associated with communism and thus banned in the name of modernization and anticommunism (Tanasaldy 2012, 200).

Development and Marginalization in the Suharto Era

Development had been a major concern of Indonesian governments since independence, but in New Order Indonesia, a specific notion of development became a hegemonic, government-driven discourse, coming to be known as the *pembangunan* discourse. Contrary to a Marxist understanding in which development is seen as a process of society's evolution conducted by a certain class (in Indonesian, the term *perkembangan*, literally "flowering," was used for this concept), the New Order *pembangunan* discourse emphasized the state's role and the need for the state to plan and conduct the process. *Pembangunan* was not something all human societies were necessarily heading toward but rather was a political choice requiring economic growth though integration into capitalist world markets, political stability though authoritarian means, and—in the regime's rhetoric—equal access to public resources, such as education, health care, and income opportunities (Arnscheidt 2009, 117–118). During the struggle for independence and in the early years of the independent nation, *pembangunan* denoted a creative process of overcoming old tradition and building a new society in a revolutionary process; however, *pembangunan* under Suharto no longer meant the process of nation-building but became a term used for technocratic development (Heryanto 1988, 10–11).

The apolitical characteristics of *pembangunan* indicate that it was the ideology of a structural coalition; its function was to maintain social stratification through social stability. The ruling class emerged in New Order Indonesia from the upper ranks of the bureaucracy and the military. The bureaucratic authoritarianism they provided lacked a utopian aim; it relied instead on seemingly pragmatic efforts at modernization (King 1982). Budiman (1988) has argued that Indonesia became a bureaucratic capitalist state, lacking a larger domestic bourgeoisie as Indonesia had no bourgeois class worth mentioning before 1965. Thus the New Order state was not simply an instrument of the bourgeoisie, nor did it represent their interests. Rather, it constituted the general interests of the new coalition "by providing political, ideological and even economic conditions for their existence and for the process of capital accumulation" (Robison 1982, 131). Only later did a domestic bourgeoisie emerge, and this was closely related to the military and the bureaucracy (Robison 1986). At this stage, the regime relied heavily on foreign investment in mining industries and agribusiness (mostly rubber to begin with, and later palm oil) and revenues from oil.

The ideology of *pembangunan* was useful for this structural coalition as it blurred the emerging class contradictions and emphasized the unity of a nation striving collectively for a better future. The concept of development carried out by the state in an apolitical way was based on the notion of a center, that is, the cities (especially in Java, South Sumatra, and Bali) on the one hand and the hinterland and outer islands in urgent need of development on the other. This dichotomy was fostered by the regime's terminology. Because the idea of the margins as the other of developed mainstream society set an important condition for the later emergence of Indigenous peoples' movements, it is worth taking a closer look at it. Beginning in the mid-1970s, the government began to apply the concepts of "isolated tribes" (*suku terasing*) and "isolated communities" (*masyarakat terasing*). The term *terasing* (estranged or isolated) was used because it was considered, at least from the regime's point of view, to be free of negative connotations (on this concept, see Koentjaraningrat 1993). The concept did not identify the communities in question as being at fault but depicted a common effort across the nation to incorporate all its citizens into the project of development (Persoon 1998, 297–288). This wording gained its meaning from what these communities had been isolated from and overcoming *terasing*-ness was the aim of the Program of the Development of Social Prosperity of Isolated Communities (*Pembinaan Kesejateraan Sosial Masyarakat Terasing*), carried out by the Department of Social Affairs. Even if it was not meant as a derogative term, the communities in question felt stigmatized as primitive. Another term used by the government and in mainstream discourses was *masyarakat terbelakang* (backward communities; Sombolinggi 2008, 377), stressing the derogative connotation even more.

In the 1990s, some research was done concerning the classification of certain communities as backward or isolated and the program's effects on these communities (e.g., Koentjaraningrat 1993; Li 1999a). In its own publications, the Department of Social Affairs identified concerns about several problems for development, namely nomadic ways of life, animism, and swidden agriculture.

This assessment implied that development required modern housing, following an acknowledged religion (Islam, Catholicism, Protestantism, Hinduism, or Buddhism), and orderly permanent cultivation. It was not until the last years of the New Order era that the term *adat* reentered official political discourse, and in 1999, the program was renamed as the Program for the Development of Social Prosperity of Geographically Isolated Customary Communities (*Pembinaan Kesejateraan Sosial Komunitas Adat Terpencil*; Duncan 2004, 86–87).

The number of people categorized as members of these "isolated communities" or "isolated customary communities" has grown from about 30,000 in the mid-1960s to more than 1.5 million at the end of the New Order era. In the late New Order era, most of these groups were identified in the outer islands, especially in Kalimantan and Papua, whereas some provinces in the center (Bali, Central and East Java, Jakarta, Lampung, and Yogyakarta) had no "isolated groups" (Persoon 1998, 288). The difference between the margins and the center was a difference between culturally backward, primitive people and the average Indonesian citizens said to be the norm (Li 2000, 154). Thus, tribal communities gained discursive difference through the ways they were addressed or interpellated. Precisely because this interpellation was derogative, it constructed passive objects of development. This derogative effect of the *pembangunan* ideology was the necessary condition for the *masyarakat adat* movement to emerge as political subjects: Although marginality was a burden imposed by the state, it later became political capital in the wake of transnational discourses of indigeneity.

Before dealing with the *masyarakat adat* movement emerging in late New Order Indonesia, it is important to look at state practices and laws concerning these communities in Indonesia's margins. The Basic Forestry Law (*Undang Undang No. 5/1967 tentang Ketentuan-Ketentuan Pokok Kehutanan*), one of the first laws of the New Order government, undoubtedly had the biggest consequences for many *adat* communities. The law marked a major change in Indonesia's policies toward rural communities by declaring most of Indonesia's forests as state forests. Fitzpatrick (2007, 138) writes that although the center, the island of Java, was less affected by the law, well over 65 percent of the land in the outer islands fell under the category of state forests and thus under the jurisdiction of the Forestry Department. According to Moniaga (2007, 279), 70 percent of the total land mass of Indonesia was declared state forest; Li (2001, 654) suggests it was as much as 75 percent. In Article 5, the 1967 Forestry Law states that the state controls all forests within the territory of Indonesia and that the state has the authority to designate areas as forests. Only forest land under private ownership was not directly under the jurisdiction of the Forestry Department. All other forests, as state forests, could be leased to companies, for instance, to establish plantations. The Forestry Department also could regulate forest utilization, the management of forest tourism, and community forest programs.

Adat ownership or *adat* institutions were ignored (Moniaga 2007, 279). *Adat* land automatically became state forest when not in permanent use. *Hak ulayat* rights were formally recognized in the Basic Forestry Law, but the law also made it impossible to convert them into property rights of an *adat* community. A general elucidation to Article 2 explains that in cases in which *ulayat* rights have ceased to exist they will not be revived and that it is expected that they will weaken anyway in the future. Moreover, all the rights of *adat* communities were subordinated to national interests. Article 17 of the Basic Forestry Law states that all "implementations of the rights of *adat* law communities as well as the rights of its members and the rights of individuals, to directly or indirectly benefit from forest, as far as these rights are based on provisions in the law and actually still exists, are not allowed to disturb the goals stipulated in this law."

These potential disturbances were specified in the elucidation of this article and included the use of land for livestock, hunting, or harvesting forest products. The elucidation concludes by stating that "it cannot be allowed that *hak ulayat* of a customary law community is used in order to oppose the implementation of public plans of the government, for instance the rejection of large-scale forest clearance for large scale projects or for needs of the *transmigrasi* program and so on."

Bedner and van Huis (2008, 182) conclude that the Basic Forestry Law had an even greater impact on *adat* communities than the Basic Agrarian Law of 1960 because the Forestry Law granted the state the power to specify what land was declared as forest and thus a domain of the state. In practice, *adat* communities' rights to farmland and use because of their customs and needs, for instance, by swiddening, was replaced by a vague recognition of *hak ulayat*, the right to collect forest products. Even this right could be restricted whenever the Forestry Department decided to grant rights of use to another party in the name of development. In some places, communities could no longer subsist on what they were allowed to take out of the forest; they were forced to work in the forestry sector, which, in places like Sumatra and Kalimantan, was increasingly dominated by large companies and large-scale plantations (Cribb 2003, 42). The new configuration of property regimes in rural areas led to a massive amount of original accumulation and, as a side effect, to a workforce of people formerly engaged in subsistence and extended subsistence economies. The New Order government also applied other means to enforce the political economy of *pembangunan* in rural areas. Although *adat* was largely ignored and *ulayat* rights were restricted, nevertheless some efforts were made to incorporate *adat* councils at district levels into centralized hierarchies. More often, however, the repressive state apparatus was used to intimidate rural communities and to force them to comply with the government's policies (Bedner and Arizona 2019, 420). A slight change unfolded, however, at the end of the New Order era. In 1995, the concept of community forestry was introduced. A community forest is a state forest that can be used by a community, but the land and natural resources on it remain the domain of the state. The community receives usage rights for only a certain period of time. This usage does not imply any recognition of *adat* forest claims; however, this concept was more inclusive because it was open to every community, not exclusively *adat* communities (Bakker and Moniaga 2010, 189).

Another law used for the expropriation of *adat* communities during the New Order era was the Mining Law (Law No. 11/1967). This law completely ignored customs and *adat* associated rights. It was designed to make exploitation of natural resources as easy as possible. Only in Article 16(3) did the law specify some restrictions. This article states, among other things, that mining is prohibited in cemeteries and holy places. Because the government did not acknowledge traditional beliefs, holy places had to be associated with one of the officially acknowledged religions. In Article 25(1), the law regulates compensation, but it limits this compensation to what is actually on the land and it does not consider the resulting inability to use the land after it is converted to a mining site. *Ulayat* rights would thus at best serve as compensation only for crops and forest products existing at the time of conversion (Bedner and van Huis 2008, 183).

For Indigenous activists these laws represented a new form of colonialization. In their view, the Indonesian nation, once an agent of anticolonial struggle, had become a colonizer under Suharto. Other New Order laws often criticized in conversations with Indigenous activists include the Regional Government Law (*Undang-Undang No. 55 Tahun 1974 tentang Pokok-Pokok Pemerintahan di Daerah*) and the Village Government Law (*Undang-Undang No. 5 Tahun 1979 tentang Pemerintahan Desa*). Both laws created uniform administrative units in Indonesia at the expense of *adat* institutions (Acciaioli 2007, 308). In Article 3, Law No. 5/1979 replaced all *adat* institutions in village government with a uniform system called *desa* (village). The law also created completely new boundaries between communities previously forming a single *adat* community. Although it was promoted as a genuine Indonesian model for village government, the *desa* system was based on the traditional Javanese model and was alien to other parts of the archipelago. The law contributed significantly to the decline of political *adat* institutions in villages. Because the new administrative institution could not always replace *adat* institutions, it left a political vacuum in some places and weakened this administrative level. It was not until the reform era that the law was abrogated (Antlöv 2003; Bedner and van Huis 2008, 172).

Long before rural communities began to organize under the banner of indigeneity in the late Suharto era, Indonesia had a tradition of rural political struggle as the struggle of politically organized peasants. This history is important to understand the Indigenous movement as a rural political force—not only because indigeneity is sometimes seen as a competing political identity to peasant movements but also because indigeneity can accommodate peasant demands.

Because of the high numbers of organized peasants in political, often left-wing organizations before 1965, especially on Java, Bali, and parts of Sumatra, peasants and their depoliticization were a major concern for the New Order regime. A variety of peasant organizations had been active in pre-1965 Indonesia. The most influential one, the Indonesian Peasant Front (*Barisan Tani Indonesia*, BTI), was associated with the Communist Party and had tried to push for land reform through unilateral actions (*aksi sepihak*) when peasants belonging to the BTI occupied the lands of large private owners. The BTI was outlawed soon after Suharto seized power, but other peasant associations—such as PERTANI (*Persatuan Tani Nasional Indonesia*, the Indonesian Peasants Union, which was associated with Sukarno's Nationalist Party, PNI) or PERTANU (*Persatuan Tani Nadhatul Ulama*, the Peasants' Union of the Islamic *Nahdlatul Ulama*)—were banned and replaced by a single, state-controlled organization. The HKTI (*Himpunan Kerukunan Tani Indonesia*, Indonesian Peasant's Harmony Association) was formally affiliated with the hegemonic party of the New Order, Golkar (*Golongan Karya*, Functional Groups), and ensured Golkar's election success in rural areas. The HKTI was organized top-down by government officials and the military, which was typical of associations in New Order Indonesia, and peasants were often forced to join (Peluso et al. 2008, 383).

This depoliticization was also applied to *adat* communities, which were meant to become part of the rural "floating mass" (*massa mengambang*; on this concept, see Moertopo 2003). Although peasant organizations were actively banned, destroyed, and forced under the umbrella of the HKTI, *adat* movements had not been organized nationwide when the New Order took control and therefore were not a concern for the regime. If, however, *adat* was used to oppose development projects, rural protestors were labeled as communists. Conversely, the New Order also adopted an approach of political containment.

The government granted official acknowledgment of selected *adat* leaders and councils willing to work in line with government policies (Tyson 2010, 32). Through this strategy, the government exploited traditional leadership for its own political capital and incorporated *adat* structures into the state apparatus, whenever possible, to control them.

This economic exploitation and political control of rural communities, which were later organized under the banner of indigeneity, came hand in hand with other forms of marginalization. For instance, traditional beliefs were not recognized. Recognition was offered only in the sense of recognition of traditional beliefs as part of the officially acknowledged religions (usually Hindu, as was the case for the beliefs of the Dayak Ngaju of Kaharingan in central Kalimantan or the Mukhdi Akbar movement in Selayar, South Sulawesi). In mainstream discourses, local religions were perceived as backward, and it was expected that adherents of animist beliefs would sooner or later subscribe to the acknowledged religions. Ideologically, this perception was underpinned by Indonesia's state ideology *Pancasila*, which stresses a divine entity (*Ketuhanan yang Maha Esa*) as its first principle. In practice, this usually meant (and continues to mean) monotheistic beliefs. The religion of each citizen was then documented on their identity card; leaving that column blank raised suspicions of being atheist and therefore a communist threat. Animism or other forms of traditional beliefs was also not an option, and as a result, the number of unaffiliated or self-proclaimed animists declined during the New Order era. In West Kalimantan, for instance, the number of people who declared adherence to "other religions" (the majority very likely to be animist) declined from more than 650,000 people in the 1975 census to about 116,000 in 1980 and to only about 16,000 in 2000 (Tanasaldy 2012, 197).

The Emergence of Indigeneity as a Political Movement

During the New Order, the government rejected the idea that some groups are Indigenous, arguing that all Indonesians (except citizens of Chinese, Indian, and Arab descent) are Indigenous. Marginality became a major marker of Indigenous identities in transnational discourses, however, and the New Order ideology of *pembangunan* contributed greatly to the idea that some groups were marginal both in spatial and cultural-economic senses.

In the 1980s and especially in the 1990s, the expansion of natural resource exploitation in Indonesia's outer islands accelerated. Based on the laws mentioned earlier, the development of Indonesia's margins was carried out through a process of original accumulation. Accordingly, this process separates the producer from the means of production (e.g., land), a process through which "social means of subsistence and of production" are transformed "into capital" (Marx 1983, 711). Dispossessed people, who now became free laborers, created new contradictions in rural Indonesia. When these processes occurred, conflicts between large-scale industries and local communities emerged, frequently involving the repressive state apparatus. In some struggles, the deprived communities emerged as political identities, referring to their tradition, ethnic identity, and *adat*. To give some examples, from the early 1970s onward, local communities at Lake Matano in South Sulawesi began to oppose their forced dispossession by a Canadian mining company by expressing their rights in idioms of nativeness and indigeneity, using the term *orang asli Sorowako* (original people of Sorowako; Robinson 1986). In 1988, Toba Batak communities in North Sumatra begun organizing struggles against a pulp company that had been granted access to the communities' forests (Moniaga 2007, 281). When large-scale conversion of customary forests began to affect Dayak communities, several nongovernmental organizations (NGOs) were founded in Kalimantan to advocate for the affected communities, using Dayak ethnicity as the conceptual foundation of their struggles. In West Kalimantan, for example, the Institut Dayakologi Development and Research was formed in 1990 under the auspices of the Catholic Church (Tanasaldy 2012, 283–284). Pan-Dayak movements emerged in Kalimantan to coordinate the local struggles of Dayak communities against dispossession and to strengthen Dayak identity within these processes (Maunati 2012). With support from environmental and human rights activists, Dayak activists in West Kalimantan also organized the *Lembarga Bela Benua Talino* (Institution for the Defense of the *Talino* Land, with *Talino* meaning "people" in a local Dayak language). In the Moluccas, an Indigenous NGO named *Baileo Maluku* was established, and in Papua, young lawyers founded the *Lembarga Pengkajian dan Pemberdayaan Masyarakat Adat* (Institution for the Assessment and Empowerment of Customary Societies). Indigenous organizations were also established in Nusa Tenggara and in West Sumatra (Moniaga 2007, 282).

Indigeneity became a political resource, and it was not only used in local struggles but eventually also on larger scales. Most important for that process was a meeting in Tanah Toraja, South Sulawesi, in 1993. The Indonesian Forum of the Environment (*Wahana Lingkingan Hidup Indonesia*, WALHI) organized a meeting attended by Indigenous leaders as well as by environmental and human rights activists. This rather informal meeting took place at the private home of a Toraja village chief, Sombolinggi, whose daughter later became the first female national chair of *Aliansi Masyarakat Adat Nusantara* (AMAN). As

Sombolinggi enjoyed moral authority, he successfully kept the police and military at bay. In this meeting, the Network of Defenders of Indigenous Peoples' Rights (*Jaringan Pembela Hak-Hak Masyarakat Adat*, JAPHAMA) was founded (Moniaga 2007, 281). It is no coincidence that environmental activists from the WALHI network helped to establish the nationwide network of Indigenous activists. They drew on the argument of the environmentally noble savage, arguing that Indigenous peoples have a proven ability to maintain sustainable and ecologically friendly ways of life. Although this argument has gained both support and criticism in academia (Hames 2007), support for Indigenous people has grown in the Jakarta activist community as an effective means to challenge the dispossession of rural communities. The concept of Indigenous peoples has not simply been deployed in the form found in international discourses. Rather, Indonesian activists set it into the context of Indonesian history and their particular struggles (Li 2000, 155). At the first meeting of the JAPHAMA network, activists vigorously debated which Indonesian term would be best to refer to "Indigenous peoples." In addition to *masyarakat adat*, some suggested *orang asli* (original people), *pribumi* (sons of the soil), *masyarakat hukum adat* (societies of customary law), or *masyarakat tradisional* (traditional society). *Masyarakat tradisional* had some negative connotations as being nonmodern and thus backward. The term *orang asli* was rejected by Papuans who feared that this term would, in the political context of Papua, evoke the notion of secessionism and therefore could be politically dangerous. The activists also agreed that *pribumi* was too general given that it referred to all Indonesians not of foreign descent—after all, the connotation of *pribumi* was the very reason why the government had rejected the concept of Indigenous people in Indonesia. *Masyarakat hukum adat*, as also used in laws, was seen as too much a state idiom (and, as I will explain, Indigenous activists' first strategies were aimed at stressing their difference from the state). Moreover, the scope of the law was too narrow: *Adat* was much more than law to the activists as it also included values, political institutions, land tenure, and other domains of human culture. Thus, the activists chose *masyarakat adat* because the communities in question had begun to use this term to refer to themselves, and it was politically acceptable in the New Order context (Moniaga 2007, 281–282).

AMAN activists also stress that the term *masyarakat adat* was chosen to counter the stigmatization of the communities in question as *suku terasing* (estranged tribe), *masyarakat perambah hutan*, *peladang liar* (derogative terms for swidden cultivators), *masyarakat primitive*, or *penghambat pembangunan* (opponents of development; AMAN n.d., 1). Although activists stressed that they aimed to counter derogative notions of Indigenous communities, they also relied on the state-driven notion of marginality. Moreover, distinctiveness between *masyarakat adat* and mainstream society was crucial. In a working definition of *masyarakat adat* that later also became the basis for the AMAN definition, the activists defined *masyarakat adat* as social groups that possess ancestral origins in a specific geographic region (referring to the principle of Indigenous people as a place-bound social entity) and possessing a distinct system of social values, ideology, economy, politics, culture, and society (Acciaioli 2007, 299).

INDIGENEITY AND THE INDONESIAN NATION II

After Suharto

In chapter 1, I outlined the dialectical relation between *adat* and the Indonesian nation until the end of the so-called New Order. In this chapter, I shed light on the *adat* movement after Suharto. Although the Indigenous movement was constituted through the political-economic contradictions of the Suharto regime, these contradictions did not disappear after Suharto, but the new political framework instead required new strategies and presented new opportunities as well as challenges for the Indigenous movement. By discussing the consolidation of the Indigenous movement, state responses, and new forms of activism and engagement, I conclude that *adat* activism in the post-Suharto era was initially characterized by a confrontational approach that nonetheless always stressed indigeneity as part of the Indonesian nation. In particular, during Jokowi's first election campaign, *Aliansi Masyarakat Adat Nusantara* (AMAN) changed its strategy. Direct involvement in political campaigns on different levels became common and institutional activism occasionally proved to be successful. It soon became clear, however, that the Jokowi administration would neglect Indigenous interests in favor of the interests of the political-economic elite. With disappointment, AMAN then again applied a rather confrontational approach on the national level, which not only made possible new alliances with other progressive organizations but also continued institutional activism, especially in the regencies. Regencies are an administrative level that became highly important because Indigenous communities now have to seek recognition from these regencies before they can apply for land titles. This shows a new unfolding of the Indigenous dialectics: Recognition, for

Indigenous communities and the Indigenous movement, depends on the recognition of the state as well as the conceptualization of *adat* communities as both distinct from the state, its land tenure, and its administration, and, simultaneously, as part of the Indonesian nation.

The Consolidation of the *Adat* Movement

With the downfall of the Suharto regime in May 1998, the thirty-two-year authoritarian New Order came to an end. The new liberal political framework that was established enabled many groups to organize freely and voice their demands in public. Indonesia had not been as free since the years before Sukarno's so-called guided democracy was introduced in 1957 and this new freedom had a tremendous impact on civil society. In the first years of *reformasi*, the reform era, political parties and nongovernmental organizations (NGOs) proliferated. Also, freedom of the press enabled activists to gather more information, including from Indonesia's periphery where the dispossession of land continued. In terms of the political economy, however, parts of the oligarchy were removed from political positions immediately after Suharto resigned, but they remained untouched in terms of economic power and overall influence. Their networks remained intact, as did their business conglomerates, and soon they managed to reestablish their power in the formally democratic Indonesia. Another important continuity in *reformasi* Indonesia was the anticommunist legacy of the New Order regime. Other political identities, such as Indigenous peoples, happened to be more effective when seeking support and funding from international donor organizations (Affif and Lowe 2007, 90). Although they did not rely on class, they nonetheless managed to articulate class-based contradictions in rural Indonesia.

In March 1999, less than a year after the downfall of the Suharto regime, Indigenous activists from various provinces met in Jakarta for the first AMAN congress. Seeking recognition by the state was the leitmotif of this congress. Therefore, the activists demanded the abolishment of all derogative terms that they viewed as constructions of the authoritarian New Order *pembangunan* regime, a regime many of the activists remembered as a colonizing force with no respect for their traditions, culture, and rights. Derogative exonyms from the New Order era that the activists opposed included "wild swiddeners" (*peladang liar, penebang liar, peladang berpindah*), "isolated/estranged tribes" (*suku terasing*), "primitive communities" (*masyarakat primitif*), "opponents of development" (*penghambat pembangunan*), and "susceptible communities" (*masyarakat rentan*). The term *masyarakat adat* was chosen as their self-ascription and defined as "communities that live on the basis of their hereditary ancestral land in a specific *adat* territory, that possess sovereignty over their land and natural resources, whose social and cultural life is ordered by *adat* law, and whose *adat* institutions ensure their enduring social life [as *masyarakat adat*]" (AMAN, n.d.; author's translation).

Note that the activists used definitions from the state-driven *pembangunan* discourse as the common base of what they rejected. The notion of sovereignty (*kedaulatan*) was meant as an oppositional stance against the state. Activists did not seek recognition as part of the official state structures but in the form of a sovereignty parallel to, although not against, the state and as an integral part of the Indonesian nation. They referred to Indonesia's national motto of *Bhinneka Tunggal Ika* (usually translated as "unity in diversity"), arguing that Indonesia should be a "plural state" (*negara majemuk*). Thus, *kedaulatan*, in this context, did not mean state sovereignty but sovereignty within the state. It is a complementary rather than an exclusive notion of sovereignty. Sovereignty as advocated by AMAN activists, is concerned with the internal order of local affairs and especially with the use of local natural resources (Acciaioli 2007, 303–305).

Although AMAN did not advocate for secessionism among ethnic groups, the notion of communities' sovereignty over natural resources nevertheless challenged the sovereignty of the state as it suggested alternative orders to that provided by the legal framework. This notion of opposition was also dominant in the famous proclamation "if the state will not recognize us, then we will not recognize the state" (Moniaga 2007, 275). This statement reveals the dialectical relationship between Indigenous peoples and the state as two distinct entities. Although the sentence is formulated negatively, the notion of *masyarakat adat* emerges through the possibility of a negation of the state. It emerges as a political subject with the ability to recognize and to deny recognition—similar to the state. The statement also means that the state served as a condition for the emergence of the political subject of *masyarakat adat*. In the proclamation, the state and *masyarakat adat* are constitutive of each other (Tamma and Duile 2020, 277). These complementary claims of sovereignty, on the one hand, and the challenge to state sovereignty over natural resources, on the other, as well as mutual (non-)recognition, marked AMAN's beginning.

In September 2003, AMAN held its second congress in Lombok. By that time, AMAN had 927 registered communities, out of which 777 had been verified as members. In the second congress, AMAN's goal was, among others, to strengthen its regional activism and to broaden its alliance with other prodemocratic groups. This second congress emphasized practical problems and implementing programs (Moniaga 2007, 283). As Greg Acciaioli (2007) has argued, the second congress marked a transition from mere calls for acknowledgment to pragmatic strategies. A leaflet from the organizing committee demanded the "[facilitation of] dialogues and negotiations among national political interests."

(Acciaioli 2007, 295). It also called for the formulation of Indigenous peoples' positions and perspectives on new relationships between them and the state to achieve sovereignty and autonomy, to improve Indigenous peoples' welfare, and to build alliances with other progressive and democratic organizations on both the national and international levels. This congress represented a more outward orientation for the movement (Acciaioli 2007, 296). These aims were important in the following congresses in 2007 in Pontianak, West Kalimantan; in 2012 in Tobelo, North Malukku; and in 2017 in Tanjung Gusta, North Sumatra. Engagement with political actors became increasingly relevant, especially after the 2013 decision by the Constitutional Court that ruled that *adat* forests were not state forest. It was at the third national congress in 2007, however, when AMAN opened the way for collaboration with the state (Arizona et al. 2019, 492), further shifting from an oppositional to a collaborative approach.

AMAN activists thus engaged in negotiations and political processes to implement the *adat* forest scheme, a process I analyze further in detail in chapter 6. In terms of membership, the organization grew enormously. In 2018, AMAN had 2,366 verified member communities and claimed to represent about eighteen million Indigenous individuals, which made it the biggest national Indigenous organization worldwide. AMAN in 2020 had 21 regional bodies (*pengurus wilyah*) and 117 local bodies (*pengurus daerah*) all over the archipelago. It has a head body (*pengurus besar*) at the national level. The head body consists of the general secretary (*sekretaris jendral*) and the national assembly (*dewan AMAN nasional*), all elected on the national congresses. These institutions coordinate AMAN's implementation strategies on the national level. In addition to the general secretary, an institution called the permanent executive committee (*pengurus harian*) represents organizational, political, economic, and cultural issues. AMAN also has wing organizations (*organisasi sayap*): the *Adat* Youth Front of the Archipelago (*Barisan Pemuda Adat Nusantara*), the Federation of Indigenous Women (*Persekutuan Perempuan Adat Nusantara*), and the Archipelago's Indigenous Peoples' Defense Committee (*Perhimpunan Pembela Masyarakat Adat Nusantara*), which is concerned with legal issues.

State Responses

Before analyzing AMANs' struggle within the context of the Indigenous paradox and its ideological content, it is necessary to shed light on the laws concerning Indigenous communities issued after Suharto's downfall, as they highlight both a continuity as well as some slight changes in the approach taken toward Indigenous peoples.

Shortly after the downfall of Suharto, the Basic Forestry Law was amended in 1999. The new law mentions the rights of *masyarakat hukum adat* in Article 67, paragraph 1, in which it is said that *masyarakat hukum adat* have the right to collect forest products for their daily needs and to manage the forest in accordance with their *adat* laws. These communities also have the right to receive assistance to improve their prosperity. Because farming is still not allowed, the rights of use are limited in the amended version. It is interesting how *masyarakat hukum adat* is defined in an Elucidation to Article 67:

> *Masyarakat hukum adat* are recognized when in reality they fulfill, among others, these criteria: a. the community still exists as a law community (*recht-gemeenshap* [Dutch for "law community"; author's translation]), b. there are political *adat* institutions, c. there is a clearly defined *adat* law territory, d. *adat* law institutions are still respected by the community, e. the community still collects forest products in the surrounding forest area for their daily needs. (author's translation)

According to this definition, land already taken from *adat* communities and converted to plantations or mining sites, for instance, cannot by definition be land to which *adat* communities have a right because the communities no longer depend on products from this land. Also, self-definition, a crucial criterion in international discourses and demanded by AMAN, is not mentioned. Most important, in Article 5, the amended law still states that the state controls the forest and the natural resources within it.

Also in 1999, a ministerial regulation was issued by the head of the National Land Agency (*Kepala Badan Pertanahan Nasional*), the Minister of Land Affairs. In this regulation, the *adat* law communities and *ulayat* rights mentioned in the Basic Agrarian Law were defined. An *adat* law community is said to be a "group of people bounded by its *adat* legal order as common members of a legal association because of a common domicile or on the basis of descent." In terms of *ulayat* rights, the first paragraph of the regulation states that

> *ulayat* rights and those rights resembling them of *adat* law communities (. . .) concern the authority that according to *adat* law a certain customary law community enjoys over a certain territory which forms the living environment for its members to make use of its natural resources, including land, within that territory, in order to survive and make a living. This authority arises from the physical as well as from the spiritual bond, inherited from generation to generation and uninterrupted, between the customary law community and the mentioned territory. (author's translation)

These definitions draw heavily on international discourses on Indigenous peoples in which the relation between Indigenous peoples and their land is emphasized. It still contains the restriction that the bond between the *adat* law community and their land has to be uninterrupted. The criterion of an enduring relation between the community and the land is also mentioned in Article 2 of the regulation, and Article 3 explicitly states that *ulayat* rights, once abandoned, cannot be revived. As Adriaan Bedner and Stijn van Huis (2008, 186) notice, however, this regulation was "the first serious sign of an Indonesian government's willingness to recognize *adat* communities and their rights"—at least as long as they still exist. Note also that this ministerial regulation was a very early example of state–Indigenous activist interaction. Despite AMAN's provocative threat that they would not recognize the state if the state did not recognize Indigenous peoples, the Minister of Agrarian Affairs at that time, Hasan Basri Duri, was present at this first AMAN congress in 1999. Because he was accused of being responsible for land dispossession, the ministerial regulation could be seen as a response to this criticism.

Another important step during the period immediately after the New Order era was when the *Majelis Permusyawaratan Rakyat* (MPR, the People's Consultative Assembly), Indonesia's constitution-making body, adopted Decree IX/2001 on Agrarian Reform and Natural Resource Management. The decree states that an agrarian reform must respect, recognize, and protect *adat* communities' rights and it is therefore not in line with the approach of conditional recognition as outlined in the Basic Agrarian Law. In the process of amending the constitution between 1999 and 2002, however, *adat* communities did not receive special attention.

The 2013 ruling of the Constitutional Court is often mentioned as a milestone for Indigenous peoples' struggle in Indonesia. In its review of the Forestry Law, the court ruled that *adat* forests could no longer be simply a part of state forests. In contrast, the judges also confirmed the validity of Article 18B(2) of the Constitution and its conditional acknowledgment of *adat* (Bedner and Arizona 2019, 424). The ruling of the Constitutional Court demanded that "state forest . . . does not include customary forest . . . and customary forest is stipulated insofar [as] the Indigenous peoples concerned remain in existence and their existence is acknowledged" (The Constitutional Court of Indonesia Decision No. 35, quoted from Affif and Rachman 2019, 459–460).

Although the Constitutional Court's decision is portrayed as a major achievement, this is only one side of the coin. It has undoubtedly initiated a process of recognition of *adat* forests. Customary forest, *hutan adat*, was given the category of "forest subject to rights" (*hutan hak*), instead of the old category as "state forest' (*hutan negara*) (Rachman and Siscawati 2016). At the same time, this decision still limits Indigenous communities' sovereignty. Recognition is possible only when it coincides with the interests of the state and in accordance with a judgment regarding the current situation of the respective community, meaning that they have not been subject to the social changes of either modernization (which would nullify the very existence of *adat*) or dispossession (which would nullify the continuity of *hak ulayat*).

In my conversations with Indigenous activists in Jakarta and Bogor, it was often mentioned how important countermapping strategies are as a means to make Indigenous land claims. In 2010, AMAN established the Agency for *Adat Territory Registration (Badan Registrasi Wilayah Adat*, BRWA). The agency was intended to be a means for their countermapping strategy. The idea of claiming *adat* territory has been part of AMAN's strategy from the very beginning; however, in the wake of transnational discourses about climate change and forest conservation, these strategies gained in prominence. The discourse on Indigenous peoples as forest defenders led to ideological conjunctures with large donor agencies such as, for instance, the Ford Foundation and the McArthur Foundation. In 2014, AMAN succeeded in persuading the national REED+ Agency to recognize the mapping conducted by the BRWA thus far (Affif and Rachman 2019, 458–459).

In 2014, a new village law was issued that recognized *adat* villages. In Article 6, Law 8/2014 states that "villages consist of villages or *adat* villages (*desa adat*)." AMAN engaged in the lawmaking process, creating a draft for a law on the recognition and protection of Indigenous peoples in 2011. Because they believed that such a law would be impossible to realize because of the resistance of influential companies with economic interests in *adat* territories, AMAN pragmatically engaged in a process of negotiation over the new village law (Vel et al. 2017, 459–460). AMAN, however, was eventually disappointed with the new law, which provided rather symbolic recognition and hardly offered a new means for opposing land dispossession (Bedner and Arizona 2019, 423). In terms of recognition by the state, the law paved the way for another option beside the acknowledgment of *adat* forest, namely recognition as *adat* villages (Arizona et al. 2019, 490).

Institutional Activism and State–Indigenous Peoples Relations

Yance Arizona et al. (2019, 501–502) argue that the recognition AMAN has achieved in post-Suharto Indonesia is the result of a development within the *adat* movement. Although the movement applied an oppositional strategy at first, it changed this strategy as it became increasingly involved in the networks of international funding organizations. Through their institutional apparatus, AMAN was incorporated into forestry management, biodiversity, and conservation projects. Within these projects, strategic partnerships became crucial, and legal recognition of *adat* forests became the most important goal of this network. As Tania Li (2016) has argued, this has led to an approach focusing on short-term projects rather than on a wider political strategy. This critique against projectization states that governance in rural Indonesia is now mostly executed in terms of projects that are limited to a certain period of time, are funded by hegemonic actors, and usually consist of short-term technical intervention. These projects are concerned with specific problems and thus neglect wider structural issues that reproduce social inequality. Indigenous activism has become increasingly involved in this framework of projectization (see also van de Muur et al. 2019, 387–388). When discussing this issue with AMAN activists in the Bogor and Jakarta offices, they found this critique unfair, stressing that they are still concerned with broader issues. They stressed the importance of bringing "real change" and specified that this could not be done with theoretical, abstract analysis. In this regard, they also mentioned some social scientists who sought AMAN's help, but they did not find their critical work helpful. It was "too abstract" and lacked empathy with Indigenous peoples' actual struggle. Conversely, they highlighted the importance of engaged researchers working together with AMAN activists on concrete cases. To prove that change is possible, they have to engage in projects. In their view, projects might enable people to imagine larger change.

The recognition of *adat* forest had been a concern of AMAN's from its very beginning. According to claims by AMAN activists, about forty million hectares (30 percent of the forest the state claimed as state forest) are *adat* forests (Butler 2013). In comparison, this is almost the size of the state of California. Joko Widodo, president from 2014 to 2024 and commonly refered to as "Jokowi" in Indonesia, triggered hope among Indigenous activists when he declared during the election campaign in 2014 that it was his aim to distribute up to 12.7 million hectares to Indigenous peoples. Later, this aim was downscaled to 4.39 million hectares. By February 2019, however, only 28,289 hectares had been acknowledged as belonging to Indigenous peoples (Arumingtyas 2019). When I talked to AMAN activists in 2019 and 2022, many expressed their disappointment about the slow process, but the activists were far from abandoning the path of cooperation AMAN had chosen since 2007.

AMAN also reached out to Indonesian academicians willing to support their struggle. One such engaged academic is Suraya Affif, an anthropologist at Universitas Indonesia in Depok. Along with Noer Fauzi Rachman, an AMAN activist who engages with political actors, she published a paper on institutional activism for *adat* forest rights (Affif and Rachman 2019). It is worth outlining the way this process works on the national level, because I later examine an example of such processes on a local scale. According to Affif and Rachman, engagement by institutional activists has occurred at a political conjuncture based on three conditions: First, the Jokowi government paved the way for new politicians willing to work together with institutional activists—this occurred during the election campaign in 2013/2014 when politicians and the Jokowi camp tried to incorporate activists into their campaign. Second, a conscious strategy within the Indigenous movement was crucial. Third, coalitions between activists and state officials ensured the—at least symbolic—success of the Indigenous movement when on December 30, 2016, some *adat* communities officially received their *adat* forests in a ceremony at the state palace.

Under the government of Susilo Bambang Yudhoyono lobbying was difficult and AMAN's demands were usually ignored, whereas Jokowi's approach to the electoral campaign opened new opportunities. In 2013, politicians from Jokowi's camp began to embed both scholars and activists into their campaign. In exchange for their support of Jokowi, the activists and academics had an input on the design of the electoral program and the visions outlined in it. The outcome was the *Nawacita* (Program of Nine National Priorities). Although these guidelines were rather general, some of the nine points had implications for policy regarding Indigenous peoples. Point 4, for instance, outlines the aim to develop Indonesia from the margins by strengthening rural areas and villages within the framework of the unitary state. Point 5 mentions the intention to conduct land reform, and point 9 emphasizes diversity (*kebhinnekaan*), a major concern for the acknowledgment of *adat* communities as particular entities within a plural state. The *Nawacita* program, however, also outlines some main ideological conjunctures of capitalist economy, development, and patriotism. In its detailed version, the *Nawacita* contained items from AMAN's agenda, namely the aim to review all land-related laws to ensure that they align with the 2001 MPR decree, the implementation of the 2013 Constitutional Court ruling on *adat* forests, the deployment of the new village law to strengthen *adat* villages, the intention to resolve conflicts on *adat* land, the establishment of a special government agency for accelerating the recognition of *adat* communities' rights, and, perhaps most important, the intention to draft and pass a law on *adat* communities that would unify existing laws and give legal certainty to Indigenous peoples (Bedner and Arizona 2019, 424).

AMAN strongly supported the Jokowi-Kalla campaign, and after success in the election, AMAN activists became involved in the formulation of the

Mid-Term National Development Plan (*Rencana Pembangunan Jangka Menengah Nasional*) in 2014. A success for AMAN, the plan contained a commitment to an agrarian reform, under which *adat* communities would also be granted land rights. To implement this plan, AMAN activists had to cooperate mainly with two ministries, namely the Ministry of Environment and Forestry and the Ministry of Agrarian Affairs and Spatial Planning. In terms of the Ministry of Environment and Forestry, cooperation between institutional activists and state officials was quite strong. The new minister, Siti Nurbaya Bakar, even recruited activists from environmental and Indigenous NGOs, either as direct advisers or as staff in a new forum, the Social Forestry and Environmental Partnership. Within this forum, a special task force was instituted to implement the *adat* forest scheme. From early 2016, AMAN activists took the general director of the Social Forestry and Environmental Partnership to field visits where he met *adat* communities. Eventually, the minister visited *adat* communities proposed by the Social Forestry and Environmental Partnership forum.

The activists also faced bureaucratic obstacles. In particular, AMAN activists rejected the proposal that *adat* communities must be acknowledged by regencies (*kabupaten*) before they could apply for *adat* forests. The activists feared that involving the regencies would significantly slow down the processes of recognition. Eventually, the activists agreed to the regulation after the minister approved the recognition of the *adat* forest of the Wana Posangke communities in return (on the Wana group in Central Sulawesi, see also Grumblies 2013). This forest was a delicate case because it was partly within a state nature reserve area. The activists successfully created a precedent, but the price was that state institutions on a local level gained much say in terms of *adat* recognition (Affif and Rahman 2019, 464). In certain ways, this allocation of procedural competencies to the regencies reflects Indonesia's decentralized political features. Law 1999 No. 22 gave local governments great autonomy over crucial services, such as public health, education, and, most important, local economic development and environmental management (Hadiz 2004, 707).

The first material outcome of the institutional activists' engagement was the acknowledgment of nine *adat* forests in a ceremony at the state palace on December 30, 2016. The ceremony represents an important symbol of recognition. State representatives sit together with Indigenous peoples expressing their indigeneity through traditional dress. This staged cooperation between AMAN and the state continued. On March 22, 2017, for instance, Jokowi again met representatives from Indigenous communities in the state palace. He greeted them in nine local languages, expressing Indonesia's diversity just as it is always stressed by AMAN. On this occasion, he also mentioned the proposed law on

Indigenous peoples (*UU Masyarakat Adat*), once again triggering hope among the activists that the law would be issued soon.

Overall, the process of Indigenous land rights' recognition was rather slow in Jokowi's first term in office. After the initial recognition of the land titles of nine communities with a total population of about 5,700 individuals, encompassing approximately thirteen thousand hectares (Affif and Rachman 2019, 454), in October 2017, the land titles of nine more communities were acknowledged. Once again, this was staged in a ceremony at the state palace. By that time, however, 16,400 hectares had been acknowledged while AMAN had mapped 1.9 million hectares belonging to 607 Indigenous communities in total (Gokkon 2017). The process continued slowly. By May 2019, forty-nine customary forest ownership certificates had been issued, resulting in the recognition of approximately 22,193 hectares of *adat* forest (Khafi 2019). Another source, the NGO Mongabay, has identified 28,286 hectares of recognized *adat* forest (Arumingtyas 2019). That was far below activists' expectations, but the process of recognition nonetheless continued. In late 2022, 105 *adat* forests had been officially acknowledged and, for the first time, this acknowledgment included some forest in the easternmost part of Papua (Keagop 2022).

Conjunctures of Capitalist State Ideologies and Indigenous Recognition

As a main obstacle for the institutional activists, Affif and Rachman (2019, 465) have identified the ideological background of the minister of Agrarian Affairs and Spatial Planning, Sofyan Djalil. Support from this ministry is crucial. Whereas the Ministry of Forestry and Environment designate forests as *adat* forests, the Ministry of Agrarian Affairs and Spatial Planning is responsible for issuing communal land titles. The ministry can slow down processes and even deny final approval of the designated land. Affif and Rachman refer to an interview with *Tempo* magazine to explain the minister's ideology. According to the interview, Sofyan Djalil favors allocating land to corporations because they are believed to be capable of better, more professional management given that they can draw on personnel and technologies. Rather than supporting *adat* communities, the minister promoted individual land title programs for rural poor populations and corporate responsibility policies. In his argument, higher productivity in the industrial-agrarian sector directly results in greater benefit to the public. In general, the minister is skeptical of land reform, and he warns that this type of reform will lead to lower productivity. He declares:

"Do not think that allocating land to the people is always good. This is not for sure. If the land in the hands of the people is not productive, we will take it" (Maulana 2019, author's translation).

The state as the legitimate owner of the land, which ensures the most effective use of land for the benefit of the people, is a widespread ideology in Indonesian politics. This argument is often applied to connect the interests of a specific class to those of the nation. In a televised discussion between Jokowi and Prabowo before the 2019 election, the ideological background of the two candidates became clear. Although they agreed on the notion of productiveness, they disagreed when it came to the question of whether the state should maintain full control over land. Although Prabowo expressed views similar to those of Djalil, Jokowi expressed a rather entrepreneurial ideology: With legalized land titles, Indigenous communities and peasants can have better access to capital. That is not the whole picture, however. To describe the ideology Jokowi represents, it is important to take a closer look at his version of developmentalism. Eve Warburton (2017) has analyzed Jokowi's new developmentalism, which emerged during his first years in office, consequently superseding his earlier progressive approaches. Jokowi's new developmentalism is twofold: On the one hand, he and his government embrace neoliberal, market-oriented policies and focus on debureaucratization and deregulation. On the other hand, Jokowi sees the state as the driving force behind economic growth. The state sector, with its state-owned enterprises as well as state-driven infrastructure programs, should lay a foundation for growth within the private sector (Warburton 2017, 306). Warburton also shows that Jokowi did not make any attempt to pursue an anticorruption agenda, to counter oligarchic structures, or to challenge the patronage distribution of resources. A shift from the rather populist, propoor approach that characterized Jokowi's campaign and first months in office toward a developmentalist agenda of growth occurred in 2016 as a result of Jokowi's consolidation of political power. At this time, Jokowi and his administration also began to abandon AMAN and engage merely in token recognition of small amounts of land rather than in large-scale land reform. In terms of Indigenous policies, this approach leads to contradictions: Should land be a domain of the state and allocated to private and state enterprises—in accordance with what Warburton (2017, 309) has called the "statist-nationalist-orientation"—or should Indigenous communities be supported by the state to unleash their potential entrepreneurial abilities?

The view that Indigenous communities should be supported by the state to conduct economic activities is, for instance, in line with that of the minister of Environment and Forestry who cooperated with the institutional activists and expressed her support for Indigenous communities, declaring that they can also be productive. In an interview with *Tempo* magazine, Siti Nurbaya Bakar stated that

> *adat* communities are pushed to get economic support. We will assist them to open enterprises, and these enterprises will not only concern timber and non-timber forest products, but also genetic resources from plants which have so far not been included in economic calculations. I have already signed the ministerial regulation on the conservation of local knowledge. This will for sure bring an economic effect for *adat* communities. (Tempo 2017; author's translation)

In accordance with liberal arguments from transnational discourses, the minister also said that Indigenous peoples have proven that they manage forests well. For Siti Nurbaya Bakar, *masyarakat adat* are forest defenders with traditional rules of sustainability.

In public, AMAN stresses its ideological conjunctures with politicians, such as Jokowi or Siti Nurbaya Bakar. A good example is an interview with Abdon Nababan in 2015. At that time, Nababan was AMAN secretary-general and the organization had just begun to strengthen its ties with the newly elected Jokowi government through their institutional activists. At the East Asian World Economic Forum in Indonesia, Abdon Nababan outlined the role of Indigenous communities in the economy:

> Nawacita, the President's nine priorities, highlights the need for protection of people's lands, especially indigenous peoples. It even emphasizes that the government is committed to continuing the moratorium on granting new forest use licenses. Indigenous peoples need to be protected. So starting now, every new investment should consider the rights of the indigenous peoples. This will also benefit the businessman since their investment will be more secure if violations of the rights of indigenous peoples are absent. Transformation of the oil palm industry should also refer to Nawacita commitments: people-based economy, recognition and protection of indigenous peoples' territorial rights and effective local governance, corruption eradication and a moratorium on new licenses until the One Map policies are in place. Production increases in the palm oil industry should not only happen in company plantations, but also within people's agroforestry areas. To boost production nationally there should be a program developed and managed in a systematic, structured and massive way. It must ensure a bio-regional approach to the development of the palm oil industry in

Indonesia. In this case there should be no more expansion of palm monoculture plantations at the expense of the natural landscape. In this approach, production increases are obtained based on recognition of the land rights of indigenous peoples through BUMMA (enterprises owned by indigenous communities). (Nababan 2015)

Abdon Nababan's argument drew on the concept of an economy in which both big business and Indigenous communities as entrepreneurs can coexist. This argument relies on the ideology of a society without conflicts as propagated during the New Order era. In this regard, Nabadan's argument is apolitical because it acknowledges the overcoming of contradictions within the given capitalist framework. This ideological conjuncture is an important precondition for AMAN's institutional activism and for the success they have achieved so far. It also limits space, however, for utopian approaches and broader alternatives of common struggles with other marginalized groups, as I argue later.

In 2020, AMAN launched a coalition to put pressure on the government to issue the Law on Indigenous Communities, the *UU Masyarakat Adat*. A total of thirty organizations from civil society, such as the Indonesian Forum of the Environment (*Wahana Lingkungan Hidup Indonesia*, WALHI) and the Indonesian Legal Aid Help Foundation (*Yayasan Lembarga Bantuan Hukum Indonesia*, YLBHI), joined the coalition to bring the government and AMAN into dialog. In a discussion session named *Talkshow RUU Masyarakat Adat* (Talkshow about the proposed law on indigenous communities), Abdon Nababan and other AMAN activists met with representatives from ministries, such as the Ministry of the Interior, the Ministry for Agrarian and Spatial Issues, and the Coordinating Ministry for the Development of Human Resources and Culture. These ministries were crucial because the further processing of the bill depended on their support. During the *Talkshow RUU Masyarakat Adat*, Abdon Nababan argued for the importance of the Indigenous peoples' law within the frame of the proposed *UU Cipta Kerja*, the controversial Law on Job Creation, also known by its former name *UU Omnibus Law* (which was, unlike the Law on Indigenous Communities, passed in 2020). The government argued that the Law on Job Creation was necessary to create sufficient new jobs for the young population and to raise foreign and domestic investment. To achieve these goals, the law aims to reduce regulatory requirements for business permits as well as processes of land acquisition.

Although Abdon Nababan saw the potential for further conflict, he did not entirely condemn the Law on Job Creation. In his statements, he pointed to the law's potential to create conflicts in the agrarian sector, therefore highlighting the need for legal security for Indigenous communities. Therefore, he argued that a law on *masyarakat adat* could even "save the nation." With a law on Indigenous peoples, "not only will the state/nation (*negara*) be present in the middle of the Indigenous communities," but also would ensure that the Indigenous communities would be present in the state/nation (AMAN 2020a; author's translation).

More critical stances exists within AMAN, however, especially after AMAN's relationship with the Jokowi government cooled down. As AMAN pursued its agenda of institutional activism in Jokowi's first term in office, it seldom engaged in wider alliances with other progressive organizations. That began to change during Jokowi's first term, and in September 2020, AMAN launched a political manifesto on agrarian reform with other progressive organizations. AMAN joined the National Committee for Agrarian Reform (*Komite Nasional Pembaruan Agraria*), an umbrella organization joined by WALHI, the Congress of Indonesian Unions Alliance (*Kongres Aliansi Serikat Buruh Indonesia*, KASBI), and the National Student League for Democracy (*Liga Mahasiswa Nasional untuk Demokrasi*, LMND), a left-wing student organization. The manifesto outlined that the continuation of the national revolution for independence and democratization, as well as realizing the prosperity of the nation and social justice for all Indonesian people, a principle of *Pancasila*, would be determined largely by the success of implementing an agrarian reform. This reform is said to be a constitutional and legal obligation, and the Basic Agrarian Law of 1960 as well as the Indonesian Constitution are mentioned as the legal frameworks of the proposed agrarian reform. The nationalistic thrust of the manifesto is underpinned by references to anti-imperialism and anticapitalism: The proposed omnibus law is said to make land, water, and natural resources once again the object of international capitalist exploitation—that is, neocolonialism/neoimperialism. The manifesto thus states that the proposed law would benefit only foreign investment and the domestic oligarchy. It calls for "cooperation between all sections of society in order to ensure that Indonesia breaks free of the shackles of capitalism" (AMAN 2020b; author's translation). The alternative to capitalism and oligarchy, however, remains vague in the manifesto. The system of liberal capitalism should be displaced by a system of mutual help and assistance (*gotong royong*), which must be rooted in local wisdom and local agrarian and maritime culture. (AMAN 2020b; author's translation). In August 2020, Rukka Sombolinggi, Abdon Nababan's successor, called the proposed omnibus law a "kind of a predator of Indigenous territories," adding that Indonesia "butchers itself with the omnibus law" (Sudirman 2020, author's translation). The Indonesian parliament issued the bill in October 2020. Trade unions, environmental NGOS, and also AMAN protested vociferously. This law revealed the homogeneity of Indonesian politics because all fractions within the parliament either supported or acquiesced to the law. In contrast, a large civil society coalition was against the law (Lane 2021). AMAN's stance, in this regard, has revealed that both cooperation with state institutions as well as possible alliances with other progressive forces are possible within the ideology of being Indigenous.

Class and Indigeneity: A Common Struggle?

The joint struggle against the omnibus law made visible the potential for wider alliances wherein AMAN could engage with leftist organizations on a common anticapitalist language. The relationship between the Indigenous movement and other class-based movements, however, is complex. As a cultural rather than a class identity, the Indigenous movement nonetheless emerged because of economic dispossession and as a means to make class-related issues in rural Indonesia visible. Already in 2003, AMAN suggested building up alliances with other progressive and democratic organizations (Acciaioli 2007, 296) as a step in the direction of a common struggle that might express class-based concerns. The aim of this coalition was rather to bring up Indigenous people's aspirations as part of a larger movement and less an expression of desire for universal redistribution. In the following, I outline the wider context of the proposed agrarian reform in Indonesia and situate AMAN within this frame to help us to understand how far the issue of class was addressed in the Indigenous movement's strategy. Despite the possibility of organizing a joint movement based on class, this opportunity has been missed so far. Thus, the general political aim of an agrarian reform that would reshape production and ownership structures in rural Indonesia has largely fallen out of focus.

In the struggle against the Suharto regime in the 1990s, independent peasant organizations and NGOs emerged. On the one hand, NGOs concerned with rural development, such as Bina Desa or Mitra Tani, operated in rural New Order Indonesia and occasionally took critical stances regarding the regime. Their ideological outlook was strongly influenced by productivist and developmentalist approaches, however, and they aimed at increasing productivity rather than addressing structural inequality and issues of political economy. On the other hand, progressive and radical NGOs, such as the YLBHI, got involved in land rights disputes that arose from the 1980s onward. Wider alliances between urban-based activists—occasionally with a concept of class in mind—and peasants emerged. The 1990s saw a proliferation of independent peasant unions, building ties on a national level with leftist organizations. The National Peasant Union (*Serikat Tani Nasional*), for instance, was associated with the leftist student organization Students in Solidarity with Democracy in Indonesia (*Solidaritas Mahasiswa Indonesia untuk Demokrasi*) and the People's Democratic Party (*Partai Rakyat Demokratik*). Also, progressive environmental organizations such as WALHI engaged in land disputes and defended peasants' rights. In the 1990s, local conflicts escalated in many places and drew nationwide attention. As a legacy of the pre-Suharto era, even direct action and mobilization were among the new political approaches of progressive organizations (Anugrah 2019, 81–82).

Anticommunist legacies made it difficult for progressive peasant organizations to establish mass movements in *reformasi* Indonesia. Given a more democratic political frame, peasant unions engaged in lobbying for an agrarian reform inspired by what was interrupted in 1965: large redistribution to landless and almost landless farmers (*petani gurem*) and the establishment of a rural solidarity economy of cooperatives. At first, the liberal zeitgeist of *reformasi* seemed to make such visionary political projects possible when the MPR passed Decree IX/MPR/2001, which suggested a revitalization of the idea of land reform. Oligarchic interests soon reorganized, however, and prevented any further steps. Not much happened until the presidency of Susilo Bambang Yodhoyono, commonly referred to as SBY. During these years (2005–2014), a so-called reform was carried out, but the result left progressive activists deeply disappointed. Rather than redistributing sufficient amounts of land to landless peasants, the SBY administration's program focused on the distribution of land to transmigrants, as had been done under Suharto, and it gave land mostly to farmers who already occupied that land (Neilson 2016, 251–251).

Although allocation of land to transmigrants appeared to be untransparent as it was subject to patronage networks, land titling as conducted under the SBY administration often led to another problematic outcome. Individual land titling had the effect of eventually dispossessing peasants from land through market mechanisms as many peasants sold their land. To some extent, the fear that proponents of the Leiden school had raised in late colonial times, namely, that market engagement would lead to greater structural inequality, came true in *reformasi* Indonesia. Indeed, the program was embedded into existing market and power structures rather than providing an alternative political frame that could challenge rural modes of production and ownership structures. The lack of class as a tool to critically assess the political-economic framework makes it difficult to provide a profound critique of the mechanisms. This critique could be expressed in the forms of traditional landownership and traditional tenure systems and their identities, however, and made possible the articulation of a class-based aim—that is, a substantial land reform that would redistribute land as a means of production to the producers. Like AMAN, some progressive peasant organizations supported Jokowi in his 2014 campaign, hoping for a more progressive land reform. The new government was, however, rather concerned with expanding the transmigration project to support large-scale food cultivation in Indonesia's margins (Neilson 2016, 253).

The political strategies of peasant activism included institutional activism as well as engagement in electoral politics. Some activists managed to obtain positions in the state bureaucracy, for instance, in the President's Staff Office (*Kantor Staf Presiden*) or the National Human Rights Commission (*Komas HAM*). They were not successful, however, in entering crucial ministries and their influence on policymaking remained limited overall. In terms of engagement in electoral politics, activists supported district head candidates (*bupati*) who had close ties to civil society organizations as well as their own candidates for local and national parliaments. These strategies are very much the same as AMAN's strategies. In terms of economic strategies, peasant organizations developed concepts of solidarity economic models, suggesting that land should not just be redistributed individually but also as communal land for common production in cooperatives. Peasant-run collective enterprises (*Badan Usaha Buruh Tani*, BUBT) should become, in their view, the cornerstone of a new rural economy. In these enterprises, landless and near-landless peasants should be incorporated into farming activities on land purchased and owned by the state but administered by the peasants. The BUBT should be directly organized and controlled by the peasants (Anugrah 2019, 87–90).

Although AMAN and peasant organizations did have a common concern, namely the redistribution of land, and although they did use similar strategies, such as institutional activism and engagement in electoral politics with limited overall success, the peasant movement and the Indigenous movement have not developed close ties leading to overarching political strategy and concepts. Although the agrarian reform did constitute a frame for a joint struggle, the movement became rather fragmented into separate peasant and Indigenous struggles. An important reason lies in their ideological foundations: Peasants made use of an economic identity, whereas AMAN often applied a cultural identity. A class-based approach—at least if it is a radical one that does not subscribe to the concept of an organicist state in which different classes cooperate on behalf of national interests—aims to dialectically sublate itself by making peasants and laborers the universal class, which, then, simultaneously disappears in its process of universalization. In contrast, an approach based on notions of authenticity and identity seeks economic and social spaces within the given political and economic order in which it can assert its identity and practice alternative economic modes, which nonetheless are embedded into a wider capitalist framework.

The manifesto for agrarian reform (AMAN 2020b) presented, in this sense, a new approach as it made visible a language of a common struggle based on class, for example, by referring to *oligarki, kapitalisme,* and *neo-imperialisme.* Even though the notion of class was not directly mentioned, the proposed alliance among different sections of the people (peasants, laborers, Indigenous people, urban poor) was in fact class based. Attempts to form larger alliances, however, still remain in a rather embryonic state. Much will depend on whether institutional activism can tame Indigenous activism or whether a common language of struggle will provide a stable base for a broader alliance of civil society in the agrarian sector.

Transactional politics in Indonesia represent a serious threat to any political movement that seeks independence from established oligarchic patterns. After 1965, a domestic bourgeoisie emerged, but it became fragmented during the New Order era. In *reformasi* Indonesia, this fragmented oligarchy engaged in the new multiparty electoral system, whereas other classes, including marginalized rural groups, lacked both the material and ideological resources to organize within the new system. The fragmentation of the sociopolitical elite resulted in transactional politics, that is, politics in which the ruling parties ensured their power through deals with other parties. In other words, parts of the political-economic elite engaged in deals with other factions, often by incorporating politicians and interests into their coalitions and decision-making processes (Lane 2019a, 6–7). This transactionalism fit well into the ideology of harmony and consensus, but what was portrayed as a consensus for the sake of the nation was actually a deliberate compromise by the ruling class to ensure the stability of the economy and social order.

In his 2014 campaign, Jokowi promised not to become a transactional leader but to rely on expertise alone when choosing his staff for political positions. This was a major reason why he managed to get support from many progressive organizations, but it soon became obvious that Jokowi also engaged in transactionalism (Lane 2019b, 5–6). As Jokowi tried to incorporate activists from the very beginning, this transactionalism was not limited to the political elite. Activists could, under certain circumstances, also enter the circle of power, and the whole strategy of institutional activism is designed to do so. This is, from a critical class perspective, however, a double-edged sword. On the one hand, classes that are now organized can enter the political realm and can express their demands. On the other hand, they depend on a wider political network that is dominated by the oligarchy and they necessarily engage in an interclass alliance that neuters any radical approach. Institutional activists seem to represent the economic and political interests of a certain group, but through their engagement, they also help to legitimize the overarching political and economic order, that is, the very order that marginalized them in the first place.

In Search of *UU Masyarakat Adat*

In many conversations with Indigenous activists in Jakarta and Bogor, the Law on Indigenous Communities was mentioned as an important political goal of state–Indigenous interactions. Through this law, Indigenous communities should receive official state recognition and legal security. The law had already been submitted to the Indonesian Parliament in 2011 when AMAN gained the support of the Indonesian Democratic Party of Struggle (*Partai Demokrasi Indonesia-Perjuangan*, PDI-P). At that time, however, the PDI-P was in opposition, and the chair of the committee in charge of parliamentary processes was from the ruling *Partai Demokrat* of President Yudhoyono, and for political reasons, he slowed the process as much as possible. The PDI-P supported the bill in the 2014 election campaign but eventually lost interest in further promotion after the election. In 2015, AMAN gained the support of Luthfi A. Mutty, a member of parliament from the *Partai Nasional Demokrat*. AMAN was not satisfied with the revised version of the Law on Indigenous Communities because it still required recognition by regency governments instead of a unified process for the entirety of Indonesia in which *adat* communities could directly apply to the national government. Another chapter in the draft attracted harsh criticism from AMAN as well. It stated that the government had the right to revoke a community's status as an *adat* community and their land rights if the community no longer fulfilled the requirements of an *adat* community, for instance when *adat* institutions disappeared. AMAN demanded a provision about rehabilitation and restitution that had been part of the first draft, arguing that it should also be included in the current draft given that it would ensure that the law could be applied to past cases of land dispossession. The Ministry of Domestic Affairs responded swiftly. The letter identified the existing laws dealing with Indigenous affairs as being sufficient and argued that the *UU Masyarakat Adat* would require large sums from the state budget for compensation to *adat* communities. AMAN activists expressed their anger and stressed that the law was part of Jokowi's election campaign; it was his promise to the Indigenous communities. Officially, the minister responded that he still supported the law, but ministry officials expressed their desire for this law to be obstructed in the legislative process because it would interfere too much with their village development programs as well as with land concession processes for corporations (Bedner and Arizona 2019, 425–426).

The Ministry of Domestic Affairs, however, turned out not to be the only problem. When discussing the issue with AMAN activists during my fieldwork, they pointed out that other ministries were also doing their best to slow down the process and even prevent the bill from being discussed in parliament. After a parliament initiative, President Jokowi issued a *Surat Keputusan Presiden* (Presidential Decision Letter) ordering six ministries to discuss their nomenclature regarding Indigenous peoples, namely the Ministry of Domestic Affairs, the Ministry of Village Affairs, the Ministry of Environment and Forestry, the Ministry of Agrarian Affairs and Spatial Panning, the Ministry of Maritime Affairs and Fisheries, and the Ministry of Law and Human Rights. They were asked to give their evaluations of the current draft of the law. In July 2018, parliament conducted a meeting with representatives from these ministries. Although they basically agreed with the proposed law, they decided to compile an inventory of problems that might occur if the bill were passed in its current form. This is where the process came to a halt, and as of 2025, this list of potential problems had not yet been released by the ministries. The activists have interpreted this as a sign that they want to sabotage AMAN's main goal of a nationwide law on Indigenous communities, their status, and their rights.

Taking the slow process of the acknowledgment of *adat* forests and the stagnant process of the *UU Masyarakat Adat* into account, AMAN's success on the national scale has been limited to date. After the euphoria over the 2013 Constitutional Court ruling and Jokowi's victory, activists were disappointed by the slow process of *adat* forest recognition and withdrew their support for Jokowi in the 2019 election (Tamma and Duile 2020, 280). Before the 2019 election, AMAN activists emphasized in conversations with me that they sought discussions with representatives from both the Jokowi and Prabowo camps but had not gained substantial support. As a result, AMAN's main project, the national law on Indigenous peoples, has not been pushed further. When the government insisted on local recognition of Indigenous communities as an essential precondition to applying for *adat* forest, this likely was designed as a means to slow down the process of land redistribution. Compared with AMAN's national project of a comprehensive law on Indigenous communities, however, processes of recognition at the regency level were, at least in some regencies, quite successful. Although some denied recognition, others issued local regulations (*peraturan daerah*), especially when Indigenous activists successfully utilized their ties with local politicians. By the end of 2016, sixty-nine *peraturan daerah* and decrees had been issued on matters related to Indigenous people and a total of 538 communities had been acknowledged as *adat* communities (Arizona et al. 2017, 1). Moreover, 133 villages had been granted *adat* village status (Bedner and Arizona 2019, 242).

The Question of Indigenous Religions

Thus far, this overview has shed light on legal processes and the political economy behind them. Being Indigenous, however, also has a cultural component:
Indigenous peoples or communities differ culturally from mainstream society,
and in many countries, this is expressed through Indigenous worldviews that
claim to be fundamentally different from hegemonic, modern, or Western perceptions and religions. In the Indonesian context, the question of religion is
especially interesting and telling, as the Indonesian state is based on the principle of a divine almighty entity (*Ketuhanan yang Maha Esa*). This is the first
principle of Indonesia's state ideology of Pancasila. The state recognizes Islam,
Protestantism, Catholicism, Hinduism, Confucianism, and Buddhism as religions (*agama*), which are all conceptualized as monotheist. This monotheist
principle of *Ketuhanan yang Maha Esa* is a fundamental principle of the Indonesian state (Sinn 2014, 231). The religious affiliation of each citizen also
appears on the Indonesian identity card. Traditional religious beliefs are usually subsumed in the notion of *kepercayaan*, which has a reputation for backwardness and even paganism. At best, state recognition is half-hearted and has
caused severe discrimination against adherents of traditional beliefs (Maarif
2017, 73–110).

Six adherents of *kepercayaan* issued a lawsuit, however, arguing that nonrec-
ognition of *kepercayaan* represented a case of discrimination (Faiz 2017). In
2017, the Constitutional Court decided in their favor. In its decision, the court
stressed Article 29(2) of the 1945 Constitution, which declares that the state
must guarantee all citizens freedom of worship according to their religion
(*agama*) and belief (*kepercayaan*). In its decision, the court argued that *kepercayaan* can be seen as a part of religion rather than something that threatens
the acknowledged religions and the principle of *Ketuhanan yang Maha Esa*.
The decision was thus an important step against discrimination (Fachrudin
2017). It was not surprising, however, that conservative religious groups protested against this decision given that they saw traditional beliefs as being at
odds with acknowledged beliefs and not in line with *Ketuhanan yang Maha
Esa*. Also in 2017, the conversion of a part of the Orang Rimba, an Indigenous
community in Sumatra, to Islam made the news and triggered controversy.
Although conservative Muslims strongly supported the step and called for
material support to establish mosques and Islamic schools for them, others
pointed out that this step could be seen as a pragmatic way of dealing with the
Orang Rimba's loss of their traditional livelihoods and simply made it easier for
them to gain access to public education and medical facilities (Firmansyah
2017; Henschke 2017; Nugraha 2017). In any case, these issues were sensitive

and emotional topics: They must be seen within the context of a general conservative turn in Indonesian Islam from at least the mid-2000s (van Bruinessen
2013) and the mass-mobilization of conservative and radical Muslim groups
for political purposes in 2016 and 2017 (Lim 2017).

AMAN was surprisingly quiet on both issues. Some AMAN activists
expressed their support for the Constitutional Court's decision and their uneasi-
ness about Islamic engagement against traditional beliefs, but they generally
refrained from public statements and did not openly advocate for recognition of
kepercayaan. There were several reasons for this. First, many AMAN members,
especially educated professionals, are usually Muslims or Christians. More
important, AMAN does not want to engage in these controversial debates
because it fears that it could incur the wrath of influential Muslim organizations, for instance the conservative Indonesian Ulama Council (*Majelis Ulama
Indonesia*, MUI), of which the vice president under Jokowi, Maruf Amin, was
the chair. Finally, a cooperative approach with the state also requires some ideological conformance with the state and any suspicions of being against the first
principle of Indonesia's state ideology could be a severe obstacle to this approach.
When I later shed light on how religious issues play a role in local processes of
Indigenous recognition in South Sulawesi, it will be important to remember
these national debates.

Indigeneity and Its Dialectics in the National Context

This analysis of indigeneity and the state has so far outlined some general features of the formation of indigeneity in the Indonesian context. In chapter 1, I
argued that indigeneity went through a dialectical process, starting in the late
colonial era when *adat* became an object to be protected against the devastating
effects of liberal-capitalist economy. It was the internal contradiction of a colonial condition that claimed universal progress and free market exchange, and
simultaneously drew on racial differentiation and the devastating effects of
colonial exploitation. In independent Indonesia, *adat* was connoted with backwardness and feudalism, and therefore was something to overcome; in contrast,
several features of *adat* also served as tools for the process of nation-building.
Consequently, indigeneity became indigenism, first in a populist-leftist sense,
and then, during the New Order era, in a conservative version of traditional
hierarchy. In both ways, it was an ideological formation of the political economy promoted by the state. Thus, indigenism triggered new contradictions.
Indonesian indigenism was concerned with development in both its populist

and demobilizing conservative versions. Although New Order indigenism claimed to serve the nation in accordance with the concept of a harmonious family, it produced culturally and economically alienated and marginalized communities, even addressing them as such (e.g., *masyarakat terasing*). This led to the formation of particular indigeneity—as Indigenous peoples—in late New Order Indonesia and especially after Suharto. This new formation, *masyarakat adat*, can be understood as both an antithesis to the nation and as a sublated legacy from the colonial concept of *adat*. Although the state, development, and modernity first appeared as the opposite of indigeneity, the developments discussed in this chapter have shown that within the context of ideologies of neoliberalism and new developmentalism, Indigenous people and the state have converged. At the same time, however, a tension originating from this ideological formation has emerged. Opposing the new developmentalism, Indigenous activists nonetheless find their connections with the state and the dominant ideologies. Self-difference is also inherent in the concept of indigeneity as used by Indigenous activists: They have to claim sovereignty and opposition to the state and its ideology, while also having to engage with it to emerge as political subjects. Indigeneity is thus a somewhat flawed identity as it is never merely outside the state and the nation, nor can it completely be absorbed into the state and its ideological frameworks. It is precisely these flaws through which indigeneity can emerge and gain its political agency.

This sheds light on how the Indigenous paradox emerged and unfolded within the Indonesian context. Engagement with the law of the very state that Indigenous peoples initially positioned themselves in opposition to eventually became their condition of existence. Bens (2020, 2–3) has described the Indigenous paradox as a situation in which Indigenous groups reject the state while relying on its laws. As understood in the Indonesian context, rejection was never unconditional but was, from the very beginning of the Indigenous movement, an option only if mutual recognition was not achieved. Indigenous activists' fight for the *UU Masyarakat Adat* is thus part of that Indigenous paradox.

The obstacles AMAN faces in that process appear at first sight to be obstacles to indigeneity in general. Taking the Indigenous paradox into account, however, they also equip Indigenous activists with a basic condition of indigeneity, that is, their identity in opposition to the state. Taking this a step further, this formation of simultaneously opposing and being incorporated also emerges in relation to the economy: Indigenous activists oppose state-centrist approaches that define land, a basic means of production, as the state's domain. In contrast, neoliberal entrepreneurial ideologies offer a potential connection with the state. As I explain in more detail later in the case study of chapter 6 and in the discussion in the conclusion, it is precisely these flaws that enable political agency and simultaneously limit it. As an expression of the self-difference of Indonesian society, however, Indigenous movements always have the potential to point out fundamental contradictions, just as they have the opportunity to play along with hegemonic ideology. In a dialectical account, this contradiction is not a dichotomy, it is not a simple either/or question: To achieve fundamental change, indigeneity might well facilitate the given ideological and political frame and explore its inherent contradictions.

HISTORIES AND IDENTITIES
IN SOUTH SULAWESI

In Indonesian academia, public events are crucial. A campus' prestige has to constantly be reaffirmed, to be displayed in public in ceremonies. This is also true for Western universities, which have their own rituals for displaying academic identities, but I often felt that at Indonesian universities, it is even more important. Not a single week goes by without large public events, each carefully and skillfully organized and executed. The Hasanuddin University in Makassar has a huge auditorium facing an artificial lake at the main entrance to the vast campus that is used for large events. One of my research partners was in charge of one such event, which I attended along with delegation from Jakarta. After a two-hour discussion, an obligatory lunch was served. Hierarchies matter a lot in Indonesian universities, and guests as well as dignitaries from the university are served special food in a separate room, which is air conditioned and much better suited to conversation. As a guest researcher from abroad, I was asked to join the lunch. In the room, my attention was immediately drawn to the much larger-than-life picture of Sultan Hasanuddin. The sultan is depicted on a battlefield with glowing eyes, expressing his desire for vengeance. Dead and dying Dutch soldiers are scattered across the scene. It is no surprise that this painting was hung up in the room used for guests from outside Makassar. It perfectly depicts the official narrative of Sultan Hasanuddin as an Indonesian hero who opposed the Dutch and as a local leader who contributed to the imagined national struggle against the Dutch. Hasanuddin is omnipresent in Makassar. Not only is the largest university in the city—and in eastern Indonesia overall—named after him, but also the airport has his name with a gigantic statue of Sultan

Hasanuddin greeting passengers at the entrance. The fight against the Dutch was subsequently narrated as a national struggle, and Hasanuddin was declared a national hero in 1973. During his lifetime (1631–1670), however, nobody had yet imagined a political entity called Indonesia, and the struggle against the Dutch was embedded in a local rivalry between Hasanddin's Gowa kingdom of the Makassarese and the Buginese kingdom of Bone. The latter aligned with the Dutch and eventually won the war. This fact, however, is often overlooked in Bugis narratives. When I once visited Bone to give a talk at the local university, my hosts proudly talked about the Buginese kingdom of Bone. My comment that they once aligned with the Dutch provoked an awkward silence.

Although the history of the Gowa kingdom is framed in a national narrative of struggle, in most cases, the Dutch cooperated with feudal rulers and also benefited from local trade, including slave trading. In 1660, Bone and the Dutch fought successfully against the Gowa kingdom. Subsequently, polities in the realm of the large kingdoms came under the jurisdiction of the Dutch, first the VOC (*Vereenigde Oostindische Compagnie*, Dutch East India Company), and later, after the VOC went bankrupt in 1777, the Dutch government (Tyson 2010, 23).

Why do such narratives on history, the nation, and ethnicity matter for an account of the ideology of indigeneity? In chapter 4, I shed light on Indigenous movements and indigeneity in South Sulawesi. To understand these issues, it is crucial to situate them within narratives and other forms of identity as Indonesians, Muslims, Bugis, or others. Therefore, in this chapter, I provide an overview of the narratives and history of South Sulawesi. My aim is not to tell a detailed history but rather to outline major features of the way history is narrated. As we will see, it is mostly the history of kingdoms and, later, national struggle—and the identities that emerge and develop from wars, trade, and cooperation in these histories—that make up hegemonic accounts of local history which usually do not encompass what later became Indigenous communities. This marginality is crucial. My overview has yet another purpose, namely, to provide insight into the region that I deal with in the second part of this book. My account is not strictly chronological, but instead develops along lines of thought on ethnicity, political/economic power relations, and narratives.

Ethnic Identities in South Sulawesi

The modern idea of ethnic groups as distinct identities based on language and customs is a concept the Dutch applied to categorize and rule their subjects. The Dutch colonial administration started its work on categorizing people along ethnic differences in Sulawesi, and the independent nation continued this approach (Aragon 2000, 47). Ethnic groups and identities, however, are not simply Dutch inventions. A sense of ethnic belonging also emerges from local history, as I outline in this chapter.

The rivalry between the Bugis and Makassarese is prevalent in South Sulawesi, and the Makassarese are especially proud of Hasanuddin. In older literature in particular, however, Makassarese and Bugis have been depicted as a single ethnic group (Mattulada 1975; Koentjaraningat 1985). They also represent the most cosmopolitan ethnic groups in South Sulawesi because of their history of maritime trade and kingdoms with complex political relationships with many parts of the archipelago, whereas the Toraja and other upland groups were involved in local trade within the island. The kingdoms of Gowa, Bone, and to some extent, Soppeng are often depicted as the culturally most sophisticated and most complex Indigenous societies in the history of South Sulawesi (Antweiler 2000, 163). The oldest kingdom in this area, however, is the Luwu kingdom. Luwu was the hegemonic kingdom in South Sulawesi until it was eclipsed by the Makassarese sultanate of Gowa in the early seventeenth century. Islam arrived in the region in the fifteenth century, but it was not before the early seventeenth century that large kingdoms adopted Islam as their official religion (Pelras 1994, 135–136). Within the realms of the great kingdoms, smaller kingdoms were incorporated into alliances through payment of tributes and intermarriage. In large parts of what later became the province of South Sulawesi, local customs were heavily influenced by hegemonic Bugis culture, especially in the lowlands.

Makassar was a notorious place for slave trading because it was the transit port for the slave trade from eastern Indonesia to Java (Vink 2003, 143). In that region, peripheral groups, most notably Mandars, Toraja, and other upland groups, became the victims of slavery (Vink 2003, 156). With conversion to Islam, former non-Muslim societies changed from "closed" slave societies—which enslaved members of the lower castes within a respective society—to "open" slave societies that were in constant need of slave supply from other societies as older generations of enslaved peoples were assimilated into the dominant group. In a closed slave society, the distinctiveness of the enslaved was continuously reinforced, usually on the basis of their descent (for these terms, see: Watson 1980; Reid 1983). In open slave societies, the enslaved were not usually determined by descent but, for instance, were non-Muslims sourced from other groups. When the Bugis converted to Islam in the early seventeenth century, hereditary Bugis who had been enslaved were emancipated from slavery and members from non-Muslim groups, especially from upland Sulawesi (Ward 2011, 172), were enslaved. The highlands thus became what one can term 'slaving zones' (Fynn-Paul 2009, 2018), namely geographic regions in which societies enslaved other inhabitants through warfare, slave raids, or slave trade.

Until slavery was officially abolished by the Dutch in 1860, slave hunting was common in South Sulawesi and wars between the larger and smaller kingdoms ensured a constant supply of war prisoners who were often sold and enslaved. Until the 1930s, however, slavery was still common in some remote places in South Sulawesi (Dutch Colonial Heritage n.d., 3). South Sulawesi societies were highly stratified at that time and consisted of three social classes. A small strata of aristocrats were at the top, with their position legitimized through their descent from divine founding ancestors. Below that strata were free men (Buginese: *tomaradèka*) and those who were enslaved (Buginese: *ata*), with porous boundaries: Free men could become enslaved because of indebtedness. Freemen, however, enjoyed a range of rights and liberties, such as security of person and property, the right to justice, freedom of commercial contract, and freedom of movement (Henly and Caldwell 2019, 244–247).

Contrary to the image of marginalized highland people primarily engaged in subsistence economy, Sulawesi's upland population was embedded in translocal trade even before the Dutch arrived, and their engagement with other parts of the island increased massively in colonial times. As lowland agriculture was dominated by wet rice cultivation, the highlands of Sulawesi were increasingly incorporated into the international spice trade. At the beginning of the twentieth century, the fertility rate increased in the peripheral regions in Sulawesi, just as it had in urban areas approximately half a century earlier. Henley (2005, 2006) has argued that this was due to changing economic conditions: Incomes increased because of market expansion, as did demand for labor. Economies reliant on bondaged labor through debt slavery disappeared, while the growth of commerce in the highlands facilitated marriage and prosperity. In Sulawesi's marginal highland, cash crops such as coffee, cloves, or nutmeg became a cornerstone of the economy. The Dutch also introduced food crops such as potatoes, tomatoes, cabbage, carrots, and onions, which found good growing conditions in the temperate climates. As early as 1820–1870, the Sulawesi highlands experienced the first small cocoa boom caused by market demands from the nearby Philippines (Li 2002, 419).

South Sulawesi remained a peripheral part of the colony, and even though Makassar had already been brought under Dutch control in 1669, the largest part of what is now South Sulawesi remained independent from the Dutch until the early twentieth century (Henley and Caldwell 2019, 243). From about 1905 onward, as Tyson (2010, 27) explains, interventions in the form of "administrative reform, agricultural rationalization, geological explorations, ethnography and cartography, set in motion a direct, deliberate process of constructing *adat* in non-threatening terms." At that time, swidden cultivation was replaced by permanent cultivation as the former was seen as an inefficient, ancient form of agriculture that now had to make room for more advanced methods (Tyson 2010, 27). In South Sulawesi, that meant an expansion of rice paddies as well as increased cultivation of cash crops, such as coffee and cloves, in the highlands.

The formation of the main ethnic groups of South Sulawesi took place in precolonial and colonial times. They were precolonial entities insofar as they established distinct polities, but colonial classification systematized and conceptualized them as distinct groups with clear boundaries of language, custom, and religion. Thus, their respective histories were systematized, too. The history of South Sulawesi began to take shape as a history of its kingdoms. One was Luwu, the first kingdom and the cradle of Bugis civilization (Schrauwers 1997). The later-emerging Bugis civilization consisted of many bigger and smaller polities, with Soppeng, Sindenreng, and Wajo as the largest social-political units. Finally, the twin polity of Gowa-Tallo represented the kingdom of the Makassarese (Henly and Caldwell 2019, 244).

When visiting Makassar's Losari waterfront, the names of the major ethnic groups are displayed in large letters (figure 3.1). In addition to Bugis and Makassarese, two other groups are present. The Toraja are a highland group that has often successfully evaded direct control by the lowland kingdoms of Luwu and Bone. They are an icon of traditional culture with their famous burial rituals and the iconic *tongkonan* (Toraja term for ancestor houses of

FIGURE 3.1.   The names of the major ethnic groups are presented at the Losari waterfront in Makassar

noble families, but also a term for larger social units). Because of their distinct culture, the Toraja uplands are among of the main tourist destinations in eastern Indonesia (Yamashita 1994). The other ethnic group represented in large letters in Losari are the Mandarese, a costal group primarily living in what was, until 2004, the northwestern part of South Sulawesi province and has since become a province of its own (figure 3.2). Bugis, Makassarese, Toraja, and (until 2004) the Mandarese are the four dominant ethnic groups in the province (Antweiler 2000, 148–160).

As noted previously, identity and history in South Sulawesi are, as in other parts of the country, closely related to the way history is constructed around the motif of a national struggle and the development of cultural entities contributing to Indonesia's national identity. In the hegemonic narratives of the New Order era, a history of a supposedly bright precolonial era was narrated in which the essence of an Indonesian nation already existed throughout the archipelago. This golden era was interrupted by a dark age of colonialism with heroic resistance, through which the political entity of Indonesia eventually appeared (Nordhold et al. 2013, 11). For South Sulawesi, this narrative has meant that groups, such as the Bugis, connected the archipelago through their trade and shaped an "Indonesian" national culture with their sophisticated local culture. The Bugis epos of *La Galigo* represents one such cultural achievement, but dynasties and material culture are also portrayed as a components of ancient Indonesian culture. Sultan Hasanuddin's struggle is a narrative of a heroic, exceedingly Indonesian uprising against the Dutch. In these narratives, any ambiguity is sidelined: Hasanuddin is narrated as the noble liberator against the colonizing Dutch. The enslavement of peripheral groups by the representatives of advanced, ancient cultures is downplayed, as is the alliance between Bone and the Dutch. South Sulawesi's idol Hasanuddin does not only appear as a fighter with an angry face in large paintings and statuary. The city of Makassar's official mascot is a friendly smiling rooster with a traditional Makassarese headpiece, which is a reference to the honorable title given to Sultan Hasanuddin by the Dutch: *de haantje van het osten* (Dutch for "the rooster of the East"). What many people in Makassar probably do not know, however, is that the term *haantje* is the diminutive of *haan*, and thus it may not be an honorable denotation after all.

Identity and history in South Sulawesi are thus centered on narratives of struggles against the Dutch, narratives of ancient, advanced Indigenous culture and, because of tourism, exoticism. This indigenist-nationalist representation not only marginalizes any narratives of repression not related to the Dutch but also marginalizes peripheral groups and their history outside the large kingdoms in general.

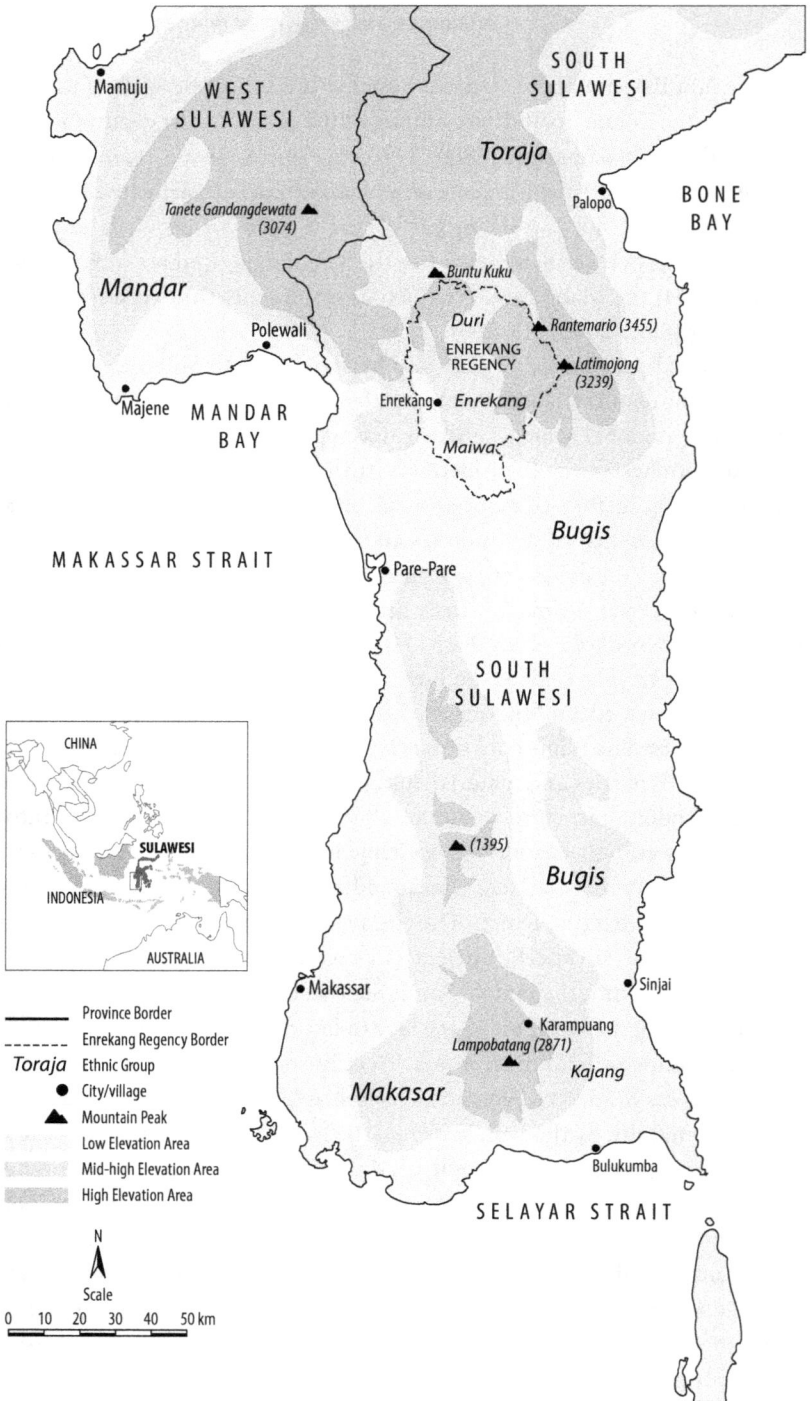

FIGURE 3.2. South Sulawesi. Map of South Sulawesi © Ruy Nubarani, illustrator

Lowland and Upland Relations in the History of South Sulawesi

Despite the New Order regime's efforts to domesticate and depoliticize ethnicity, ethnic identity has remained important in South Sulawesi because it determines the way people construct their ways of belonging and think about other groups of people. During my stays in southern Toraja, for instance, I often came across the narrative of Toraja land being lost to Bugis. Lowlanders, some Toraja used to say, are eager to buy land in Toraja to marginalize the Toraja economically in their domain as losing land means lost of control. As in other parts of Indonesia, ethnicity is an important marker for claiming space and expressing loyalty in everyday life. When I was new to the region, people often helped me to buy bus tickets for my travels between Makassar and the uplands. When Bugis or Enrekang friends bought me tickets, I traveled in buses owned by Bugis, adorned with Islamic symbols and stopping at Bugis- or Muslim-owned restaurants. When Toraja friends organized my transportation, I found myself in buses owned by Litha, a Torajan bus company. Christian gospel music playing during the journey and a little chapel at the main station in Makassar—in addition to the obligatory *musholla*—marked the space as a Torajan, Christian domain. Good and peaceful relations between the ethnic groups are stressed in official discussion, but when it comes to informal talk, one can hear many prejudices. They usually reflect the different narratives of history in which advanced Bugis culture is sometimes highlighted, but in other cases, predatory invasions into the uplands are referenced.

In South Sulawesi, just as in many parts of Indonesia, the concept of marginalization has often developed along a lowland-highland axis (Li 1999b). Whereas the dominant groups, the Makassarese and, especially, the Bugis, are inhabitants of the lowlands, the Toraja are the main upland inhabitants in the province. Just as language divides the three groups, religion divides the lowland and upland. Makassarese and Bugis became adherents of Islam in the early sixteenth century, whereas the Toraja were Christianized from the early twentieth century onward. Dutch Protestant missions arrived in Rantepao in 1913, but relations between the Dutch and the Toraja were troublesome in these years as Protestant missions tried to outlaw rituals (Torajan: *aluk*) that they saw as being at odds with Christianity (Volkman 1985, 35–36). It is not just the distinction between Christianity and Islam, however, that separates lowland and upland South Sulawesi culturally. The Toraja are also associated with their traditional religion (Torajan: *aluk to dolo*) and their elaborate rituals, including their cave funerals conducted sometimes as long as a year after the death of the person being buried (Nooy-Palm 1986). More than any other major group in Sulawesi, the Toraja have maintained an image of an exotic, marginal, and traditional group and have deployed that image in the tourism industry (von Vacano 2010). The term *Toraja* derives from the Buginese *to* (person) *ri aja* (of the interior) and therefore is based on the coastal-interior distinction. In Makassarese, *raja* means person of the north and was applied at least from the seventeenth century onward as a term for the upland groups they raided and enslaved. The Dutch adopted this term, and in the 1970s, it became the self-designation of what is now known as *Tana Toraja* (Land of the Toraja) (Volkman 1985, 2–3).

Relations between the lowland and the upland in South Sulawesi are, as in many parts of the archipelago, characterized by a long history of invasions and raids by lowlanders into the uplands as well as by marriage alliances, trade, and cultural exchange. Different perceptions of each other are common, and they are also depicted in the myths of the respective groups. The Bugis, for instance, explain their relations with the Toraja in regard to the royal genealogies of Luwu. According to them, Batara Guru, the first heavenly being to descend to earth, came to Luwu accompanied by forty cousins. Although Batara Guru became the ruler of Luwu, the navel of the world, his cousins were sent to other parts of the island, including the highlands. From that ancient time onward, marital links were established between high-status Toraja and Bugis. Another narrative of the ties between the Toraja and Bugis is outlined in Toraja mythology. A Toraja myth tells that Karaeng Dua, a handsome young man, married a Luwu princess. When the princess found out that Karaeng Dua's mother was actually a large white pig, she abandoned Karaeng Dua in disgust and ordered the Luwu to get rid of all pigs. Torajans are proud of this myth, but Bugis strongly reject this narrative (Volkman 1985, 20–21). In this myth, some basic ways of perceiving the other come into light: The lowlanders think of the highlanders as relatives but of a lesser status. The Toraja myth is a means to narrate the betrayal and arrogance of the lowlanders.

Once the Dutch established their ties with the lowland kingdoms, raids into the uplands became increasingly common. After the Dutch established their rule in cooperation with Arung Palakka, the king of Bone who had defeated Hasanuddin, the Bone sultanate became the hegemonic force in South Sulawesi. Arung Palakka's raids are an outstanding feature in the collective memory of the uplands as almost all Toraja groups united for the first time in history to repel the invading forces (Volkman 1985, 24). In the late nineteenth century, relations between the highlands and lowlands intensified. Not only Bone, but also the sultanates of Sidenreng and Luwu, increased their trade with the Toraja while seeking to enslave inhabitants of the uplands. This was the period of the coffee and slave wars.

Coffee, a commodity introduced to the highlands in the seventeenth century, had become a cornerstone of the economy. Around 1870, prices for coffee were increasing and coffee became a contested resource. Makassar, Pare-Pare, and Palopo became transshipment centers for the commodity, which was grown in the highlands thanks to the suitability of its climate for coffee (Pelras 1996, 316). The lowland kingdoms competed for control of the coffee trade. Luwu, with its port of Palopo in the east, and Sidenreng, with its port of Pare-Pare on the west coast, became the main rivals. Sidenreng took the lead after sending groups of armed forces into the highlands and terrorizing the population. The long-distance coffee trade routes were also utilized for slave trading and whenever coffee was in decline, those who were enslaved filled this trade gap. As the Toraja elite often cooperated with the invading forces from the lowlands and took the benefits of trade in coffee and slaves, ordinary highlanders became the victims. The intertwined coffee and slave economy imposed a large degree of uncertainty and exploitation on them. Growing labor shortages in the lowlands, and especially on the coast, were compensated for with enslavement, whereas the coffee economy led to a short supply of land in the uplands (Bigalke 2005, 18–55). The coffee war between 1885 and 1897 established Sidenreng as the new hegemonic force in the region, controlling the coffee trade with their Duri allies for the next twenty years (Pelras 1996, 316).

Slavery had theoretically been abolished in 1818, but that did not apply to the inhabitants enslaved by natives. When in 1860 slavery was made illegal in the Netherlands Indies, Bugis traders clandestinely moved those who were enslaved to other parts of the archipelago and even overseas, mostly to Arabia. In these final days of slavery, the majority came from the uplands, most of which were lower caste people from Toraja. Even though this issue is sometimes framed as an inversion of the lowlands into the uplands, in reality, Luwu and Sidenreng traders cooperated with Toraja and Duri dealers to enslave other people (Pelras 1996, 309). The Dutch gained control of Toraja in 1906 after they successfully seized power over all the major lowland kingdoms in South Sulawesi. The slave trade was eventually abolished, but to exercise power, the Dutch military killed or imprisoned many powerful Toraja nobles (Hollan and Wellenkamp 1996, 10). Although this development marked progress toward a more egalitarian society, in the Indonesian collective memory and national narratives, these events were remembered as a tragedy. Pong Tiku, a Toraja noble, led an armed resistance against the Dutch for months. In 1960, he was declared a national hero, and thus the Toraja people inherently became associated with the anticolonial struggle (Volkman 1985, 27–28).

Forces of Modernity

When the abolition of slavery was put into force in 1911 by the colonial government that had now established its control of the region, about one-third of enslaved Torajans returned home from the lowlands. As the Dutch aimed to establish indirect rule, however, they had to keep basic social structures and hierarchies intact. The cash crop economy expanded between 1906 and 1942 in the South Sulawesi uplands. A new class of free labor emerged, but aside from these forms of modernization, traditional ritual systems as well as traditional hierarchies remained in place (Volkman 1985, 30–32): Modern forms of paid labor, colonialism, and traditional hierarchies existed side by side. The nationalist thinking increasingly common among educated groups in Java had not yet made an impact on ordinary people in South Sulawesi, especially not in the remote highlands. The seemingly stable system of colonialism and indirect rule came to a sudden end in the wake of World War II. In 1942, Japanese forces seized control of Sulawesi and ruled for three years. This time was a traumatic period in the uplands. The Japanese armed forces were eager to extract as much wealth as possible: Rice, pigs, sugar, salt, and everything that could be sold on the market, most of all coffee, were cultivated by force or taken away from the producers. There were shortages of the most essential goods, even clothes. The Japanese imposed high quotas on the villages for the production of basic commodities. Also, forced labor was used to improve the poor infrastructure to transport the goods to the lowlands and thus were moved to wherever they were needed to feed the Japanese war machine. Compared with the Dutch period of relatively stable economic conditions under Dutch authority (sometimes referred to using the Latin term *pax neerlandica*), the Japanese occupation was a brief era of uncertainty, shortages, and violence. Traditional institutions and power structures were forcibly unraveled by the Japanese. After the Japanese were defeated, the Dutch aimed to reestablish their colonial rule. In Toraja, a small and brief nationalist uprising occurred, but it was quickly crushed (Volkman 1985, 38–40).

Overall, the independence movement was rather weak in South Sulawesi. After the declaration of independence on August 17, 1945, Ratulanggi, a nationalist from North Sulawesi, was appointed as the governor of Sulawesi (which was a single province at that time) on August 19, 1945. The Royal Dutch Indies army took power in Sulawesi without meeting significant resistance. Ratulanggi's Sulawesi Revolutionary Fighters of the Indonesian Republic lacked weapons and substantial support from ordinary people in many places. Before he was caught and sent to prison in Java in April 1946, Ratulanggi obtained promises from some traditional authorities that they would support an Indonesian republic, but most of them collaborated with the Dutch soon after as they realized that their power positions would be best reinstated under Dutch rule. Kahar Muzakkar, an anticolonial fighter from Luwu, managed to organize further resistance against the Dutch. His military organization, the Indonesian Republican Army for the Preparation of the Liberation of Sulawesi, operated in remote areas of the uplands where it was more difficult for the Dutch to establish sustainable control. Dutch operations, led by Captain Westerling, once again brought suffering to the people in the affected areas. Through killings of hostages and collective punishments for communities who supported the independence fighters, Westerling gained control over large parts of South Sulawesi. The remaining fighters only sporadically attacked from their bases in the uplands. As the Indonesian Revolution caused much trouble for the Dutch on Java, the Dutch government eventually agreed to Indonesian independence but demanded to have a say in the kind of state that its former colony should be transformed into. The Dutch insisted on a federal state as they hoped to maintain close ties to the provinces of a federation. Sulawesi was incorporated into the Dutch-sponsored federal state of East Indonesia with Makassar as its capital. The state was supported by many conservative aristocrats, but eventually it was integrated into the Indonesian Republic in 1950 (Pelras 1996, 279–282).

This new peace in South Sulawesi did not last long. Conflicts emerged within the republic's new leadership about the foundation of the country—some

FIGURE 3.3. Resistance Monument in Enrekang town. The monument shows local resistance against the Japanese, but many locals also interpret it as a resistance against the Dutch

demanded a constitution based on Islam and some a secular country. Finally, a compromise was achieved by adopting the principle of *Ketuhanan yang Maha Esa* as the first pillar of the national ideology of *Pancasila*, but without declaring shari'ah law mandatory for all Muslims. In the eyes of conservative Muslims, however, this compromise was a betrayal. After sovereignty was officially transferred from the Dutch to the independent republic in 1949, Sekarmadjin Maridjan Kartosuwrijo, who previously fought against the Dutch, refused to acknowledge the compromise of *Pancasila* and started a rebellion, known as the Darul Islam rebellion (the term denotes the Muslim regions in the world). The Darul Islam rebellion was particularly strong in West Java and Aceh as well as in South and Central Sulawesi. In South Sulawesi, the charismatic Kahar Muzakkar deserted from Sukarno's presidential guard and led the rebellion in Sulawesi from 1953 onward.

In the first years, Darul Islam brought considerable parts of Sulawesi's south under control, and it was not until 1956 that the Indonesian army consolidated and eventually started their offensive. In the following years, large parts of South Sulawesi became a warzone. By 1962, the Armed Forces of the Indonesian Republic again controlled substantial areas of South Sulawesi. Darul Islam managed to survive in remote upland areas, however, until Kahar Muzakkar was killed in 1965 and the remaining pockets of the rebellion surrendered (for a detailed study on the Darul Islam movement in South Sulawesi, see van Dijk 1981, 156–217). The Darul Islam movement took strong stances against anything that they saw as being at odds with 'proper', orthodox Islam. Pre-Islamic components in popular religion were eradicated brutally. In Bugis societies, for instance, people who adopted traditional genders other than male and female (in Buginese *bissu, calabai,* and *calalai*) were killed (Andini 2017, 29–30). Generally, the Islamic forces aimed to wipe out all animist beliefs, which they considered dangerous superstition. There was pillaging by both armies as well as forced conversion and slaughtering of pigs by Darul Islam troops (Volkman 1985, 41). As a consequence of the war, trade dropped. The Darul Islam soldiers smuggled cash crops, most of all coffee, to the lowlands where they were sold. Shortages of everyday goods, such as salt and rice, occurred until the Indonesian army took complete control. Darul Islam also applied new ideas of an egalitarian society. It not only sought to abolish traditional hierarchies but also introduced land reform. Therefore, it gained the support of many ordinary peasants.

When hundreds of thousands of members and sympathizers of the PKI (*Partai Komunis Indonesia*, the Communist Party of Indonesia) were killed between 1965 and 1968, South Sulawesi was not among the most affected parts of the country. In the lowlands, however, the communists had some support among the farmers organized in the Indonesian Peasant Front (*Barisan Tani Indonesia*, BTI). In October 1965, many of them were arrested. In Toraja, people were also arrested and killed, leaving a permanent fear of being labeled as communists or atheists. Communism had become influential among the Toraja during the years before the anti-PKI operations. It was not communism, however, as an elaborate political-philosophical system that was popular among the Toraja, but instead it was the PKI's effort to redistribute land and establish communal agrarianism. The rapid change in a highly stratified society embodied the idea of a utopian, egalitarian society. To prevent bloodshed in Toraja, peasants rephrased communist ideas in Indigenous agrarian terms (Tyson 2010, 84).

After 1966, South Sulawesi experienced an era of stability and peace. Infrastructure that had been seriously damaged during two decades of war was repaired, reconnecting the uplands and lowlands (Volkman 1985, 43). Coffee farming expanded and, in the 1970s, clove tree plantations emerged. The climate in the uplands was especially suitable for clove trees. The 1980s saw an expansion in cocoa farming in South Sulawesi (Pelras 1996, 325–319). In the New Order era, however, the egalitarian approaches advocated by the BTI or Darul Islam disappeared. Traditional elites who had survived the turmoil of history were able to reorganize.

Local Histories and the Making of Identities in South Sulawesi

Just as in other parts of Indonesia, an economic and cultural distinction between the lowlands and the uplands developed through the history of South Sulawesi. In the hegemonic perception of culture in Indonesia, the lowlands were home to sultanates connected to other parts of the archipelago and bore civilizations with rich bodies of culture, whereas the uplands remained the hinterland and were regarded as backward. They did develop, however, a rich body of culture as well as political agency. Their relations with the lowlands took various forms, ranging from cooperation and collaboration to resistance and the endeavor for autonomy. The highlands often served as a reservoir of resources, in the form of both natural resources and human labor. Exchange between upland and lowland societies was common throughout history in manifold forms: Trade and intermarriage among nobles were common features of lowland-upland relations just as much as warfare and enslavement. In South Sulawesi's stratified societies, modernity came in steps, through the advent of Islam in the sixteenth century and, in the upland, Christianity in the twentieth century. Neither religion nor colonialism, however, brought abrupt change. Traditional elites proved in many cases to be conservative and came to terms with change from outside. Traditional leaders were incorporated into nationalist narratives as agents of resistance. Sultan Hasanuddin became the main icon in these narratives in South Sulawesi. Given that Hasanuddin was Makassarese, other groups also developed their own icons of resistance. The Toraja have marked Pong Tiku as a national hero, and among Bugis, the Bone Wars between 1824 and 1906 represent their attempts at a patriotic uprising against the Dutch. The fact that the then-ruler of Bone, Andi Mapanyukki, refused to acknowledge the Dutch after they returned in 1946 is often portrayed as a case of traditional resistance against colonialism. In most cases, however, traditional elites cooperated with the Dutch, even after the declaration of independence (Pelras 1996, 280). In addition, the alliances between them were the backbone of a larger feudal system in South Sulawesi.

The largest and most sudden change, at least in some places, was brought about by the Darul Islam movement. Traditional hierarchies, beliefs, and non-Islamic culture were crushed in only a few years. After the rebels surrendered and the hunt for communists ended, South Sulawesi's history of wars and struggles became more peaceful. Although Suharto's New Order era was one of economic growth and increasing mobility, it also meant depoliticization, including the depoliticization of those who struggled for an egalitarian society and the depoliticization of ethnicity. The main ethnic groups were, as elsewhere in Indonesia, domesticated as merely cultural units, contributing to Indonesia's cultural diversity. As cultural icons, the Toraja, Bugis, and Makassarese were depicted in terms of folklore with their distinct cultures, such as dances, food, and rituals.

It was not until the 1990s that political activists in South Sulawesi discovered *adat* and tradition as tools for political struggles, and they had to apply tradition in a different manner from nationalist narratives. As I explain in the following chapters, they did not apply indigeneity as ethnicity. As in other parts of Indonesia, Indigenous activists utilize traditional ethnic features to show their difference from modern mainstream society, but they do not refer to ethic groups. Instead, it is communities that are, in their account, Indigenous: small communities within much larger ethnic entities. As the history of South Sulawesi usually is narrated as a history of kingdoms, wars, and rebellions, these groups had always been present in history, but they usually never emerged as subjects. They were the groups who suffered war, looting, dispossession, and enslavement by kingdoms, colonizers, armies, and others who claimed their grand position in history. In this sense, *making indigeneity* means assembling the painful and scattered past of those who often have been no more than a footnote in the official history but indeed have had their own ways to remember their histories. The following chapters shed light on Indigenous struggles in South Sulawesi. Using the example of Duri communities in the highlands of Enrekang regency, I explain in more detail how they became Indigenous with regard to their history and their current political and economic conditions.

THE POLITICS OF *ADAT* AND TRADITION IN SOUTH SULAWESI AFTER SUHARTO

In different parts of Indonesia, Indigenous activists work on different scales: In Jakarta, for instance, they lobby for national legislation; in the provinces, they strengthen ties with other movements; and, at the grassroots level, they collect data from communities applying for recognition. On many occasions, these activists meet and interact with each other, and these events are especially interesting when determining how indigeneity comes into being. During the Indigenous Alliance of the Archipelago (*Aliansi Masyarakat Adat Nusantara*, AMAN) Congress in South Sulawesi in November 2019, I had plenty of opportunity to talk to AMAN activists. In Sinjai, I met some activists from AMAN's Jakarta and Makassar offices. Rukka Sombbolingi, the AMAN chair, came to the meeting because she is originally from South Sulawesi and is grateful for any occasion that allows her to visit her home province. As in many such Indigenous congresses, Indigenous groups showed their products, including handicrafts and foods from Indigenous production. The delegation from Toraja was the largest, and they sold not only coffee, spices, cassava chips, and sugar from their villages but also Torajan handicraft, such as necklaces. I stood at the booth learning more about Torajan necklaces, Rukka approached me and told me not to wear the particular necklace that I was looking at because it was supposed to be for women—Torajans would consider me a *bencong* (transvestite) if I wore a necklace with that specific pattern. People at the booth laughed; probably imagining me as a *bencong*. I spontaneously decided to challenge Rukka, saying that I might wear the necklace on purpose to express my solidarity with LGBTQ+ people, a group that had been facing massive state-sponsored discrimination in Indonesia for a few years. Rukka, however, was not affronted by this idea. Rather, she expressed approval of my idea and shared a story from her childhood:

> When I was a little girl, I loved to play drums, but this was absolutely forbidden for women by *adat*! My mum, however, encouraged me to play. She said that we must challenge these rules and overcome them since they are a symbol of injustice, a symbol that puts women in a lower position. So, I played the drums and everybody in the village knew it. Nothing happened to me, but that was because my family had a high status. If an ordinary girl did that, she would be punished based on *adat* law for violating the *adat*.

Rukka was able to challenge *adat* because of her family's social position. I found this quite surprising. Was she not the chair representing *adat* communities and the idea of *adat*? For Rukka, *adat* was something that can and should be criticized, most of all from within the customary communities. It is not something written in stone but something always in progress. Most of all, Rukka told me, "*adat* is not just law. In many cases, there is indeed *adat* law that is quite feudal. That is why we always say that *adat* is not just law, it is not even essentially law. Seeing *adat* as law is a very conservative view because people think that they are laws, and all Indigenous people do is follow these ancient laws, and they are only Indigenous if they do so." What I learned from talking with Rukka was that for her, challenging tradition is a crucial part of indigeneity. Tradition, I realized, unfolds in a dialectical movement. It is something Indigenous people rely on to consolidate as a political identity struggling for land rights, for instance, but it is also something they must challenge when they do not want to rebuild a new kind of feudalism: They apply indigeneity for equality, but tradition might enhance social hierarchy. Therefore, in the Indigenous activist's struggle, indigeneity is both something to be preserved and something to overcome. This is quite at odds with the state approaches to *adat* that I explained in previous chapters. On many occasions, I heard Rukka talk about the threat of feudalism. In a meeting in the Makassar office, she argued for a law on the provincial scale that should be based on AMAN's notion of *adat*. This law should not only provide a basis for other local regulations but also must make clear that feudal structures, such as kingdoms and sultanates, are not *masyarakat adat*. *Masyarakat adat*, for Rukka, are people who always have been defeated and exploited and include those who have been subject to discrimination and heteronomy throughout history. Within AMAN, these suppressed people at the margins have, since 1999, organized to struggle for their dignity including the struggle against the political structures that have oppressed them, whether the colonial state, kingdoms, or Suharto's New Order. Rukka was also aware that the structures oppressing Indigenous peoples reached into these very communities. Traditional elites all too often cooperated with hegemonic forces from outside. This internal tension—the egalitarian claim of being marginal people and traditional hierarchies of power—is always present in the politics of indigeneity.

It is no wonder that in *reformasi* Indonesia, *adat* and tradition have become contested political resources, applied by reactionary local elites, opportunist politicians, and progressive activists. Often, these groups have been in opposition to each other, but sometimes they have cooperated to reach particular political goals or to allocate resources. In this chapter, I outline and discuss some examples of the deployment of tradition and *adat* from the province of South Sulawesi. My aim is to show how *adat* is applied in different contexts and constellations, unfolding within the Indigenous paradox, that is, between indigeneity as the other of the state and, at the same time, as a part of the state and state institutions. Indigeneity as an ideology can emerge in quite different forms, representing people's different relations to their political and economic circumstances. Rukka's understanding of *adat* is only one possible way of thinking about *adat*; other ways of understanding *adat* compete with this progressive approach and sharpen the political discourse and legislation on indigeneity as well. The following section is based on conversations with members of *adat* communities, activists, political scientists, and politicians, but most of all, the discussion is based on close readings of legal texts, in this context, local regulations (*peraturan daerah, perda*) dealing with *adat* issues.

Adat in Local Legislation After Suharto

The first legal document concerning *adat* to be issued in South Sulawesi after the New Order period was the local regulation No. 8/2000 in the regency of Jeneponto, an area inhabited by Makassarese in the very south of the province. The *perda* on Empowerment, Preservation and Development of Custom-Tradition and Customary Organizations (*Pemberdayaan, Pelestarian dan Pengembangan Adat Istiadat dan Lembaga Adat*) was, as Tyson (2011, 662) writes, unilaterally implemented by the local government without any meaningful participation of or consultation with customary communities or even *adat* authorities. Similar *perda* were adopted in other regencies in the following years, for instance, in Gowa and Majene, but all without delivering substantial effects on the acknowledgment of *adat* that would appease Indigenous activists. A closer look at these documents reveals rather superficial references to *adat* and shows the thrust of these *perda*, which were more concerned with embedding *adat* under the domain of the state, even though some hints were made in favor of limited sovereignty. In paragraph 2, the 2000 regulation in Jeneponto, states that the empowerment, preservation, and development of custom and tradition (*adat istiadat*) is intended to enable *adat istiadat* to "encourage and designate the continuity of development and national resilience in the archipelago" (Pemerintahan Kabupaten Jeneponto 2000, 4; translation by the author). The local regulation borrowed much of its terminology from the New Order by referring to development and resilience, but it also stressed the importance of the marginal setting as the archipelagic perspective is mentioned in the *perda*. This reference to development indicates that *adat istiadat* is seen as a part of Indonesia and its archipelagic culture—that is, as an integral part of the nation.

Consequently, the next paragraph of the regulation states that the "empowerment and preservation of tradition must be directed toward fostering solid national stability in the fields of ideology, politics, economy, culture, and national defense" (Pemerintahan Kabupaten Jeneponto 2000, 5; translation by the author). This embedding into the nation can be found throughout the *perda*. In paragraph 4, two criteria are outlined for *adat istiadat*: It has to be alive and it has to be useful in development. The notion of tradition still existing clearly has similarities with the amended version in Article 18 B(2) of the Indonesian Constitution in which the ongoing existence of *adat* is a crucial feature. *Adat* cannot be revived after it has disappeared and lost importance for a specific community. The notion of being useful for development once again reproduces the New Order ideology of development, but it is interesting that this development is carried out within *adat istiadat* and not against this tradition. Also, in paragraph 10 on the authority and obligations of *adat* institutions, one can find at least a partial recognition of *adat*: *Adat* institutions have the authority to restrict activities that contradict *adat* in a certain place, and they have the authority to settle all disputes over customary/traditional issues. This grants *adat* institutions partial sovereignty over their internal affairs, once a major concern for Indigenous activists (see on the issue of Indigenous sovereignty more generally, Acciaioli 2007, 305).

In the early 2000s, the first wave of *adat* (or, as in the *perda* of Jeneponto, *adat istiadat*) recognition on the local scale in Sulawesi through local regulation was highly influenced by the New Order idea of development and of *adat* as a domesticated part of the archipelagic national culture. Land rights and land tenure were still not mentioned in the Jeneponto, Gowa, and Majene regulations, and the whole process of debating and issuing the regulation was top down, with little effect on *adat* institutions and communities. These regulations were important insofar as they put *adat* onto the political agenda and thus created a common political language of *adat*, recognition, customary institutions, rights, and obligations through which activists could start to communicate with local policymakers. It was not until 2015, however, that local regulations acknowledging *adat* communities were issued in South Sulawesi.

In the next section, I outline some examples of how *adat* and tradition were applied politically in different parts of the province. This is not an overview of all aspects and cases. I provide these examples to discuss how *adat* was deployed in different ways and how these processes shaped the relations between Indigenous people and the state, as well as how indigeneity as an ideology emerged through these processes.

Negotiating Indigeneity in the Toraja Uplands

As outlined in chapter 3 on identities and history in South Sulawesi, the Toraja in the uplands have become an iconic symbol of tradition. The Toraja ethnic group in the northern part of the province is a well-known group that made use of tradition to attract tourists especially from the late New Order era onward; however, tradition and *adat* are also crucial in Torajan politics. Torajans were incorporated into the New Order state through what Schefold (1998) has called the domestication of culture: Folkloristic elements were actively used by the state and promoted as parts of national culture. This was part of a strategy to not only depoliticize ethnicity but also develop cultural tourism. The scenic landscape of the uplands, exotic burial rituals with *tau tau* statues in the rocks marking burial sites for nobles, iconic *tongkonan* houses, and relatively good infrastructure all have made this area a major tourist destination in South Sulawesi.

The traditional icons are now an important means through which ethnic identity is expressed, but the Toraja have existed as an ethnic group only since the Dutch gained control in the region after 1906 and introduced boundaries between what they identified as ethnic groups. The Toraja, who had not been Islamized at that time, thus became an object for missions. Missionaries as well as Dutch officials dreamed of a Christian upland Sulawesi, seeking to prevent these groups from falling into Islam (Roth 2005, 493–494), and the Toraja represented the main target for their efforts. The term Toraja, meaning "people from above" in Buginese, was initially not a self-ascription. Instead, mission groups in the late nineteenth century made the term popular among the respective groups. It was during the late colonial period that administrative boundaries united distinct Toraja-speaking groups that had never before shared a common consciousness as an ethnic group (Tyson 2010, 82–84). This administrative unit later became the Toraja regency in independent Indonesia. Christianity, language, and traditions, such as the *aluk to dolo* religion and the related ceremonies and material culture, became important markers of Toraja identity. The era after independence was characterized by a rejection of traditional elites as populist elements gained some influence and advocated for a less hierarchical society, but the New Order provided opportunities for traditional elites to restore their power. *Adat* leaders engaged with and supported the hegemonic Golkar Party as a way to regain power. Their traditional *lembang* governance system was replaced in 1985 by the Indonesia-wide administrative unit of *desa*, which divided the *lembang* into smaller administrative units. *Adat* was reframed as culture (*budaya*). Some traditional leaders remained in influential positions, whereas others felt marginalized by the new *desa* system (de Jong 2009, 274–276). Thus, *adat* was, on the one hand, depoliticized and, on the other, strengthened through a cultural approach and traditional elites maneuvered within the new administrative system.

Whereas the New Order regime incorporated the Toraja into national culture as an ethnic group, ethnic identity engaged in a new relation with the state in *reformasi* Indonesia. As Indigenous activists often criticized administrative units as being forcefully imposed on ethnic groups outside Java, they demanded a return to the traditional administrative system of *lembang*. The *lembang* system, they argued, should replace the administrative units of *desa* that were alien to Torajan culture. Seeing an opportunity to restore the power they had gradually lost since the introduction of the *desa* system, parts of the traditional elite joined the campaign for the *lembang*. Local political elites also sought legitimation through the tribal slot. The decentralization process opened up new opportunities for this endeavor. According to law No. 22/1999, village units in Indonesia could be based on local forms instead of the *desa* (de Jong 2009, 276). This new opportunity triggered a dynamic process in the regency of Tana Toraja where Indigenous activists from the local AMAN branch, activists from the Indonesian Forum of the Environment (*Wahana Lingkungan Hidup Indonesia*, WALHI), and the *bupati* (district head) advocated for a return to the traditional *lembang* system. The local regulation No. 2/2001, which introduced the traditional administrative unit of *lembang* in the regency of Toraja, was issued only a few months after Law No. 22/1999 was put into force. This quick process was driven by local political elites as well as by nongovernmental organizations (NGOs), which were later disappointed by the results. A former AMAN director, for instance, declared that the new *lembang* system was a matter of symbolism, serving to promote and maintain the authority and power of the traditional noble class. The local AMAN branch complained that the *lembang* regulation did not support substantive autonomy or inherent rights to control *lembang* affairs democratically, and it also did not address the issue of land titles. Indigenous activists and environmental groups rejected the revised local regulation issued in 2004: They saw it as not being in accordance with local ecological wisdom, customary land tenure, and autonomous governance (Tyson 2010, 88–94).

Lembang has been defined as a "geographical area inhabited by a group of people who share the same ancestral origins over generations and a concomitant sociocultural set of laws and values as well as a 'traditional' form of government organization" (de Jong 2009, 277). The *lembang* government has an elected leader (*kepala lembang*) who is the head of the executive. In accordance with *adat*, only people from the highest strata of society are eligible for candidacy. The *lembang* as a political body that came into existence through the local regulation also consists of a *lembang* committee as the parliament of the *lembang* with a secretary and heads of affairs, such as development and economy. The members of *lembang* committees are elected by the inhabitants of the *lembang*, but they should be descendants of traditional *adat* leaders, all of whom are from the highest strata in Toraja's traditional caste system. Not surprisingly, the new *lembang* system triggered competition within the Torajan elite. Elites began to influence election processes from behind the scenes and made claims regarding their genealogies and associations with different traditional houses (*tongkonan*).

Because key positions within the new *lembang* system have been occupied by representatives from the highest caste, it is not surprising that it is most of all their interests that have been best facilitated by the *lembang* system. This has significantly weakened the checks and balances between the executive and legislative, as representatives in both bodies were elected but often came from the same noble families. Although the official salary for high positions in the *lembang* is small and initially was not even paid, the position of *kepala lembang*, in particular, became highly desirable and contested because of the large amounts of money they were able to gather through, for instance, slaughtering taxes to be paid directly to the *lembang* head. Moreover, they enjoyed a large amount of autonomy from other administrative and political institutions. As a result, *lembang* heads became "little kings" (*raja kecil*) in their territories, while the interests of the ordinary people, including access to land, were not addressed. Although Indigenous activists, environmental organizations, and other progressive NGOs had hoped for a new form of grassroots democracy, they now criticized the *lembang* system for having brought back feudalism instead. Some activists even began to advocate for a return to the *desas* (de Jong 2009, 277–281). Indigeneity as a political tool was increasingly incorporated into the social stratification and became an "outspoken claim of political hegemony" in Toraja, as Klenke (2013, 163) notes.

Most Indigenous activists still insisted on their version of tradition, positioning themselves against the elitist approach outlined in the *lembang* governance. In 2008, Tana Toraja split into two regencies: The part in the south kept the name Tana Toraja, and the northern part became the new regency of Toraja Utara (North Toraja). In the wake of the local regulations for the acknowledgment of Indigenous communities, AMAN activists lobbied for such a *perda* in the Toraja regencies as well. As the *lembang* system did not facilitate the interests of the majority of Indigenous peoples, AMAN activists hoped that communities could gain control over customary land through acknowledgment by the regency. Local AMAN activists were able to establish ties with the government of Toraja Utara and lobbied for a local regulation. In 2019, the *bupati* of Toraja Utara eventually issued local regulation No. 1/2019 on the Recognition and Protection of the Rights of Customary Law Communities (*Perdaturan Daerah tentang Pengakuan dan Perlindungan Hak Masyarakat Hukum Adat*). Given that this local regulation was the outcome of AMAN's local struggle for recognition, it is worth looking at in detail.

The introduction of the *lembang* system was disappointing, and local regulations were seen as much better tools for proper recognition to all those who subscribed to a more progressive understanding of indigeneity. This was due to the fact that through the process of the acknowledgment of Indigenous communities, a certain distance could be maintained between the state and Indigenous people. On the one hand, in the *lembang* system, state and indigeneity fall into the same category: The *lembang* is an Indigenous institution *and* a state institution. In the local regulation, on the other hand, Indigenous communities are recognized as communities distinct from the state and are granted protection by the state.

The first part of the *perda* No. 1/2019 outlines considerations of local regulations. It is stated that the customary law communities in Toraja Utara actually exist, and this existence is expressed in the life of the society, their customs, territory, genealogy, cultural norms and values, local wisdom, and traditional law, which are acknowledged and are developing in accordance with the principle of the unitary state of Indonesia. It is also stated that the following paragraphs of the regulation apply to customary law communities that still exist (meaning there is no room for a revitalization of abandoned customs) and have *adat* institutions, a system of changing *adat* leaders, natural resources, cultural norms and values, and customary rules based on local wisdom that does not contradict provisions in laws. At the very beginning, then, the relationship between Indigenous communities and the state is made clear. Acknowledgment is granted within the framework of the unitary state and its laws. Customary law communities are therefore not separate political units. Conversely, criteria are mentioned that do make them distinct social units, and these criteria are further elaborated in the first chapter of the regulation.

Paragraph 1(6) states that customary law societies are groups of people who have been living in specific geographic regions from generation to generation within the unitary state of Indonesia, which have ties to the origins of their ancestors and strong relations to their land, territory, natural resources, institutions, customary government, and customary law. These features are clearly taken from international discourses. The emphasis is on Indigenous relations with their land, genealogy, and otherness in terms of self-government. What also stems from international discourse is the criterion of self-identification outlined in paragraph 1(10): The identification of a customary law society is a process of definition concerning the existence of customary law communities that is conducted by the customary law community. This self-identification has to be verified, as stated in paragraph 1(11). The regulation does not say more about the process of verification, but in paragraph 1(13) and 1(14), it is written that the recognition and protection of customary law societies are provided by the local government. The regulation tries to reconcile the principle of self-identification and the supremacy of the state. Although Indigenous people are portrayed as already existing entities with distinct features, they nevertheless depend on the state for their existence in legal terms.

The first paragraph defines some Toraja-specific feature of customary law societies, starting with the term *tongkonan* in paragraph 1(8). A *tongkonan* is defined as a source of values, norms, and rules of life for a specific community, which organizes all aspects of life of the families in a *tongkonan*, including social relations, culture, traditional beliefs (*kepercayaan*), environment, and natural sustainability. The traditional social unit of the *tongkonan* is depicted as a basic entity of *adat* communities in Toraja and is thus related to the aspect of nature. This is done in line with international discourses on Indigenous peoples as the notion of sustainability is brought in. Moreover, two important terms are defined in paragraph 1(9): *siambe'* and *puang*. These terms denote people from the lineages of traditional leaders who can be elected as customary leaders. They are symbols of the customary order, are appointed as the highest customary functionaries, and are associated with a *tongkonan*. Interestingly, the institution of *puang* is described as the highest level in traditional hierarchies, which in theory means that they are higher than the *kepala lembang*. *Lembang*, however, is not mentioned at all in the regulation, which suggests that *lembang* falls not into the realm of indigeneity but that of the state. In contrast, the *tongkonan* represent original Indigenous social units distinct from the state. The social status of the *puang* depends on an electoral process, and Indigenous activists emphasize the democratic nature of this process. The fact that only certain people are entitled to become a *puang*, however, clearly contradicts the principle of an egalitarian society—and, in reference to the similar issue of the *kepala lembang*, this is exactly what Indigenous activists have criticized as feudal structures not in line with authentic Indigenous principles. The *puang*, however, is clearly a traditional institution, and Indigenous activists do not necessarily interpret them as symbols of feudalism, arguing that the *puang* has to commit him- or herself to the benefit of the *tongkonan* and not to a specific group. For the purpose of indigeneity, traditional power relations are blended out and the image of a rather egalitarian community is evoked, despite the undemocratic principle of leadership.

In paragraph 1(17) and 1(18), customary forest as well as customary territory are defined, respectively. Customary territory is a geographic, social, and cultural entity with defined boundaries, which is owned, inhabited, managed, and used in accordance with *adat* rules. The term *customary forest* is used in a Toraja-specific manner: *Hutan tongkonan* is a forest that is established, maintained, and cultivated to fulfill the needs of development and maintenance of the *tongkonan*. This is crucial because a main purpose of the process of acknowledgment of Torajan customary communities (termed as *tongkonan*) by the local government is the acknowledgment of their customary territory by the state.

The local regulation mentions in paragraph 14(1) that land in the customary territory can be individually or communally owned. In paragraph 15(1), it is explained that customary forest is land communally owned by the *tongkonan* group, and it is written that neither the ownership nor the usage status can be changed. *Adat* regulations appear to be static. In paragraph 15(3), the regulation states that the customary forest also covers the resources within it, such as plants, animals, and springs. A static notion of *adat* is also expressed in paragraph 16, in which the duties of customary law societies are outlined: It is their duty to adhere to, maintain, and conserve *adat* values, norms, and rules. Paragraph 16b calls for a standardization of customary dress, rituals, and local wisdom. Paragraphs 17 and 18 again concern resources and land issues. Paragraph 17(1) specifies that customary law societies have rights over their land, forest, and natural resources, and paragraph 18(1) states that these rights can be either communal and collective or individual. These rights are specified, for instance, in paragraph 18(3), which confirms that personal landownership in customary territory is transferable only through *adat* rules and processes (and not through state laws). Moreover, paragraph 18(4) states that communal land can be used by other parties only when a joint decision is made by the community. Another interesting feature of the regulation is the way it refers to internal affairs. Paragraph 23(1) states that customary law societies have the right to manage themselves independently in accordance with *adat* institutions. This applies to internal affairs as well as to external issues when their collective rights are concerned. In sum, this approach comes quite close to what Indigenous activists have outlined as Indigenous sovereignty. This sovereignty is an autonomy for smaller customary societies applying mostly to internal, local ordering, but also including Indigenous communities' rights to deal with economic penetration from the outside (cf. Acciaioli 2007, 305–306).

The *lembang* government and the autonomy outlined in the *perda* in Toraja Utara contain some similarities with the way the Dutch dealt with *adat* during the late colonial era. During this period, some principles of Western law were added to a foundation of customary law. *Adat* was the basic law for everyday issues, and the Dutch had supervisors in regency court rooms who intervened only when case decisions diverged too widely from Dutch law (Pelras 1996, 277). Today in the 2020s, *adat* law is again dominant and acknowledged on the local scale. In the local regulation in Toraja Utara, paragraph 24 states that the customary law communities have the right to apply *adat* within their territory. *Adat* is the basic law only insofar as it does not contradict Indonesian law and the principles of the unitary state of Indonesia. The state, colonial or independent, is a sovereign entity that permits *adat* sovereignty in local matters.

The question of whether the revival of *adat* is a progressive development driven by Indigenous and environmental NGOs, striving for grassroots democracy and giving people access to their land, or a conservative backlash strengthening the power of traditional elites is not easy to answer. NGOs have criticized *lembang* governance and AMAN's struggle for local regulations to acknowledge Indigenous communities, which clearly showed that profoundly distinct approaches to indigeneity were at work in Toraja. The *lembang* governance system aimed to integrate indigeneity into the state, whereas the *perda* facilitated Indigenous communities' recognition by the state as distinct entities. It has been argued that, under the cover of liberal democracy in which people are formally equal in terms of their right to vote, the outcomes of elections in Indonesia have been heavily influenced by traditional hierarchies and oligarchic structures (e.g., Buehler 2010; Aspinall and Rohmann 2017; Choi 2017). This is also true for Toraja Utara for which, in practice, only noble people from the *puang* caste occupy powerful positions and voting is a matter of expressing one's loyalty to a certain *tongkonan* (Sukri 2018, 153–192). AMAN activists, on the one hand, oppose feudalism but, on the other hand, promote traditional governance in which hierarchies play an important role. To portray Indigenous communities as egalitarian, this has to be challenged, and in this case, tensions emerge between AMAN activists and traditional elites in the *lembang*.

During my stay in Rantepao, the capital of Tana Toraja regency, I met with several *adat* leaders who expressed the need for traditional forms of government. For them, AMAN is a force from the outside that does not understand *real* Torajan culture. These traditional leaders are not necessarily satisfied with Torajan politics, but their dissatisfaction usually originates from the fact that they believe the wrong people are in power. *Lembang* leadership is a contested issue, and different factions seek support from *adat* leaders. AMAN activists have told me that these *adat* leaders are incorporated into interelite struggles, and they are certainly right. The grassroots-populist version of indigeneity that they support also seeks support from traditional leaders, but these leaders have to be progressive and willing to share power with other castes. Applying indigeneity to egalitarian issues is nothing new in the Toraja highlands. In the early 1960s, a large part of the peasantry subscribed to communism—less because they believed in the overall idea of communism and more because the communists provided a political approach for land redistribution.

After the regime change, Torajan peasants reacted pragmatically and dropped their communist affiliations, expressing their aims for land redistribution in indigenist terms (Tyson 2010, 84). AMAN's approach is aligned with peasant activists in the 1960s. As the traditional elite restored their positions after the banishment of communism, AMAN activists had more opportunities now in democratic Indonesia to pursue their versions of indigeneity. AMAN activists achieved at least a partial success in Toraja Utara when the local regulation was issued; however, Tana Toraja regency does not yet recognize *adat*, even though it implemented the *lembang* system. What shines through in AMAN activists' debate is that they claim to argue for tradition but they struggle to define a specific notion of this tradition. As a result, they introduce the egalitarian approaches mentioned at the start of this chapter. In regard to the Indigenous paradox, although AMAN activists closely work with government representatives on all scales, they do not promote the idea that the state and *adat* should fall into the same category of the *lembang*. Their disappointing experiences of *lembang* call for a structural separation from the state and its institutions.

Adat and Politics in Gowa

Another configuration of *adat* and the state in South Sulawesi developed into a latent conflict in the regency of Gowa in 2016. This conflict emerged when the head of the regency (*bupati*) tried to set himself up as an *adat* leader to strengthen his political legitimacy. This did not happen out of the blue. This political move has a long history reaching back to the early days of the independent republic. In

1946, the king of Gowa, Andi Idjo Karaeng Laolang, officially relinquished his territory to the Republic of Indonesia, which had declared independence only a year earlier and was still involved in military struggles with the Dutch. Whereas many traditional leaders remained open to the idea of Dutch supremacy, some supported the idea of an independent Indonesia, and the king of Gowa was among them. In return, he became the first *bupati* of the Gowa regency. The current *bupati* of Gowa, Adnan Purichta Ichsan Yasin Limpo, therefore argued that "there is no king after Andi Idjo Kareng Laolang, because he relinquished his title and became a *bupati*. This means that whoever becomes the *bupati* in Gowa, his position is the same as that of the king during the era when Gowa was a kingdom" (Djumena 2016, author's translation). This statement is a bit self-contradictory because it is first argued that there is "no king in Gowa anymore," only to then claim that the *bupati* holds this position. In other words: The king has relinquished his rule; long live the king! To be more precise, the *bupati* claimed the status of king, which is referred to in the local Makassarese context as *sombayya* (Sastrawati 2018, 363). In his account, the transition from a monarchy to the Indonesian republic did not make the status of the *sombayya* obsolete, but rather transferred it from a position based on kinship to one based on an electoral regime within the state (Aminah 2016).

Indeed, there is a local juridical framework in Gowa on this issue in which the relation between *adat* and the state is regulated. The local regulation No. 28/2016 on the implementation of the local regulation No. 5/2016 concerning the arrangement of customary institutions states in paragraph 1(3) that the *bupati* of Gowa is the chair of the customary council, which was interpreted as correspondent to the position of the *sombayya*. In any case, the *bupati* claimed a crucial *adat* function that comes with a significant amount of political prestige. Some people in Makassar and Gowa with whom I spoke noted that this *perda* was probably a reaction to King Andi Maddusila Andi Idjo's own aspirations to become *bupati*. The title of king of Gowa remains a heredity title without any political power. The king hoped that, in the wake of the revitalization of traditional power structures, he could also claim the political position of *bupati*. After the king was unsuccessful, the power struggle continued, and the *bupati* saw his chance to seize the *adat* position.

Tensions grew between the government, the *Lembaga Adat Daerah* of Gowa, and between the supporters of each camp. In September 2016, dozens of the king's devotees fought with the police when the *bupati* and his allies carried out an *adat* ceremony in the *adat* palace. During the ceremony, the *bupati* ritually washed important *adat* utensils. The king and his supporters called this a violation of *adat* because only the king is allowed to conduct the ritual. Andi Maddusila Andi Idjo's supporters disrupted the ceremony equipped with traditional weapons, but the government seemed to be well prepared because the police and dozens of security guards with the support of vigilante groups were brought to the palace to protect the ceremony. As the protestors tried to enter the palace, the police used tear gas and eventually the king's supporters withdrew.

When I visited Makassar in 2019, however, the conflict had not been resolved. It remained a latent tension between traditional nobles and the government, both of whom claimed to represent *adat*. This conflict also was and is of great symbolic meaning because the Gowa kingdom is one of the historically important kingdoms in eastern Indonesia and is a symbol of resistance against the VOC (*Vereenigde Oostindische Compagnie*, United East India Company). Sultan Hasanuddin, the sixteenth king of Gowa, led the revolt against the Dutch and their allied kingdoms between 1666 and 1669, known as the Makassar War. In modern Indonesia, Hasanuddin was raised to national hero status in 1973 to construct a seeming continuity of Indonesian history reaching far into the past. The government's claim regarding the position of the king demonstrates the government's eagerness to use *adat* as a supplementary resource for legitimacy. In that sense, the *bupati*'s attempt to be regarded as the king was an attempt to indigenize local democracy. According to the *bupati*'s claim, indigeneity is both preserved and also obsolete: The genealogy of the Gowa kingdom came to an end with the integration of the kingdom into the state, but at the same time, the essence of the Gowa kingdom was preserved in the state position of the *bupati*. This makes sense only when one accepts the Gowa kingdom as a predecessor of the modern Indonesian state, Andi Maddusila Andi Idjo, who was involved in the dispute that started in 2016, however, insists that state and *adat* are two distinct political entities. These represent the two extreme positions on indigeneity: Indigeneity and the state are either intrinsically linked or form distinct spheres within which the respective other should not interfere.

These attempts to reinstall kings are not uncommon in Indonesia after Suharto. In some cases, like in West Kalimantan, the revival of tradition and the revitalization of traditional kingdoms fueled ethnic violence because the kings are tokens of ethnic identification against outsiders. Only the kingdom of Mempawah, however, has aimed directly at political power (van Klinken 2007, 155–157). Probably the most prominent case, however, is that of the North Moluccas where the king of Ternate, Mudaffar Sjah attempted to fill the position of the provincial governor of the North Moluccas. This conflict occurred in the wake of decentralization when the North Moluccas became a separate administrative unit from Ambon, the provincial capital, a process that was accompanied by ethnic and religious conflict. Mudaffar Sjah used his position as king for his political aspirations, but it has to be stressed that he and his family had already been politically active in the Golkar Party for a long time. Later, the king changed sides and ran as deputy governor for the United Development Party (*Partai Persatuan Pembangunan*, PPP). In 2002, he was unsuccessful in the election, but this case revealed how traditional elites have made power claims, especially in politically unstable environments (for a detailed analysis of this case, see Bubandt 2004, 16–23).

Cases of revitalization of local nobility differ throughout Indonesia: Not always are they directly aimed at political power, and in cases in which they are, local circumstances differ, such as in the degree of ethnic conflict and formal political affiliation. For instance, in the North Moluccas case, ethnic and religious identities played crucial roles, whereas the conflict in Gowa was entirely Muslim and Makassarese. We can also observe some general patterns, however, in different parts of Indonesia, including South Sulawesi. In general, the phenomenon of the revival of nobility has shown that the egalitarian and antifeudal thrust, which had been a crucial feature of Indonesian politics during the struggle for independence and before Suharto, had faded. This is important to keep in mind when discussing AMAN's concept of indigeneity, which is outspoken against hierarchical orders and traditional nobility as they conceptualize *masyarakat adat* in rather egalitarian terms. Also, the revitalization of kings and their attempts to gain political power point toward the contradictive relations between the state, political power, and *adat*. Can or should they be part of formal politics to make political power relations Indigenous, or should they be separated to make political institutions more Indonesian, that is, formally equal for all citizens? Are the issues of traditional revitalization a cause for the people, as they are often framed that way, or are they interelite struggles? Whereas the *lembang* regulation in Toraja was the outcome of efforts by both state officials and *adat* leaders as well as activists (although activists were later disappointed with the outcome), the *perda* in Gowa was merely a claim by a state official in the name of *adat*. Land issues were not at stake but rather were symbolic capital for political purposes. In this sense, this conflict also had a material foundation, as resources were at stake. As such, the conflict in Gowa was a conflict within the elite that was carried out through the state apparatus and the supporters of each group. It has been shown that patron-client relations as well as traditional political structures and ancestry have played a crucial role in power claims and struggles for political influence in South Sulawesi (Tyson 2011, 654). In this respect, the revival of *adat* and tradition is a tool for intraelite struggles, both within the traditional elite as well as within the wider elite formation encompassing both traditional and political elites.

The Gowa kingdom and the local *lembaga adat* is not an AMAN member. As a historically dominant group, the Gowa lack the crucial criteria of being marginal. Historically, the Gowa kingdom had oppressed marginal groups in South Sulawesi, and therefore, the kingdom is depicted as an oppressive force to Indigenous peoples by AMAN activists. This does not mean, however, that smaller communities of Makassarese or Bugis cannot apply for recognition as AMAN members. Not surprisingly, AMAN activists frequently expressed their dissatisfaction when the government referred to kingdoms, such as Gowa, as *adat* communities. The idea that the state and Indigenous communities should combine in one institution is contrary to AMAN's approach.

AMAN's Early Success: The Recognition of the Ammatoa Kajang

An Indigenous group that is iconic as *masyarakat adat*—in the sense that AMAN activists understand the term—is the Ammatoa Kajang group in Bulukumba regency in the south of the province. In historical chronicles, the Kajang have been portrayed as a part of the Makassarese for political reasons, but they use different languages (Mountain and Coastal Konjo). The Kajang are formally mostly Muslim. They strongly argue that they are a distinct ethnic group (Maarif 2012, 28–34). Unlike the Gowa kingdom, the Kajang have always been marginal and therefore are representative of the ideal type of an Indigenous community. The Kajang are divided into the Inner and Outer Kajang. In parts of the territory, modern devices, such as motorbikes, cars, smartphones, and even shoes, are not allowed. The Ammatoans depict their territory as the realm of *kamase-masea* (Konjo: simplicity or modesty), which means a way of life of self-reliance and sufficiency (Maarif 2012, 113). Being iconic also means, in the age of indigeneity, to enter the spotlight. Because of their traditional appearance, AMAN activists presented the Ammatoa Kajang community as a typical Indigenous community to the minister of Environmental Affairs and Forestry, Siti Nurbaya Bakar, to persuade her that recognition of Indigenous communities is an important issue (Afiff and Rachman 2019, 462).

In 2015, the regency of Bulukumba issued the first *perda* on the acknowledgment of Indigenous communities in South Sulawesi. This was due to AMAN's efforts and the iconic features of the Kajang, and it represented a crucial step in AMAN's struggle in the province. Other *perda*, including the previously analyzed *perda* in Toraja Utara, borrowed definitions and arguments from the 2015 regulation, but there was an important difference: Whereas other local regulations in South Sulawesi have provided general criteria for communities applying for *kommunitas masyarakat adat* status and outline the processes of acknowledgment, the Bulukumba regulation directly acknowledged the Ammatoa Kajang community and did not offer this acknowledgment to other communities (paragraph 2).

The Ammatoa Kajang community has been depicted as a community with special features. Their *adat, pasang ri Kajang*, is the source of all values that are meant to regulate the principles of life in the community. In paragraph 18, it is written that the community enjoys the right to follow and practice their traditional religion (*kepercayaan*), although the Kajang are officially adherents of Islam. Difference is also, and maybe most important, evoked through their traditional knowledge on land tenure as stated in paragraph 11: The tenure and land use system in the Ammatoa Kajang customary law community area is determined based on the Indigenous *pasang*. Consequently, the Ammatoa Kajang community is obliged in paragraph 14 to comply with, maintain, and preserve *pasang* and to maintain the customary forest. In paragraph 13, the customary forest is defined as land that is owned collectively in the community's territory, and its status cannot be changed in terms of ownership or use. *Adat* land, however, can be subject to both collective and individual ownership, based on *adat* regulations as written in paragraph 16. In paragraph 17, the right to development is outlined. The community not only has the right to development but also the right to information and to make an informed decision about whether development projects should be rejected or approved. Paragraph 17 deals with interventions from outside and, along with the paragraphs on landownership, forms the cornerstone of the community's sovereignty.

Although the local regulation allows only for the recognition of one specific community, it contains crucial features that are important for Indigenous activists, most of all the "internal ordering of local control" (Acciaioli 2007, 305). *Adat* is de facto acknowledged as the prime law regime for internal issues, which indicates a high degree of autonomy. The community is sovereign over their customary forest and the natural resources within it. In this respect, the *perda* was a major success for AMAN, even though the term *masyarakat hukum adat* was used and not the favored term of *masyarakat adat*, which does not limit *adat* to matters of law. As a compromise, however, the regulation stresses the aspect of *pasang* as an encompassing worldview that goes far beyond the realm of law. Indeed, the Ammatoa or Inner Kajang, in particular, have preserved their traditional worldviews against many attempts at religious modernization. Both the Darul Islam movement and Islamic organizations who visited the community during the New Order era have largely failed (Maarif 2012, 56). The New Order also categorized the Ammatoa Kajang as *masyarakat terasing* (estranged community), but all efforts to modernize the community have been unsuccessful. Among environmental scientists, the Ammatoa Kajang are well known for their successful preservation of their forest. They divide their forest into three categories: *borong karamak* (Konjo for "powerful forest"), *borong bat-tasayya* (Konjo for "demarcation forest"), and *borong luarak* (Konjo for "outer" or "ordinary forest"). The powerful forest is regarded as the home of ancestor spirits and nonritual activities, such as extracting timber or other resources, are forbidden. Under certain circumstances and with the permission of the community, the demarcation forest can be exploited to a certain degree, but people usually take resources only from the outer forest (Maarif 2012, 36–37).

In some respects, it is not surprising that the Ammatoa Kajang was the first group whose rights were officially acknowledged in South Sulawesi. The Ammatoa Kajang group is an icon of indigeneity not only because of its traditional ways of life but also because of their struggle against the agro-industrial complex. In 1982, the Kajang engaged in a juridical conflict with PT Lonsum, which had begun to establish rubber plantations in the area. A lawsuit was issued by 253 households from the outer Kajang community claiming that 350 hectares were taken illegally from their customary land in 1981 when the company began to operate in the region. In 1983, the District Court in Buluk-umba ruled in favor of the litigants, but the court decided that they only had the right to 200 hectares. PT Lonsum, however, took the case to a higher court and in 1987, the Provincial Court in Makassar ruled that PT Lonsum had a right to the land, nullifying the claims of the litigants. The Kajang families took the case to the highest court, the Supreme Court of Indonesia, which finally ruled in 1990 in favor of the Kajang litigants and reinstated the 1983 decision by the District Court. As the litigants made their land claims on the basis of their *adat* rights, the Supreme Court found that Article 5 of the Basic Agrarian Law had to be applied. This was the only way to claim the land rights because only oral *adat* land laws existed. According to Article 5 of the Basic Agrarian Law, *adat* law should be the law applied to land issues as long as *adat* law does not conflict with national interests. This case endorsed the concept of *adat* rights after these rights had been neglected throughout the New Order era. The case showed, against many other cases, that it was generally possible to apply *adat* rights to successfully make land claims (Tyson 2010, 135–138).

Implementing the Supreme Court's decision, however, proved to be difficult. Whereas the company already had released 143 hectares after the District Court's decision, the additional 57 hectares became the subject of contestation as PT Lonsum employed a delaying tactic. The Kajang families received support from community lawyers and several NGOs, and some organized in local NGOs to express their demands. Tyson (2010, 139) called these NGOs "chameleonic" as they carried out activities and engaged in protests until they were blacklisted by the government only to reorganize as another NGO. In 2001, the Kajang were increasingly politicized because of unsatisfactory progress and

NGO engagement. As their indigeneity became the political identity on which they made their land claims, Kajang activists became radicalized and claimed further land that they now perceived as ancestral lands within the natural borders of the Kajang community, an era of about 540 hectares in total.

When tensions grew in 2001, PT Lonsum applied an appeasement policy, providing compensation money for crops farmers had lost during land resettlement. The company also offered jobs to recalcitrant farmers. The politicization on behalf of *adat* and the delaying tactics with appeasement offers fragmented the Kajang community. Some villagers perceived other Kajang as troublemakers, while local politicians also engaged in the struggle, mostly allying with the company. The conflict became violent in 2003 when direct actions were carried out by Kajang activists. Villagers and activists camped in front of the Bulukumba parliament demanding the implementation of the Supreme Court's decision. After ten days of protest, they eventually occupied the contested land. Local and provincial police forces violently ended the occupation, with at least two protestors dying in shootings, while forty-six people were injured and forty-three were arrested.

The *bupati* blamed outside intellectuals and NGOs for turning the conflict violent with false claims, and it became increasingly clear that the local government was unable to solve the conflict. Only after the *bupati* asked provincial authorities for support was a mediation team able to settle the conflict. After about two years of mediation between the conflicting and increasingly fragmented parties, the mediation team published their recommendation with the approval of the parliament of the South Sulawesi province. The team requested that PT Lonsum release a total of 414 hectares, which included an additional 271 hectares, and requested that the company commit to this decision in a written form. PT Lonsum agreed under the condition that the process of land release was monitored to prevent any further land claims in the future. This agreement included a statement from the Kajang community as well that no further land claims would be made within PT Lonsum's concession zone. On January 10, 2006, a peace agreement based on the recommendations of the mediation team was signed, and this time, the land release was secured though common efforts of lawyers, judges, government officials of all levels, the security apparatus, and the NGOs. After more than two decades, the conflict was settled to a large extent, and *adat* had proven to be a powerful resource applied by the Kajang and their supporting NGOs. The events after 2001, however, showed that frictions existed within the Kajang community. Although *adat* served as a common base for land claims and community identity, it did not cover all the particular interests of the groups and individuals within the Kajang community (Tyson 2010, 145–153).

To constitute as an Indigenous community, the image of a harmonious, traditional community was evoked as a political strategy. Micah Fisher and Willem van der Muur (2019), however, suggest that communal territory eventually became contested within the Kajang community and conflicts emerged over who could legitimately claim cultivation rights. *Adat*, therefore, should not be viewed as an ideal means to organize land tenure. Although this is certainly a valid argument, it is questionable whether the problems they raise would also occur in other *adat* land tenure sites given that the Kajang community had become internally fragmented during the years of struggle as politicians and PT Lonsum sought to fuel and exploit internal fragmentation. Moreover, as I have argued, *adat* can display both traditional hierarchies and egalitarianism. What *adat* actually is as both a political-economic praxis and as an ideology is subject to contestation, not only between NGOs like AMAN that advocate for an egalitarian approach and the adherents of kings and sultans but also within the marginalized groups. It is precisely this image of the egalitarian *adat* community advocated by progressive NGOs that challenges *adat* and causes these conflicting land claims within a community. This process, however, is valuable from an emancipatory perspective because it shows that *adat* is changeable and that, in some cases, traditional hierarchies can be challenged—precisely in the name of *adat*.

Indigenous Ideology and Its Paradox in South Sulawesi

Having discussed the examples of Toraja, Gowa, and Bulukumba in detail, it is important to note that *adat* in South Sulawesi has played, and still plays, a crucial role in many other conflicts. The conflict between the Indigenous people of Sorowako and the company PT Vale, which established a nickel mining pit in 1968, is a well-known case and has been the subject of academic research (Robinson 1986, 2019; Tyson 2010, 101–128). Instead of giving a complete overview of contemporary deployments of *adat* in South Sulawesi, however, the three cases discussed so far illuminate the different modes of how indigeneity has come into existence through its engagement with the state.

These three examples shed light on how the Indigenous paradox unfolds in local contexts in South Sulawesi. The Indigenous paradox is a contradictory formation in which indigeneity comes into being when native communities engage with the law of the nation-state while simultaneously claiming to be sovereign and thus outside this very law (Bens 2020, 2–3). This is the case in settler colonies, and in this book, I have investigated how indigeneity emerged in the context of Indonesia. As indigeneity was domesticated during the New Order era, it became mere folklore in some respects, whereas some native features of a supposedly harmonious society without class contradictions and with clear hierarchical structures became features of the Indonesian nation in New Order ideology. Indigeneity was inscribed, to a certain degree, into the state, and in democratic Indonesia, this was applied within the context of decentralization when local governments gained more authority.

In the cases of Toraja and Gowa, state institutions applied indigeneity (a concrete, local form of indigenism expressed in terms of *adat*). In ideological terms, this was similar to what was done under Suharto (Bourchier 1998, 204). Indigeneity was a paradoxical formation as the state was Indigenous, claiming native features, but nonetheless was denying special rights for particular Indigenous communities. In the wake of decentralization, indigeneity traveled to the margins within the state apparatus. Not only was the concept of indigeneity applied by activists, as I argued in chapter 4, but the state also applied the idea of indigeneity. In Toraja, indigeneity became a conjuncture of the interests of both activists and state officials, and eventually the new "Indigenous" *lembang* system became the domain of the traditional elite and politicians. In Gowa, the *bupati* directly claimed the position of king. In both cases, *adat* became a resource of the state, rather than something to be applied against the state and state sovereignty. At stake here was the political capital of traditional authorities. Indeed, the paradoxical formation of indigeneity was not apparent, because policymakers always stressed that *adat* and tradition were inherent parts of the nation and therefore must be represented in state institutions. This was the thrust of the local regulations in South Sulawesi (discussed at the beginning of this chapter). In these cases, indigeneity was even a tool for the state and the nation. Indigeneity, in this sense, is a state project. It relies on state laws, but it does not claim any profound sovereignty. This project was driven by local elites, however, and the local state apparatuses prepared a common language of tradition and *adat* through which activists could eventually formulate their claims. The case of Bulukumba revealed that it was possible to make *adat* claims successfully in New Order Indonesia even though implementation was difficult. After decades of conflict, Bulukumba was the first regency in South Sulawesi to officially recognize an *adat* community.

The questions remain: Is there a paradoxical formation within the local regulations? Do they express the contradictions of indigeneity to produce indigeneity? To a certain degree, the local regulations offer political autonomy for *adat* communities regarding their internal affairs. Paragraph 21 of the *perda* of Bulukumba, for instance, states that the Kajang community has the right to manage its internal affairs and external affairs concerning the existence of the *adat* community and their rights. These rights of autonomy and self-government based on indigeneity are guaranteed by the state. This paragraph is embedded into the context of other paragraphs, many of which deal with economic issues, such as the right to development (article 17) and the right to land and natural resources (article 16). Indigenous sovereignty only in terms of cultural distinctiveness would not require such a local regulation.

The local regulation acknowledges an *adat* community to enable it to gain land rights at the national level. It is therefore clear that political indigeneity is overdetermined in the sense that the economy and struggles over resources are the determining factors in the latter instance, but they never appear to be independent from cultural factors (cf. Althusser 2005, 112–113). Indigeneity is an ideology that cannot be explained merely in regard to the economy. Rather, the national and local context of existing *adat* institutions—a history that largely precludes other forms of political identity for peasants—and processes of decentralization are the relatively autonomous superstructures through which indigeneity came into being in Bulukumba. Economic conflicts based on the separation between producers and land resources were the last determining instance of the conflict given that they were the initial reason for political action. The conflict and the formation of an Indigenous identity in Bulukumba never asserts itself merely through this latter action. The paradoxical formation in which the state guaranteed rights against the state and thus enabled a certain degree of autonomy was overdetermined, too. This formation was an outcome of the economic struggle between peasants and PT Lonsum, but it would have been unthinkable without certain notions of indigeneity and Indonesian law.

The cases I highlight in this chapter demonstrate how the relationship between indigeneity and the state developed in different ways. The cases of Gowa and, to a certain extent, the Toraja can be categorized as attempts by local elites to claim state positions. In the case of Gowa, the traditional position of the king (*sombayya*) was transformed into the state position of the *bupati* when Indonesia became an independent nation. Traditional hierarchies were affirmed in a democratic context, and identity based on *adat* was adjusted with citizenship: People should recognize the *bupati* as the *sombayya*, whereas the *sombayya* now argued that he was the legitimate *bupati*. In both the argumentation of the *bupati* who claimed the position of the *sombayya* and the argumentation of the *sombayya* who claimed the position of the *bupati*, indigeneity based on *adat* was used to affirm a traditional hierarchy. The Toraja elite had the same motives when advocating for the *lembang* system. This notion of indigeneity and *adat* is conservative in its nature because it does not aim to change anything in terms of economic conditions but instead further strengthens the existing order. Indigeneity is thus a tool for interelite struggles and does not represent struggles or contradictions between classes. In both cases, the argument is that *adat* should be part of the official state structure as an attempt to indigenize local politics and state institutions. What might appear as a shift in the way Indonesian politics emerges is, in fact, not that much different. In many parts of South Sulawesi, it has always been common that only traditional nobility could successfully run for higher political offices. In this regard, indigenization by traditional elites does not introduce any cracks in the foundation of the political economy or in the way society and the state are organized. Indigeneity is not much more than new paint over a structure that has endured throughout the so-called New Order and *reformasi*.

In contrast, indigeneity, as it emerged in Bulukumba, represented a distinct approach: It was a rejection of new ownership structures, a project the New Order pushed in many places throughout the archipelago. Indigenous activists in Toraja had the same objectives, and they hoped that in places where an Indigenous political structure was applied that the concerns of ordinary people would be considered more readily. In Bulukumba, indigeneity is related to the changing economic conditions of land dispossession. As the ideology of indigeneity came into conflict with economic conditions, and the local government did little to implement the Supreme Court's decision, this ideological cohesion was disrupted. The state (the regency government, to be more precise) did not have an ideological apparatus to ensure cohesion between the ideology of indigeneity and the interests of the economically dominant formation (i.e., PT Lonsum and the local political elite). Therefore, the government had to rely on the repressive state apparatus. In the 2015 local regulation, the ideology of indigeneity, as it emerged from this political struggle, was inscribed into a legal document—including all its inner contradictions—which led to internal struggles within the Kajang community. Although some have suggested that indigeneity implies the notion of a harmonious society, within the actual deployment of *adat* as a system of self-governance in land tenure issues, conflicts became manifest (Fisher and van der Muur 2019). Indigeneity as an ideology that was applied to defeat a threat from outside covered up internal conflicts based on traditional hierarchies, divergent claims on land titles, and notions of egalitarianism. AMAN activists, however, are well aware of these frictions within *adat* communities. Therefore, activists constantly keep in touch with *adat* communities to promote their rather egalitarian notion of indigeneity in workshops and projects. Indigeneity is indeed a contested concept even within *adat* communities. Indigeneity has never represented the existing relations of production but instead the peoples' relationship with these relations of production and the social conditions deriving from it. Therefore, indigeneity is not a coherent set of rules about how these relations should be organized (e.g., in land tenure), but instead is an ideology that expresses general stances on economic conditions, in many cases wrapped in cultural, noneconomic terms. Internal contradictions that could lead to conflicts about land tenure in Indigenous communities often are not directly addressed by the ideology of indigeneity: It is not (at least not in the first place) an ideology deriving from an economic approach.

Activist Strategies and Concepts of Indigeneity in South Sulawesi

In 2014, the AMAN office in Makassar became a center for volunteers supporting the Jokowi-Jussuf Kalla presidential campaign. Outside the office, large stickers were put on the windows and a banner in support of Jokowi was hung up in front of the office. In 2015, when Jokowi was elected, activists in the office were euphoric and expressed their hope that a new chapter in relations between Indigenous peoples and the state had begun. They were optimistic that, within a few years, the Indonesian Supreme Court's 2013 ruling that *adat* forest could not automatically be considered state forest would be followed by processes of acknowledgment of Indigenous communities and their land. At that time, it had not yet been decided that Indigenous communities that had applied for land titles had to obtain formal recognition as *komunitas masyarakat adat* from the governments of their respective regencies first. Activists hoped that the Jokowi government would pave the way for a general acknowledgment of Indigenous communities on the national scale.

In late December 2016, however, institutional activists in Jakarta agreed with proposals that would require Indigenous communities applying for land titles to first obtain recognition in their regencies. In return, they secured the transfer of land in a state nature reserve to an Indigenous community, which created an important precedent for the activists (Affif and Rachman 2019, 464). Indigenous activists in the regencies, however, with support from their provincial counterparts, were now in charge of lobbying for local regulations on acknowledgment. Jokowi had also promised a national law on *masyarakat adat* that would ensure their juridical status and Indigenous communities' rights. This law was delayed by certain ministries, and by 2019, activists in Makassar had become deeply disappointed. The Jokowi stickers were faded and someone had tried to remove them from the campaign office. Some activists said they would vote for Jokowi as the lesser evil—after all, Prabowo had openly declared that he favored a policy in which the state would hold a strong position on land issues, and they feared a resumption of New Order approaches. AMAN's goals, they felt, were more compatible with Jokowi's ideas, which were built on strong nationalism but also assigned a less dominant role to the state. Because Jokowi promoted entrepreneurs and a more liberal economic environment, activists thought this could be helpful for their Indigenous aspirations, as Jokowi did not think that the forest would be best managed by the state. Others said that they would not participate in the election at all because they did not feel represented as Indigenous peoples. Educated activists, in particular, became increasingly aware of the close relationship between the oligarchy and the Jokowi government—a relationship that had been established when Jokowi first ran for president (Winters 2013, 13–15).

This sense of resignation concerning national politics, however, did not change AMAN's cooperative approach on the provincial and regional scales. During my stay in Makassar, AMAN activists were in constant contact with politicians on the provincial scale and notably on the local scale of the regency. When in Makassar, the vice *bupati* of Sinjai, for instance, would visit AMAN's office. Expressing her sympathies for AMAN's goals, Andi Kartini Ottong was a central figure in the process of issuing a *perda* in Sinjai in 2019 on the acknowledgment of Indigenous communities. In other regencies, the activists' lack of access to such influential politicians has made it difficult to pursue their goals.

Institutional activism has become especially important in regencies. This "local turn" (Tamma and Duile 2020, 270) is a direct result of both limited progress on the national scale and the mechanism of recognition that relies heavily on the regency level. In this sense, activists are still highly embedded in state processes but are faced with highly variable degrees of support in the respective regencies. Although they achieved success in Bulukumba, Enrekang, Sinjai, and Toraja Utara, they did not manage to gain support in other regencies, such as Tana Toraja, Gowa, Bone, or Maros. In regencies where success has been limited to date, it is often the case that *adat* and indigeneity are already applied by political actors to refer to their status within traditional hierarchical systems. *Adat*, in this context, often refers to kingdoms, sultanates, or traditional nobles who seek to maintain or regain their traditional political power. These actors try to monopolize their notion of tradition and thus are eager to keep alternative notions of *adat*, as promoted by AMAN activists, at bay. *Adat*, in this sense, becomes a contested notion, an empty signifier that is given meaning not only in discourses but also in political practices. As we have seen (and as I illuminate in chapter 5 on the processes in Enrekang), local regulations define crucial notions of indigeneity and put them into practice. Indigeneity gains meaning within the political processes of debating, negotiating, and issuing local regulations on the basis of the acknowledgment of Indigenous communities. AMAN activists, therefore, are not simply activists who fight against the state, as they demand acknowledgment. Above all, they engage with state institutions and struggle against other notions of tradition. As these other notions are often more entangled with the state—and this chapter has discussed this issue in regard to the *bupati*'s claim to be the king in Gowa and the traditional elite's aspirations in the *lembang* system in Toraja—AMAN activists are trying to occupy that very position within the state: Their version of indigeneity should be the one that is acknowledged in preference to other versions.

Since the late 2010s another crucial issue for AMAN activists in the Makassar office has been the indigenization of economies in communities acknowledged as AMAN members and by the regencies. This indigenization of local economies builds on the strategy of promoting Indigenous enterprises (*Badan Usaha Milik Masyarakat Adat*, BUMMA). During visits by government officials, for example, that of the vice *bupati* of Sinjai, economic potential is a much-discussed issue. Indigenous recognition, as the activists argue, can strengthen local economies. An Indigenous enterprise benefits from local populations' strong identification with their Indigenous community, and access to means of production (most of all land) can contribute to rural development, which has been a key issue for many politicians in rural South Sulawesi. By arguing for the BUMMA, Indigenous activists can engage deeply with the state, not only through lobbying but also through their demands: They demand access to *adat* forest for economic purposes and explain why local government should support Indigenous communities with capital (which can also take the form of machines or seedlings).

In my discussions with AMAN activists, however, the concept of Indigenous enterprises remained vague. One afternoon after lunch, I talked with Pak Ari, an AMAN activist from a Duri village about his understanding of and ideas about BUMMA. Pak Ari gave a general idea of what many other Indigenous activists had in mind when the topic of BUMMA arose. As the main criteria, he referred to the principles of local knowledge and customary rules, which should enter into the management of BUMMA. Pak Ari described normal cooperatives as being associated with the government, whereas BUMMA, in his view, were something outside the realm of the government and thus different principles should be applied. He explained this with the analogy of education: Although the government builds public schools, AMAN is eager to escape the grip of government education and has set up schools with *adat* curricula. Customary principles of management are, in his account, equal to the alternative curricula of *adat* schools. Pak Ari was eager to distinguish the BUMMA from other forms of enterprise that he associated with the government and the state. *Adat* values are at the core of both customary enterprises and schools, and these values make them different from normal schools and enterprises.

I thus asked Pak Ari to identify these values. Interestingly, Pak Ari spoke first of the value of mutual help, which should be strengthened in BUMMA. This was a surprising response insofar as *gotong royong* is often depicted as a core value of Indonesian forms of economy and is frequently referred to in state-driven discourses: It is something entirely Indonesian and by no means a value that serves to distinguish Indigenous enterprises from the state or other enterprises based on state ideology. Throughout Indonesian history, the ideal of cooperatives has been associated with the genuine Indonesian value of *gotong royong*, which has found its way into laws and state-driven discourses (Henley 2007). In other words, portraying indigeneity in terms of *gotong royong* and *gotong royong* as a symbolic resource for the Indigenous economy does not make a distinction between indigeneity and the Indonesian state; rather, it symbolically connects indigeneity, the nation, and the economy.

Pak Ari also pointed to other ascriptions regarding Indigenous enterprises— for instance, self-sufficiency/self-reliance (*keswadaan kedayaan*), which should make Indigenous communities less dependent on markets. Production should not only concern market demands but also produce value for the community. This idea, however, is also rooted in Indonesian political thought—for instance, that of Sukarno, who said that the Indonesian peasant (*marhaen*) should become independent as they own their own means of production and produce for their own consumption. The vague idea of *keswadaan kedayaan* seems to contradict notions of state-driven capitalization (through original accumulation) but also relies on the nationalist idea of an Indonesian peasantry. Just as with the notion of *gotong royong*, Pak Ari was referring to older, leftist-populist Indonesian notions and was claiming that they were represented in the idea of Indigenous economies.

When it comes to *adat* criteria, Pak Ari also remained vague as he emphasized only sustainability. *Adat* management, he explained, must avoid overcapitalization of *adat* territory. The aim is not only to ensure a prosperous society but also to maintain the functions of the ecosystem. This aim does not specifically refer to Indonesian values, but it does provide an argumentative structure against unsustainable use by large companies. Pak Ari, however, next explained the process of ensuring such sustainable Indigenous resource use. He was well aware that if a community was given land, the exploitation of natural resources as well as the furthering of individual interests within a customary community could occur. Although he did not mention the case of the Kajang in Bulukumba, I assume that he might have had that specific case in mind. Although BUMMA could ensure that all members would benefit from these natural resources, according to Pak Ari, such an enterprise was a long way from being established. As Ari explained, "BUMMA cannot be directly established. First, the capacity of the community has to be strengthened, as well as their critical awareness and their awareness of social issues."

The Indigenous community must be in a certain condition, which Pak Ari referred to using the passive forms of being in a condition (*ter-*): Awareness has to be awakened (*terbangun*) and social institutions have to be integrated (*terintegrasi*) to establish a BUMMA. Using the passive voices revealed that these communities were not currently operating according to this condition. For this reason, AMAN regularly conducted days-long workshops in these communities, which suggested that Indigenous communities were not yet able to conduct Indigenous economic activities. AMAN activists thus have had to engineer indigeneity as they engage with the community. This is not, however, simply a matter of teaching. In the eyes of Indigenous activists, this process is an uncovering of Indigenous principles that have been corrupted by individual interests and aspirations of overexploitation. In fact, activists have been eager to introduce principles of sustainability and social responsibility and equality. By "engineering" indigeneity, AMAN activists have created a new notion of indigeneity, but for this notion to emerge as indigeneity, it must appear to be original and authentic.

Pak Ari stressed the importance of self-reliance, but he eventually talked extensively about market integration. After all, BUMMA should integrate Indigenous communities into markets because they should ensure production according to market demands. Production standards should not simply be imposed on Indigenous communities but should be developed along with them (the producers) and should be monitored by them. At first sight, this approach of Indigenous communities developing Indigenous standards alongside NGOs would seem to provide agency to these communities. Autonomy of Indigenous certification, however, is possible only within the frame of market demands: Indigenous communities do not step out of the market but utilize indigeneity as a means to compete because certifying products as produced by Indigenous peoples might add value. Indigeneity therefore becomes a label, a brand: Capitalization of natural resources is partly compensated by the capitalization of indigeneity.

Indigenous activists in South Sulawesi aim at market integration but, at the same time, emphasize Indigenous autonomy and difference against capitalization and against the state. Indigeneity is evoked against and with the nation. A vague and general notion of Indigenous values is counterpositioned against other forms of enterprise, but Indigenous values always make reference to both Indonesian values and hegemonic concepts, such as sustainability. The same is true when it comes to the market: Pak Ari stressed self-reliance as an Indigenous value, but BUMMA aimed to incorporate Indigenous communities into markets. It is the rejection of the market as a self-reliant, autonomous community that constitutes indigeneity as a source of capitalization. Production under Indigenous standards increases exchange value, but this requires indigeneity as a set of supposedly authentic values that are produced through the process of awareness building that AMAN activists conduct in AMAN's member communities. This structure, in which the result (indigeneity) appears to be a precondition and original feature is not only paradoxical but also is indigeneity in its purest form in a dialectical sense: Both original and an identity in the making. In other words, the outcome of the process of becoming Indigenous and making indigeneity must appear to be the foundation of that very process. In economic terms, this means, most of all, an awareness of egalitarian principles (against individual interests) and overexploitation. Indigeneity is projected into the past as something original while departing from a critique of present conditions. When Pak Ari says, for instance, that Indigenous enterprises can be established only as awareness becomes present in a community, this process appears to be unveiling a concept of indigeneity that is obscured by individual interests and market integration. The idea of indigeneity as promoted by AMAN activists points to a social critique as it imagines indigeneity to be general equality, sustainability, and self-reliance. As such, the ideological content of indigeneity as a representation of people's relations to their material conditions becomes evident: Indigeneity represents a stance toward the state and the economy but never appears to be only a stance. Instead, it claims to refer to authentic ideas. This stance thus appears to be part of an essentialist identity. It is easy to say that this is mere imagination. Taking a critical notion of ideology into account—which argues that ideology does not simply represent existing socioeconomic conditions but rather people's imaginary relation to these conditions—indigeneity is necessarily contradictive because it posits a general explanation or approach to contradictive conditions. Indigeneity thus has to reject the nation and the market and represent a critique of these entities while, at the same time, it has to refer to and rely on them because no other sphere or language exists for the expression of indigeneity: Concepts of the state, the nation, *gotong royong*, market production, and self-reliance thus are the conjunctions between contradictory notions of hegemonic conditions on the one hand and indigeneity on the other.

In this chapter, I investigated the deployment of *adat* and, more generally, the notions of tradition in several cases in South Sulawesi and explained how Indigenous activists shape, negotiate, and refer to indigeneity. I analyzed the general contradictions that exist between distinct concepts of *adat* within political processes as well as AMAN's ideas about indigeneity. In chapter 5, I examine in more detail the case of Enrekang, the regency that adopted the second *perda* for the acknowledgment of Indigenous communities in South Sulawesi. I outline the political process, the content of the local regulation, and cases of Indigenous Duri communities seeking recognition. I also shed light on their economic aspirations. Many case studies focus on conflictual patterns, but I deliberately chose a setting in which the process of recognition went relatively smoothly. These cases are often neglected, but when it comes to exploring ideological constellations of indigeneity, it is worth examining how indigeneity is evoked in these settings.

ENREKANG AND THE DURI HIGHLANDS

Enrekang is a regency that has escaped researchers' attention. Much research has been conducted among the dominant ethnic groups in South Sulawesi, such as the Bugis, Makassarese, and Toraja, leaving Enrekang in a marginal position. Enrekang is home to three smaller ethnic groups, namely the Maiwa, Enrekang, and Duri. Historically, they formed a confederation of lesser sultanates called Massenrempulu, meaning "at the foot of the mountains," indicating the geographic features of the confederation and the present-day regency: Located between the Bugis-dominated lowlands in the south, the Toraja highlands in the north, and the Latimojong massif with Sulawesi's highest summit in the east, the area is a transitional zone. If one travels by bus from Makassar or Pare-Pare in the direction of Toraja, the flat landscape of the Bugis heartlands dominated by wide rice paddies eventually changes into a landscape of small but sometimes steep hills used for dry rice and as pastures for buffalo. This is the homeland of the Maiwa, the smallest ethnic group in Massenrempulu. Some Maiwa also inhabit the neighboring Sidenrang regency. This area is still part of the lowlands with its hot climate. Following the Sadan, one of Sulawesi's largest rivers, one eventually enters the area inhabited by the Enrekang group and the regency's capital of the same name. The town Enrekang lies at a low elevation but already at the foothills of the larger Latimojong massif. Hills and mountains surround the town, which has approximately thirty thousand inhabitants and depicts a local center of trade and public facilities. The Enrekang ethnic group occupies this transitional area between the lowland and the upland, and as soon as one leaves the town heading north, one reaches areas of higher elevation. The road eventually bends around the slopes with spectacular views into the deep valley of the Mata Allo River. This area is a destination for local tourists enjoying the cooler climate and the views. Restaurants and cafes can be found along the road, especially near the *gunung nyonya* (woman mountain), the geographic features of which symbolize a vagina. In Duri and even Toraja mythology, this geographic feature symbolizes fertility. The road winds at about six to seven hundred meters above sea level and the mountains, with their large rock formations on both sides of the road, reach up to fifteen hundred meters. In local mythology, these rocks on the high mountains are the remains of a cosmic ladder that once connected the earth and heaven. Just as in Torajan mythology (cf. Nooy-Palm 1969, 165–166), local myths in Enrekang explain that the world is divided into an underworld, the earth, and the sky. After a violation of a divine law (some informants mentioned a violation of the incest taboo by a noble), the stony ladder between earth and the sky through which humans had been able to meet with deities was destroyed and the earth was flooded by the gods as revenge. Only the remnants of the gigantic staircase can now be found as rocks within the landscape.

If one travels farther along the road, the view to the north eventually opens out onto a large highland plateau with gigantic rocks and hills, and large mountains to both the east and west: This is the land of the Duri. Living mostly on elevations between five hundred and twelve hundred meters above sea level, the Duri are a highland group. Their language is, to some degree, mutually intelligible with the Torajan language. Remnants of burials in caves similar to those in Toraja as well as paddy storages similar in shape to the famous *tongkonan* reveal similarities with Torajan culture. The Duri, however, just like the other groups in Enrekang regency, are almost entirely of Muslim faith. This explains why in some contexts, for instance in Makassar or outside Sulawesi, the Duri often refer to themselves as Bugis. In this sense, Bugis is mostly a synonym for a Muslim from South Sulawesi, but outside South Sulawesi, even the Toraja might refer to themselves as Bugis-Toraja (Mattulada 1982, 8).

The Duri, Enrekang, and Maiwa have their own languages, but these languages are mutually intelligible to some degree so that interaction, for instance at markets, is often possible without using Indonesian. The Duri farm rice only in the lowest parts of their territory because the climate is too cool for rice cultivation in higher areas. In those higher-altitude areas, onions and cabbage are the main crops, and like the coffee that is grown on the flanks of the Latimojong massif as well as the western mountainous parts of the area, these crops are mainly exported to other parts of Sulawesi and even other Indonesian islands. Most Duri live along the road between Enrekang and Makale, which is also where the largest towns, Cakke and Kalosi, are situated. Another town is Barakka in the eastern part of the Duri area. Duri from remote villages frequently visit these towns to buy food, clothes, and household articles or to sell their agricultural products.

Like the Enrekang and Maiwa, the Duri have a long history of smaller sultanates that united with the Masssenrempulu federation to strengthen their position in relation to the larger Bugis kingdoms in the lowlands. The Massenrempulu federation existed from the fourteenth century onward and throughout the colonial period. In Duri, the main sultanates were Malua, Alla, and Buntu Batu. Several smaller sultanates, such as Anggeraja, Baroko, and Banti, were vassals but largely autonomous in their internal affairs. The Dutch gained control relatively late; they established their rule between 1906 and 1912. The sultanates remained formally intact but debt bondage and other forms of slavery were abolished. In nationalist narratives, the population of Enrekang engaged in the struggle against the Dutch when they returned to Indonesia after World War II. A monument in Enrekang town depicts this struggle by nationalists against the colonizers (figure 3.3). The truth is that Indonesian nationalism was at that time something alien to a large part of the rural population. It was the educated youth who had been in contact with nationalist ideas in Java who engaged in a guerilla war against the Dutch; but, overall, resistance in Sulawesi was quite weak. Modern ideas were brought to Enrekang primarily through Islam. The sultanates and their hierarchical order had largely been destroyed during the Darul Islam rebellion when Darul Islam troops occupied large parts of Enrekang from the mid-1950s to the early 1960s. Before we deal with the current situation in Enrekang and especially in the Duri area, and their struggle for Indigenous rights and indigeneity, it is important to discuss in more detail how the Duri remember their history given that this history—and the way it is present in narratives—can greatly affect society and thus the concept of indigeneity in a given place.

The Duri have their own ways of making sense of their past—much of this chapter relies on what Duri interlocutors have told me, from ordinary farmers and Indigenous activists to Duri academics in Makassar. Their history—and the way they remember this history—is the very frame in which indigeneity has emerged as an ideology.

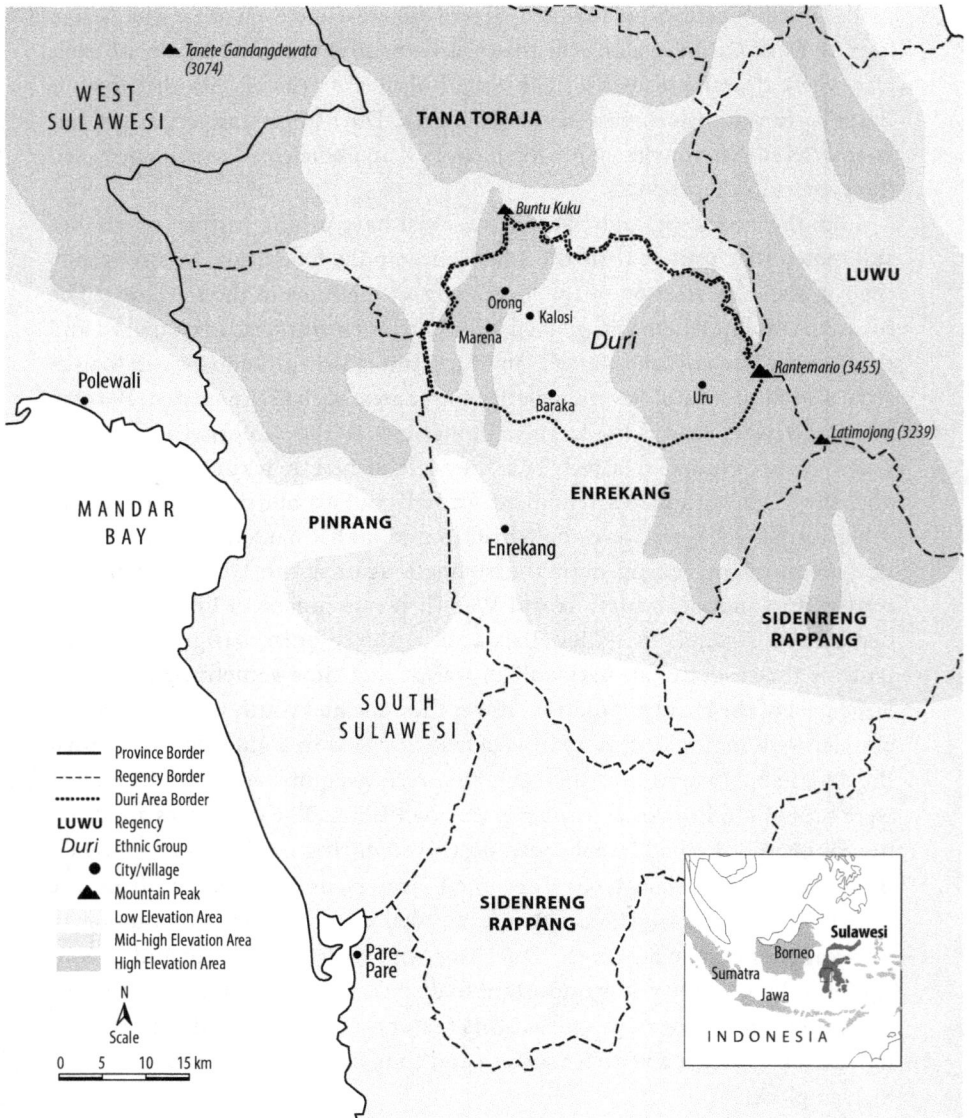

FIGURE 5.1. Enrekang Regency and the Duri highlands. Map of Enrekang Regency © Ruy Nubarani, Illustrator.

Duri Histories and Memories

History is always present for people in the Duri highlands. It is present in myths about the origins of nobles, in stories told in the evenings about the violent past, and in the landscape where not only were foreign trees and vegetables planted for food and cash crop production but also where bandits, freedom fighters, and rebels have dwelled. They came, brought ideas, politics, unrest, progress, and threat, and eventually they went away, leaving burned villages and fear as well as new crops, ideas about equality, and memories shaping the Duri identity. What appears in the 2020s to be traditional and to be the *adat* of the Duri has been subject to profound changes, especially since 1906 when the Dutch established their control throughout the province of South Sulawesi. The biggest change, however, occurred during the time of the Darul Islam rebellion between 1952 and the early 1960s. The Duri were quite used to violence. Slave traders, bandits, and rebels had come and gone since the days of the large lowland kingdoms. The Duri society of these times was stratified into slaves, ordinary people, and a complex system of ranks among the nobility. Islam had been incorporated into this system and, as in other parts of South Sulawesi, the advent of Islam changed the institution of slavery, as being enslaved by descent was abolished and people were enslaved through debt-bondage and the slave trade in other societies. "Slaving zones" (Fynn-Paul 2009, 2018) of non-Muslim population emerged in the highlands. Lowland societies enslaved people through the slave trade. In the formation of these slaving zones, political organizations were crucial because larger and more stable states were generally more successful in preventing their population from being enslaved. The petty sultanates with its part Islamic, part animist population and the small Toraja kingdoms were, in this regard, slaving zones for the lowland kingdoms, but most of all, religion as an identity marker determined these slave zones (cf. Fynn-Paul 2018, 3–4).

In Enrekang, Islamization was, as in many parts of Sulawesi, an Islamization from above: The rulers converted to Islam to strengthen their ties with the larger kingdoms in the coastal areas. Islam was introduced into the petty kingdoms in Enrekang at the beginning of the eighteenth century (Sitonda 2012, 101). Duri societies also gradually changed into open slave societies, whereas their northern neighbors, the Toraja, remained a society in which slaves were acquired from within the Toraja group. Conversion from the Indigenous Duri religion, *aluk tojolo* (which was similar to the *aluk to dolo* of the Toraja) was another means to avoid enslavement by raiders from the lowlands. Eventually, some Duri engaged in slave raiding among highland groups not yet converted to Islam and sold those they had enslaved to the lowland kingdoms.

Another change occurred during the colonial era when the Dutch established control in the early twentieth century. On the one hand, the Dutch cooperated with the majority of the traditional elite. In the Duri area, petty kingdoms were incorporated into indirect rule. On the other hand, the Dutch began to treat people outside the higher nobility as equals with little respect for traditional hierarchies among the unfree people, ordinary peasants, and the lower ranks of the nobility. Pelras (1996, 276) emphasizes this change also occurred among the wider Bugis societies in which the Dutch had introduced a clear-cut distinction between high-ranking nobility and all others. The lower nobility thus had to pay taxes and contribute compulsory labor, most of all for developing infrastructure, as did those who were formerly enslaved, many of whom became free in the wake of the establishment of Dutch control. In Duri, the majority of the population thus became formally equal, although unequal access to resources, most of all land, persisted. The Japanese continued the system of compulsory labor and even introduced a system of forced labor, which was applied to the entire population. Even today, many Duri remember which roads were first built under Dutch and Japanese rule and where people had to pay for them with their lives. After the Dutch retuned, however, the basic division between nobility and ordinary people was reintroduced.

The biggest change for Duri society took place just after Indonesian independence when Kahar Muzakkar and his Darul Islam movement ruled the area for several years, and a war between Darul Islam troops and the Indonesian Armed Forces took place in the Duri highlands. "At that time," Bang Nur, a young AMAN activist, told me, "the life of a human did not have more value than the life of a chicken." People were slaughtered on many occasions and whole villages were burned down. "The Duri used to have their own traditional architecture," he explained to me, "but everything got lost in the days of Darul Islam." Bang Nur did not blame only the rebels, however. Rather, the Indonesian army was the bad guy, as soldiers of the Siliwangi Division from Java punished entire villages that had supported the rebels. These rebels were often locals. The Duri built only simple, temporary houses in those days, and after the rebellion, they adopted Bugis-style houses from the lowland. It was common practice among both the Darul Islam and the Siliwangi Division to burn down villages to punish communities that were loyal to the enemy. To save themselves, some villages destroyed their houses on their own. When troops came to punish a community for their alleged alliance with the enemy, they were able to claim that the enemy had already burned down the village and that they had no affiliation with that respective enemy. This saved some entire villages, Nur explained.

Another AMAN activist told me that, in his home village close to the Toraja border, Darul Islam soldiers had destroyed the native religion because they saw it as conflicting with Islam. The Indigenous *aluk tojolo* religion had been pre-served, however, especially in the very north of the Duri highlands. In most parts of the Duri area, this religion was wiped out during the Darul Islam rebellion. *Aluk tojolo* adherents knew the concept of a creator, Puang Matuna, but also acknowledged the existence of a variety of deities. These deities were said to live in the sky, and in ancient times, humans used a huge stairway to visit the deities. Another metaphysical category in *aluk tojolo* are the *to mem-bali puang*, or ancestor spirits, which hold a similar status to the deities (Hadrayani and Karim 2019, 285). The notion of place-bound spirits is also common among the Duri. These spirits are associated with places like large trees, rocks, or springs. They have human-like characters and can protect or turn vengeful, and therefore, they have to be given offerings such as sweet food, fruits, meat, or *ballok* (alcoholic beverage made from fermented rice). If not treated with respect, these spirits can cause harm, for instance, by keeping ani-mals away from hunting humans or drying out springs (Sitonda 2012, 6). This resembles what Kaj Århem (2016, 296) has labeled "owner spirits," a concept widespread in Southeast Asian animism. These beliefs and the corresponding practices, however, were subject to strict punishment under Darul Islam rule. Not only were the adherents of animism punished but also the sites where spir-its lived were destroyed (e.g., by cutting down large trees). In the times of Darul Islam, it was not uncommon for those among the Indigenous population who had refused to abandon their traditional faiths and adhere to the teachings of Islam to flee into the jungle or to be forced into refugee camps (Robinson 1983). The large part of the Duri, however, abandoned their traditional beliefs and complied with Darul Islam rule.

I expected that Indigenous activists would regret the loss of traditional reli-gions because traditional religions can be a constitutive element of indigeneity as an ideological formation. AMAN activists in Enrekang, however, did not paint the Darul Islam era as a bad or dark period as it was portrayed in the offi-cial narratives of the Indonesian state. Other interlocutors in the Duri area also had perceptions of Kahar Muzakkar and Darul Islam that were different from the official narratives. A Duri peasant with whom I spoke one evening while sitting in the central village square described Kahar Muzzakar as "a rebel, a troublemaker, so they say," with "they" indicating the Indonesian government. He made it quite clear that it was neither his nor the village's perspective that Kahar Muzakkar was the bad guy. Other interlocutors admitted that their fam-ilies had helped the Darul Islam forces in economic terms by cultivating coffee trees and handing the beans to the rebels who then smuggled them to the port of Palopo and sold them. Although this endeavor has been depicted as forced disappropriation in the official narratives, I heard from educated people in

Makassar that, in Duri memories in the villages, it was entirely voluntary: They helped the Darul Islam movement because they were considered their troops. The Duri also shared food with the rebels. Although times were rough—and shortages of basic needs, such as salt, are still remembered—this bad situation was not seen as being the fault of Kahar Muzakkar and his troops but that of the Indonesian army. The Darul Islam rebellion still occupies a prominent position in the Duri's collective memory. I was astonished by the rather positive perception held by many Duri I talked to. Especially after they got to know me better, people expressed their acknowledgment of the Darul Islam movement quite openly. But did the movement not bring suffering to the people here? In official state narratives, the Darul Islam movement was a betrayal of the nation: They were dangerous extremists bringing death and injustice. This view is also prevalent in some scholarly accounts. Tyson (2010, 54), for instance, writes that "militants from the Darul Islam movement were terrorizing the highlands." This raises the question of what was behind the Duri's support and recognition of the Darul Islam movement and why their memories are so different from official views.

Darul Islam's basic rules were outlined in the Makalua charter, named after Kahar Muzakkar's stronghold at Latimojong Mountain near the Duri region. In official narratives, the gruesome *hudut* punishments (which included stoning of adulteresses and hand amputations for thieves) were stressed, but for the Duri people, these aspects were rather important insofar as an equal law for all was established. Moreover, other aspects of Darul Islam rule were certainly more important than the punishments. Pelras (1996, 284) summarizes Darul Islam's political project as

> a kind of Islamic socialism, to be expressed in measures including a moderate land reform; the suppression of social inequality and of all ostentation of dress and behavior, such as the wearing of gold, jewels, and silks or sumptuous feasting at weddings; the eradication of all traces of "feudalism," such as traditional political offices and aristocratic titles, and of "paganism," such as pilgrimages to sacred places and the performance of pre-Islamic rituals. . .

Kahar Muzakkar joined the Darul Islam movement only after coming into conflict with the Javanese-dominated elite of the Indonesian Military, which paid little to no respect to fighters from Sulawesi. Muzakkar had been a religious man from his early days when he was educated in schools run by Muhammadiyah, an Islamic organization representing the modernist-orthodox branch of Islam (which often opposed traditionalist and syncretistic currents represented by the Nahdlatul Ulama, the other Islamic mass organization in Indonesia).

He had also criticized the feudal system since his youth and had come into conflict with local *adat* chiefs in the Palopo area, aiming to abolish the aristocracy. The local population in rural Sulawesi associated the Darul Islam movement with the forest and the interior, in contrast to the "city army" of the Indonesian armed forces, also labeled the "Javanese army," which only had the support of the aristocracy (van Dijk 1981, 155). The Dutch had proven that traditional hierarchies could be changed in the early twentieth century and the Japanese regime had been even more radical. It was Darul Islam, however, that tried to establish a utopian society of equals among the adherents of Islam. Although equality was a crucial value in the Indonesian revolution, nationalism was a concept too abstract for people in remote areas in Sulawesi at that time. The Duri were accustomed to Islam, however, which now became the basic ideology of social equality.

Note the short period of time in which social change happened in the Duri area. Changes that had taken centuries in Europe occurred within half a century. Whereas slavery was still common at the end of the nineteenth century, a regime of social equality was in practice by the mid-1950s. Kahar Muzakkar emerged as the Robespierre of Sulawesi, the Darul Islam movement as a Muslim version of the Jacobins: They brought not only terror but also the social change that most of the population benefited from. Ordinary people were thus not simply passive objects: When actively supporting Darul Islam, they took sides against both feudalism and against the Indonesian Army, which was perceived as another invasive force. This view revealed a clear wish for social change toward an egalitarian society. The social change that had begun at the turn of the twentieth century was a promise to the peasant, a promise of modernity, that is, the promise of equality. People in the Duri highlands, however, were not able to enforce that change on their own. Not equipped with a sense of being active agents ready to change the flow of history, Kahar Muzakkar appeared as a *ratu adil* (just ruler), which at that time was a necessary precondition for change. When his reign ended after about ten years, Duri society never went back to how it had been.

The end of the Darul Islam movement came shortly before the so-called New Order, Suharto's development regime. As the Communist Party had never been strong in the Duri area, the regime change happened without much impact. The area was now free of rebels, and the state began to exercise its control. The traditional elite, however, did not manage to fully reinstate their positions. Where they maintained their *adat* positions, they did so in a now more equal society. Ideologically, Muhammadiyah filled the gap that Darul Islam had left. As Muhammadiyah also promoted a modernist understanding of Islam, it was also at odds with traditional pre-Islamic hierarchies and practices.

It was only in the post–New Order era when, in the wake of the general revival of tradition in South Sulawesi and Indonesia in general, the Duri nobility staked their claim for recognition. They sought acknowledgment as *masyarakat adat*, but AMAN did not recognize them as an Indigenous community. This denial of recognition was a result of their feudalistic features. In the Duri highlands, there are three petty kingdoms, namely Alla, Malua, and Buntu Batu. The kingdom of Buntu Batu in the village of Pasui near the town of Barakka applied for AMAN membership. Two crucial issues made it impossible for the sultanate to be recognized as an Indigenous community: First, there was no clear *adat* territory. The kingdom had a sphere of influence over Indigenous communities in the surrounding area, but it did not have any borders that could be clearly defined. As a small mandala state, it lacked clear-cut borders. Only at the very margin of the mandala, namely between Indigenous communities, is it possible to define these borders. Another issue was its feudalistic hierarchy. According to AMAN activists, Indigenous communities must be rather egalitarian. As AMAN uses egalitarianism against feudalism as a criterion for indigeneity, this egalitarianism was also a product of the anti-*adat* efforts of the Darul Islam movement. In other words, the foundation of indigeneity as promoted by AMAN also was rooted in the anti-Indigenous movement of Darul Islam. The sultanate of Buntu Batu in Pasui has a *puang* as its head, which in Duri and Toraja societies denotes high nobility. In contrast, *komunitas masyarakat adat*, as they are acknowledged by AMAN, are led by *pakke*, which are lower in the local hierarchies. This type of leadership is closely related to Indigenous activists' narratives about colonialism: According to them, the petty sultanates helped the Dutch in their colonial project as they collaborated closely from 1906 onward. This narrative contradicts other views that emphasize the resistance of the kingdoms, among others Buntu Batu, against the Dutch. Butu Batu gained the status of a *zelfbesturend landschap* (Dutch for "self-governing area"), which meant that the Dutch applied indirect rule with the help of the kingdom (Sritimuryati 2013, 35–39). Subsequent resistance against the colonizers thus came from Indigenous communities, and this narrative helped to establish a close link between Indonesian nationalism and indigeneity. AMAN Enrekang eventually denied Buntu Batu membership after they found it to be at odds with AMAN membership criteria as a result of these two issues. The kingdom accepted AMAN's decision and sought membership in another organization that used *adat* but did so as a feature of kingdoms and sultanates.

The New Order state aimed to civilize its margins, and the Duri area was no exception. As infrastructure was rebuilt, trade between the Duri highlands and the coastal areas began to flourish again. The cool climate was ideal for the cultivation of vegetables, such as garlic, red onions, cabbage, and tomatoes, which now could be taken to Makassar and other lowland towns through the road between Makassar and Tana Toraja. This network of trade expanded especially during the late New Order era and today vegetables cultivated in the Duri highlands are brought to faraway places, such as Kalimantan and Java, as some of my interlocutors proudly told me. In the forests, coffee and cloves were cultivated. Much of the forest was declared state forest in New Order Indonesia, however, and the Duri have distinct memories of how these state forests were approached. In some areas, the state established timber or resin plantations and rented land to timber companies, but much of the state forest was poorly used. It was forbidden to take resources from these forests, but because of the lack of state control, many communities made use of them anyway, especially in the more remote areas, such as the flanks of the Latimojong massif. In Uru, for instance, people even planted coffee and cocoa trees in state forests, maintaining and harvesting them regularly. Monitoring by the Ministry of Forestry was rare. In some villages, people established ties between local authorities to get information about when authorities were about to investigate state forests. Occasionally, however, people searching for resources within state forests were caught and punished. This has been emphasized by Indigenous activists in the area who use this narrative as an argument for Indigenous control. The state was far from a strong force in the region. By maintaining resource extraction from the forests, Duri communities also maintained the concept of *adat* forest as an area to which all members of the communities had access, at least in their view. They were aware that the state had claimed that land, too, and therefore resource extraction was rather limited. Just as the Duri learned to live a provisional life in simple housing during the Darul Islam era, their forests were also provisional given that they could be claimed by the Ministry of Forestry at any time.

After the Dutch and Japanese regimes, the struggle for independence, and the Darul Islam movement, the New Order represented an era of stability, both in economic and political terms. Consequently, the periods of abrupt social change came to an end. What eventually became "indigeneity" in the post–New Order era was anything but merely traditional; it was a social formation shaped not only by the marginality of an upland people threatened by invasions from the lowlands but also by exchange with the lowland and other upland societies. It was shaped by new revolutionary ideas of equality brought and prevented by the Dutch, brutally enforced by the Japanese, and eventually put into practice by the socialist-Islamic forces of the Darul Islam movement. Throughout their history, the Duri were accustomed to the presence of forces from outside their homeland, and the history of the Massenrempulu federation provides only a vague idea of being independent. Although the feudal order of the petty kingdoms, in practice, specified everything but independence for ordinary lower-caste people, the sultanates themselves were not independent in the modern sense of sovereignty. The petty sultanates of the Massenrempulu federation and *adat* communities were incorporated into larger kingdoms and tribute systems of the lowlands. Eventually, they were ruled by people from overseas, the Dutch and the Japanese. It is thus not surprising that the Indonesian forces were perceived as an alien force as well. Indonesian nationalism did not take root in rural Duri life. The Darul Islam movement, in contrast, was a movement of the people. After they were gone, however, the Duri found themselves in a situation they knew well: The ultimate place of power lay far beyond their reach. A force out of reach and out of control, the rural communities had to rely on their capability to organize social life in the villages.

When I stayed in Uru, a Duri community on the southern slopes of the Latimojong massif, I often talked about the past with both Indigenous activists and villagers. As I show in chapter 6, their way of narrating descent became an important tool for constructing their indigeneity as the area's original people. I often heard another story as well, and because that story sounded very strange to me first, I did not pay much attention to it. The story stayed with me, however, probably because it sounded so unbelievable. Uru, locals and activists told me, had been located at the seashore some hundreds or thousands of years ago, and the village had been an important port. At that time, people in Uru built large boats and took goods from Sulawesi to all the other places in the archipelago. As the sea level dropped, however, it became a mountain village. Rock formations and sediments in rocks are taken as proof that the shoreline was once just below the settlement of Uru.

This sounded like a strange and far-fetched myth to me given that Uru is situated at an altitude of about eleven hundred meters above sea level and undoubtedly has never been on the shore during human lifetimes. Later it occurred to me that this story did make some sense as a narrative if not taken literally: Being at the shore is, in Sulawesi just as in many other parts of the archipelago, a synonym for not being marginal. The coastal *pesisir* is where civilization happens, where exchange, trade, and culture blossomed throughout the history of Nusantara. It also appeared that the people in Uru and the AMAN activists were applying a narrative from the *La Galigo*, an epic Bugis myth and an icon of Indigenous sophisticated culture in South Sulawesi. In the myth, the former shoreline is said to be at the foothills of Enrekang and Rappang (Pelras 1996, 8)—although not as high as the people in Uru claim. In other words, the Uru myth is a tool to think of a past in which Uru and the Duri highlands were not marginal places in the mountains. It is a means to imagine the Duri as having any kind of history at all as history was always narrated as the history of the centers and the lowlands.

What other opportunity did the people have to claim that they had a history? In narrating their history in their stories, they had to rely on the way history has appeared in discourses of the historic center as contrasted with the margins, which do not have their own history. The deeper meaning of the myth, I concluded, is that the Indigenous community of Uru might appear to be marginal, but it has some kind of history—at least for the people of Uru who believe in this myth. Although Indigenous peoples need to be marginal, they are required to have a history of their own. AMAN activists influenced by transnational discourses on indigeneity are well aware of the discursive setting in which Indigenous peoples have to position themselves. The myth of being at the coast, in this sense, sheds light on an otherwise dark and murky past. To narrate their history, to reach out into the past, the villagers nevertheless have relied on the very opposite of the *pesisir* (coastal realm) versus *pendalaman* (interior and the highlands)—an opposition that makes them marginal in the first place. This opposition is thus a crucial means for making history—and indigeneity. In chapter 6, I address the question of how indigeneity came into being in Enrekang and in Duri communities.

THE MAKING OF INDIGENEITY IN THE DURI HIGHLANDS

In previous chapters, I have argued that indigeneity is always an identity in the making. The politics of indigeneity are therefore always politics of "becoming indigenous" (Tyson 2010, 154). This, however, is just one side of the coin. A crucial notion of indigeneity is that when it does appear, it appears from the very beginning as original and prior. For those who act, think, and apply indigeneity, indigeneity is not simply a matter of "becoming" but rather of expressing an identity that always existed: This identity could be distorted, corrupted, or disregarded, but in any case, the ideology of indigeneity implies that it has always-always existed. Indigenous activists, although they actively engineer indigeneity and stress their specific and particular notions of indigeneity, always refer to something that already exists and that has always existed, whether in social practice, land tenure, or memories. Acknowledged indigeneity, then, means the acknowledgment of existing practices, memories, and the engineered identity, and usually all of these processes are intertwined. Thinking indigeneity as a dialectical concept that comes into existence only with and against its other (the state, its institutions, and discourses as well as the dominant political economy) means that indigeneity is not simply a reactionary category. It can also emerge as progressive or contested category, as I have argued in regard to several cases in other parts of South Sulawesi. Indigenous dialectics suggest that indigeneity indeed appears to be a political identity that plays along with the given conditions, but it holds the potential to undermine it precisely by playing along.

The example of Enrekang and especially the Duri communities in the northern part of the regency can provide a deeper insight into these processes.

It illuminates the development of Indigenous–state relations at a local level, a development through which indigeneity emerges *and* is acknowledged as an original identity. This is a process of an ideology coming into existence. The local level illustrates well the relational character of indigeneity. In this process, sociocultural marginalization leads to an emphasis on cultural distinction (Merlan 2020). This distinction, however, is sometimes less dominant on the local scale than on the national scale: Although Indigenous peoples distinguish themselves culturally from hegemonic parts of national society, they can portray themselves as rather ordinary citizens in their own territories, as integral parts of the local population. Cultural distinctiveness is thus also a feature of the local place, and it can even contribute to the uniqueness and identity of a certain place. In this chapter, I explore these local processes in Enrekang. I shed light on the political process of recognition and point to ideological conjunctures as well as frictions among between populations, politicians, and Indigenous activists.

In this chapter, I outline how Indigenous activists successfully play along with local state institutions and their hegemonic notions of economic growth, entrepreneurship, and original local identities. As I argue, this playing along does not mean simply reproducing neoliberal ideologies and practices. It also offers a means to introduce cracks in the foundation of the very way that politico-economic systems work, at least at a local level: First, this playing along with local state institutions paves the way for local economies in which land (and even other means of production) is owned collectively. Second, the ideology of indigeneity as it has emerged in the Duri highlands as a result of playing along with state institutions picks up egalitarian notions, as it rejects the aspirations of traditional elites.

In South Sulawesi, Enrekang was the second regency after Bulukumba to issue a local regulation (*perda*) for the acknowledgment of Indigenous communities. Indigenous activists proudly referred to Enrekang as a trendsetter for Indigenous recognition because the Enrekang regulation was the first that not only recognized a particular Indigenous community (like the Kajang in Bulukumba) but also provided general rules and procedures for the recognition of Indigenous communities. Generally, the *perda* enables communities from all ethnic groups in the regency (Duri, Enrekang, and Maiwa) to be recognized if the requirements are fulfilled.

The Local Regulation on the Recognition of Indigenous Communities in Enrekang

In 2015, I visited Enrekang for the first time when I accompanied a friend to his hometown. Pak Munsi, a political scientist at Hasanuddin University in

Makassar, was invited to a hearing held by one of the regency parliament's committees. He was involved in the making of the *perda* as an academic expert on Indigenous issues and invited me to attend the hearing in the Enrekang parliament building. The day before the hearing, I noticed that Pak Munsi was quite nervous, but it was a few days until I found out that discussions about the *perda* on the acknowledgment of *masyarakat hukum adat* had caused some controversy in the town. The hearing was businesslike and no one became emotional. After the hearing, my friend spoke privately with representatives of the Islamic Justice and Prosperity Party (*Partai Keadilan Sejahtera*, PKS), and afterward, we all went to a restaurant north of the town with spectacular views over the rugged Mata Allo Valley. The politicians and Pak Munsi prayed together in a nearby mosque and after the hearing and the trip, things calmed down in the town.

A few weeks before the hearing, Islamic groups had started to organize protests after they discovered that a local regulation for the acknowledgment of Indigenous communities was in the making. As in other parts of South Sulawesi, modernist Islam, as represented by Muhammadiyah, is strong in Enrekang, and some modernist Muslims became adherents of orthodox Salafi groups. These conservative organizations and individuals are aligned with the PKS, which at that time occupied three seats in the legislative (out of thirty in total). The National Mandate Party (*Partai Amanat Nasional*, PAN), which represents the modernist branch of Islam, was particularly strong, with seven seats. Orthodox Muslims, who organized in one of the major mosques in town, feared that recognition of Indigenous peoples would come at the expense of Islam because it would promote traditional animist beliefs and practices. The specters of *aluk tojolo* and animist rituals haunted the town, and for conservative Muslims, they were all simply *shirik* (idolatry, superstition, and polytheism)—in any case a serious sin.

The nearby Kaluppini village is a symbol of traditional Enrekang culture. Even though it is only a forty-minute car ride from the town up to the mountains, in the imagination of orthodox Muslims in the town, Kaluppini is occasionally depicted as a place of animist practices, which they consider paganism. People in Kaluppini have a self-image as ordinary Muslims, however, and they do not see a contradiction between Indigenous rituals and Islam, because all traditional rituals are always embedded into Islamic contexts (Muhaemin et al. 2019). Kaluppini is the closest but far from the only place orthodox Muslims assume to be rife with *shirik* practices. In the very north of the regency, in Duri villages close to the Torajan border, animism is said to be alive (Hadrayani and Karim 2019, 284). In fact, conservative Muslims in Enrekang town have constructed their identity on the basis of this distinction from inappropriate Muslims or pagans in Enrekang's margins. This view stems from the dichotomy between proper Muslims and paganism introduced by Darul Islam in the 1950s. As this view reemerged in recent processes of Islamic revitalization, the proposed *perda* soon came under attack. Protests of dozens of pious Muslims were carried out in front of the regency's parliament, and the PKS faction represented these concerns inside parliament.

It would have been easy to simply outvote the PKS and the few Islamic representatives in the parliament. The PAN faction supported the *perda masyarakat hukum adat* for reasons that I will discuss. Political culture in Enrekang—as in many other places in Indonesia—is characterized by the search for broad consensus, and this is especially true when sensitive issues, such as religion, are involved. No politician wanted to develop an infamous reputation as someone who pays less attention when it comes to Islam. Deliberations have been held between legislators, politicians in the local executive, academics, and Indigenous activists, and the hearing as well as the informal talks after the hearing were part of these discussions. Through deliberation with Islamic politicians, it was possible to reduce the pressure from orthodox Muslims who initially opposed the *perda*. These politicians were eventually able to persuade their community that the proposed *perda* was not seeking to revitalize animist beliefs in the villages: The *masyarakat hukum adat* to be acknowledged were not distinct in religious terms (*agama*) but merely in terms of culture (*budaya*), which consists of folklore, land tenure, or customary law with no reference to anything connoted with animism.

The intervention of Pak Munsi was important because he gave academic credibility to the argument that the acknowledgment of Indigenous communities would not undermine Islam. In the hearing, he made frequent references to international definitions of Indigenous peoples. Thus, he showed that recognition of indigeneity is not unusual in other countries and had improved the political and social situations of the local populations. In the context of Indonesia, such recognition, he stated, would first of all underpin the cultural diversity of the nation. As someone originally from Enrekang and a pious Muslim, his appearance at the hearing emphasized that indigeneity was not something alien to the local conditions in Enrekang.

A major actor in the process of the making of the *perda* was Pak Budi. Already in his fifties, he was a well-known notary in the town, and his work, which was related mainly to land issues, had convinced him that local communities needed better access to land. A Duri from the north of the regency, Pak Budi had studied law in Yogyakarta in the 1980s and 1990s and came back to Enrekang after he obtained his degrees. His office on the main road in the northern part of the town also served as AMAN's local office for a few years. In 2018, AMAN Enrekang built a training center on the road between Enrekang town and the Duri highland plateau, about a thirty-minute ride by car, but the location was too far from the town and was used only for workshops. Pak Budi's office, in contrast, has been a meeting point for neighbors and friends, and many of them have been involved in politics or occupy positions in religious institutions. Pak Budi became a member of PAN in 2012. His religious affiliation with modernist Islam and his hopes for a democratic Indonesia encouraged him to work for PAN in Enrekang, and since that time he had held strong ties with local politicians as well as with religious authorities. The latter included not only Muhammadiyah-affiliated figures but also some clergy affiliated with *Nahdlatul Ulama* (NU). Whenever I was in Enrekang, I would spend some time at Pak Budi's office, which also had a little room for guests in which the generous owner allowed me to sleep. In terms of ethnographic research, this serene place was an excellent place to stay. It never got boring in the office because it was frequently visited by clients, local AMAN activists, politicians, and other public figures, and they were happy to talk with me about the Indigenous communities in Enrekang. Pak Budi's engagement with his network was a primary reason why concerns regarding the local regulation could be overcome among religious networks. He did not directly engage with *Salafi* networks, but instead he maintained close ties with both PAN and Muhammadiyah on the one hand and NU on the other, and he even was in touch with PKS functionaries. Muhammadiyah and PKS did have some affiliations with orthodox groups and, as they had been persuaded that the proposed *perda* would not come at the expense of Islam, they transmitted this view to those orthodox groups.

One frequent guest at the AMAN office was Pak Suleiman. Pak Suleiman was also an important figure in the negotiations between activists and religious forces because he was both an administrator of one of the largest mosques in the town and a member of the customary council of his village close to Enrekang town. In our discussions, he told me about his negotiations with orthodox groups that objected to the proposed local regulation. He stressed that the object of acknowledgment was the community's rules on the order of life, which did not contradict their pursuit of becoming better people—the latter phrase was clearly connoted with the pursuit of becoming more religious. Orthodox groups, in his account, feared that that acknowledgment of customary communities was an expression of their wish to return to a former or original situation. According to Pak Suleiman, however, that was not what customary communities actually wanted. In his view, at the core of this acknowledgment was the acceptance of these communities' recent ways of life. The problem, he continued, was that rural communities have often been blamed by outsiders, which has affected their self-esteem. Telling them that they were not real adherents of Islam was one way of accusing them of being wrong. Religious authorities, he argued, must be close to the people. Islam, in his account, usually had local forms of expression and unfortunately some in Enrekang rejected this. They were "allergic to *adat*" and saw *adat* as something that contaminated proper religion. Pak Suleiman called these people *wahabi*, and according to him, they were a new phenomenon in Enrekang, with their white dress and exclusivist behavior.

At the core of this problem, according to Pak Suleiman, lay a religious dispute: Some people say that everything that is not forbidden in Islam is allowed, and *adat* rituals fall into this category because *adat* rituals are not about engagement with other deities. The other faction, the *wahabi*, claims that if there is not a clear instruction in the religious texts to perform a ritual, this ritual must be considered a sin. Pak Suleiman objected that the *wahabi* instruction to live exactly as Prophet Muhammed did is impossible because we do not have sufficient knowledge of what life was like at that time. Rather, it is important to adapt Islam to local conditions. The first faction did not want to sin, and the other faction was driven by the fear of loss. Although these sound similar, there was an important difference. The *wahabi* faction was mainly driven by fear, whereas Pak Suleiman has argued that sins occur only when people do something that is clearly considered a sin. *Shirik* is without doubt sin, but for Pak Suleiman, *adat* was not *shirik*.

Pak Budi emphasized that the Darul Islam movement successfully eradicated *shirik* practices in Enrekang, and Pak Suleiman agreed. Pak Budi mentioned sacred trees that were cut down by Darul Islam troops and their commands not to worship spirits. Although people might still believe in spirits, they do not engage with them. For both Pak Suleiman and Pak Budi, indigeneity had nothing to do with the worshipping of spirits or any belief that contradicts Islam. Therefore, indigeneity and Islam had the same spiritual foundations. Pak Budi did not think that Darul Islam harmed indigeneity when they outlawed traditional animist practices. Indigeneity, in his view, consisted of rituals, but these rituals are always embedded in larger Islamic contexts and should be conducted in an Islamic framing. It is indeed common in rural Duri communities to carry out *adat* rituals with Islamic clergy and Islamic prayers. Allah is always addressed, and when people try to contact ancestor spirits, they do not worship them in the way they worship Allah. Darul Islam introduced proper Islamic rules in Enrekang, and Indigenous activists did not construct their identity against this history. In short, the 2015 controversy concerning the local regulation showed the importance of narrating indigeneity in accordance with socioreligious conditions in Enrekang and not against them.

In some respects, the controversy between *adat* and Islam in Enrekang can be interpreted in light of broader debates arising in Indonesia at that time, most prominently in the *Islam Nusantara* controversy. The concept of *Islam*

Nusantara roughly describes Islam in the context of the Indonesian archipel-ago, and as such, it is opposed to Arabic Islam. Proponents of *Islam Nusantara* stress the importance of incorporating local customs into Islam and the cul-tural diversity of the archipelago (*Nusanatara*) as the field into which Islam has entered. This concept was meant to be used as a tool to counteract ortho-dox influences from the Arab world as well as the threat of terror. It was therefore promoted by parts of the Indonesian government, but at the same time, it remained controversial even within NU, Indonesia's largest Muslim organization, which is often said to be a supporter of *Islam Nusantara*. At the core of this controversy is the question of whether faith is subject to indi-genization or if indigenization and cultural plurality can be expressed in Islamic jurisprudence:

> Islam Nusantara, opponents argue, enters the realm of belief (*akidah*) to which there can be no compromise. Supporters, meanwhile, believe that Islam Nusantara operates more in the realm of *fiqh*, or Islamic jurisprudence, which can be more flexible. So the two groups are deadlocked: opponents say Islam Nusantara as an understanding is flawed; supporters say opposition to Islam Nusantara is because of a failure to understand. (Hosen 2016).

Clearly, Pak Suleiman, as a representative of the Nahdlatul Ulama, argued for the latter viewpoint, while the structural dominance of modernist Islam in the regency contributed to the fear that *akidah* was at stake. *Fiqh* and *adat*, however, are not mutually exclusive realms as long as *adat* jurisprudence does not contra-dict Islam and as long as *adat* rituals are incorporated into an Islamic frame.

After this dispute was settled, the local regulation was approved by all fac-tions within the parliaments of the regency. The local regulation on the guide-lines for recognition and protection of customary law communities in the regency of Enrekang was the first regulation issued in 2016 in the regency. To explain how this relationship between the state and indigeneity emerged, a closer analysis of this document is warranted. This specific regulation is impor-tant insofar as it was the first regulation in South Sulawesi, and it was one of the first local regulations throughout Indonesia that did not directly recognize a specific community, like in Bulukumba, but instead provided guidelines for a process of recognition. Because the ideology of indigeneity was eventually man-ifested in this document, analyzing this regulation is crucial for an account of indigeneity as an ideology.

In the considerations at the start of the document, the recognition of *adat* law communities is said to be an important step that is carried out with the mandate of the Indonesian Constitution and an order to fulfill the requirements of human rights. The legal framing that situates the process of recognition in both domestic and international law is mentioned. This recognition is also clear in the second paragraph of the preliminary consideration in which it is written that everybody in the customary law communities must be acknowledged along with their human rights, which are acknowledged in both international and national law. In the third paragraph, recognition is said to be important as a sign of respect for the existence of the traditions, history, and ways of life of customary law communities, which are special in communal matters and are part of the overall population of Enrekang. The distinctiveness of the Indigenous communities is mentioned as it contributes to Enrekang's identity and as it is a part of the conditions of Enrekang's population. The Indonesian national motto of *Bhinneka Tunggal Ika*, usually translated as "unity in diversity," mirrors this consideration.

The first chapter of the *perda* outlines important definitions. *Masyarakat hukum adat* is defined as Indonesian citizens who have special characteristics, live in communities in a harmonious way according to their customary law, and have ties to their ancestral origins. It is also written that *masyarakat hukum adat* have strong relations to the land and environment as well as a value system that determines economic, social, political, cultural, and juridical institutions. Finally, it is a characteristic of customary law communities that they use a particular area of land from generation to generation. In this definition, difference prevails. The vague term "special characteristics" is followed by notions common in international discourses on indigeneity: Harmony within the Indigenous society, the principle of ancestry as a means to argue that customary law communities have a right to the land they have "strong ties" to, and a special relationship with the environment are all markers of indigeneity. A particular "value system" is mentioned with an emphasis on the difference from other segments of society. At the very beginning of the definition, these people are identified as Indonesian citizens. Through this explanation, difference cannot transgress the frame of the state: There is no difference of indigeneity beyond their preliminary identity as Indonesians.

The *perda* thus describes the identification of customary law societies as a process that is carried out by the *bupati* through the subdistrict head (*camat*) by involving the customary law societies. The state identifies Indigenous communities but, interestingly, the right to self-identification is considered to be a crucial issue for Indigenous activists as the people in question are incorporated into the process of identification. The recognition or acknowledgment is thus defined as a written statement on the existence of customary law communities in accordance with the verification and validation of the customary law societies committee. This committee is formed by the regency government. The third chapter of the *perda* specifies that the committee should consist not only of government officials but also of assistants and experts on the characteristics of customary law societies. In practice, academics as well as representatives of Indigenous communities have been incorporated into the committees: *Adat* recognizes itself through the state. The verification is thus a process of assessment of the identification process in which it is verified that the communities in question have their own history, territory, law, cultural artifacts, and institutions. These serve as markers of difference, and these markers, once verified, are validated by the government. This process is further illuminated in the third part, paragraph 8, of the *perda*. The criteria for acknowledgment include a history of being a customary law society, customary territory, customary law, precious or customary artifacts, and institutions and customary government systems. In paragraph 9, it is written that the committee both verifies and validates the results of the identification process, which is carried out under the administration of the subdistrict head.

In practice, the committee always includes AMAN members, which means that AMAN has a great deal of say in who is and who is not recognized. Effectively, this means that communities who apply for recognition by the regency must be AMAN members as well. Academicians who are members of these committees can come from different fields, and their backgrounds usually determine which features are highlighted. From the Hasanuddin University in Makassar, academicians from social science as well as the forestry department have been members. The social scientists have stressed indigeneity as a matter of local political features of *adat* institutions, whereas the academicians from the department of forestry have emphasized the Indigenous communities' sustainable land use. In both cases, the academicians had close relations to AMAN but had gained the trust of the local government as well. Whereas academicians are familiar with international discourses on Indigenous peoples, members from regency departments are concerned with technical issues based on their background and the department they are working in. A committee usually includes members from the social department; the Department of Village Community Empowerment; the Department of Youth, Sport, and Tourism; the Environment Department; and the Forestry Department.

The main marker of Indigenous identity in Indonesia is, as I have argued throughout this book, the notion of *adat*. Because *adat* was codified during late colonial times by scholars who were concerned with Indigenous law, *adat* has most of all meant customary law, although many Indigenous activists in Indonesia who use the term *adat* to denote their indigeneity stress that *adat* is not just law but also encompasses norms, values, and distinct worldviews, even an all-compassing cosmological order (Acciaioli 1985, 152). Because Indigenous communities were defined as *masyarakat hukum adat* (societies of customary law) in paragraph 18B(2) of the Indonesian Constitution and because *adat* as law is mentioned in paragraph 5 of the Basic Agrarian Law of 1960, the term *hukum adat* has become an Indonesian legal term. It is also used in local regulation No. 1/2016 of Enrekang. Note, however, that the definition of *hukum adat* in the local regulation uses the notion of law in a general manner. *Hukum adat* is defined in the local regulation as a set of norms and rules, both written and unwritten, which exist and apply to regulate human behavior. This set of norms and rules contributes to the cultural values of the Indonesian nation. It is passed down from generation to generation, is always obeyed and respected in justice and public order, and applies legal consequences or sanctions.

Thus, the definition starts by describing *hukum adat* as a set of norms and rules and mentions the juridical dimension only at the end. Norms are more general than law, but the definition does not go beyond the realm of social norms. For instance, worldviews or cosmologies that lay at the root of norms, human behavior, or law are not mentioned as they potentially might conflict with Islam. In contrast, however, the definition applies a general notion of *hukum adat* in which *hukum* is only a consequence of a more general social order of *adat*. The definition also accommodates the fact that most *adat* rules or laws are not written and that they are a matter of heritage. The latter notion emphasizes the crucial claim of indigeneity: genealogy and ancestry. *Hukum adat* is thus an expression of a history of particular groups, which in practice are acknowledged politically, namely *adat* law communities (*komunitas masyarakat adat*), not whole ethnic groups or peoples. As in the general considerations at the beginning of the local regulation, indigeneity is embedded into the context of the Indonesian nation. The formulation is quite interesting as *hukum adat* contributes to Indonesian values: *Bersumber pada* denotes a process of "sourcing" from *adat* values to (*pada*) contribute to the cultural values of the Indonesian nation. Similar ideas were prevalent in discourses on the relation between *adat* and Indonesian-ness during the early years of the Indonesian republic, as I argued in chapter 1. This line of thought, in which the Indonesian nation draws its cultural identity from traditional communities is, on the one hand, a reactionary argument, given that it was applied against modernist and revolutionary notions of a new nation leaving tradition-cum-colonialism behind. This argument was often used to justify authoritarian and hierarchical approaches as originally Indonesian. In the local regulation, on the other hand, the argument that the nation and *adat* norms are inherently interconnected provides a legitimation of recognition. At the same time, this argumentation ensures that *adat* is not used to make any claims against the Indonesian nation.

Two more crucial terms are defined in the local regulation, one of which is customary territory. Customary territory is both a geographic and a social entity, inhabited and managed in a hereditary way through agreement with other customary law societies or ownership of land subject to traditional rights of avail (*tanah ulayat*) or customary forest (*hutan adat*). This definition urges *adat* communities to settle any conflicts with other *adat* communities and to seek agreement concerning *ulayat* rights. The aim is to prevent any conflicts based on land claims in the name of *adat*. Furthermore, the rights of customary law societies are defined as communal rights that stem from the communities' origins and are supplied by their social and cultural systems, especially the right to land, territory, and natural resources that are in their customary territory. As in transnational discourses on indigeneity, Indigenous rights derive from their origin.

The local regulation outlined the mechanisms and the criteria for recognition by local state institutions, a necessary process for applying for customary land rights. Six customary communities gained recognition in the regency in 2018, namely Orong, Marena, Pana, Patongloan, and Tangsa (all Duri), and Baringin, a community in the southern part of the regency inhabited by the Maiwa. Marena and Orong became the first communities in Enrekang to gain their *adat* forest from the Ministry of Environment and Forestry in late 2018: Marena was granted 155 hectares and Orong 81 hectares. I next shed light on the processes of the practice of recognition, both recognition as an Indigenous community and recognition of Indigenous land.

Indigenous Grassroots Activism and the Making of Indigeneity

Bung Nur, although already in his early thirties, is a member of AMAN's youth organization. He joined AMAN a few years ago when he learned about the issue of indigeneity. Nur felt that recognition of traditional ways of life and land tenure in the Duri area had huge potential for improving the local population's lives. Nur is well known among the communities in the foothills of the Latimojong in the eastern part of the Duri area. In 2018, he built a house made of local materials, most of all bamboo, and turned it into a public library. In his view, the children of the nearby villages needed a place where they could read books. Reading, focusing on a topic, he said to me, can give you more knowledge than all the information people can find on the internet, because when you read, you pay attention. Young people needed a place to contemplate. Bung Nur is also a passionate hiker and environmentalist; he organizes trekking tours to the summits of the Latimojong massif as well as small-scale forestation programs in the nearby villages. When I was in the area, I stayed in his large house where he had a room for guests. Some stickers on a cupboard that were critical of the World Trade Organization (WTO) and environmental destruction hinted that he has been in touch with transnational discourses on social justice. The collection of books in the bamboo house library had an emphasis on alternative Indonesian history, especially covering the struggle for independence and the early years of independent Indonesia when leaders such as Sukarno applied a populist, anti-capitalist, and anti-Western approach. These big issues, however, seldom came up in our conversations. Nur was always more concerned about local issues.

When the local regulation on the acknowledgment of customary law societies was issued in 2016, AMAN had already verified some member communities, but the local regulation persuaded more communities to apply for the status of customary community. In practice, AMAN and the local state apparatus engaged in an alliance for the process of recognition: It was AMAN and its members that collected data on the communities applying for recognition in the field. Nur and other activists went to numerous villages in the area and sought evidence of indigeneity. Being an AMAN member is, in practice, a necessary requirement for a community to gain recognition from local state institutions. AMAN activists like Nur who collect data on history, social and economic conditions, customary institutions, and *adat* law help the community to prove their status as Indigenous as required in the local regulation.

One day, Bung Nur took me on a motorbike trip through several villages near the Latimojong. He was able to tell stories about most of the villages, about which criteria for an Indigenous community they fulfilled and which they did not. Some villages north of his home, for instance, were promising. In the fields, we saw rice barns with roof structures similar to the famous *tongkonan* in Toraja. The inhabitants also obeyed *adat* laws, but for Nur and his friends, it was impossible to clearly identify *adat* institutions. They were not simply absent, but different people made claims to represent *adat* institutions. This would, Nur told me, inevitably lead to conflicts if the community were to be officially recognized as an *adat* community. In most cases, the lack of *adat* institutions that could be clearly identified was the main problem. Nur attributed the disappearance or ambiguity of *adat* institutions not only to the Darul Islam rebellion but also to the growing influence of modernist Islam. As Islamic jurisprudence became more important in settling social conflicts, *adat* was weakened, especially over the preceding two decades. Being a devoted Muslim, Nur always stressed that Islam is not problematic for *adat* as long as Islam does not aim to destroy tradition. For Nur, *adat* is a local way of life, a form of land tenure, and a way of applying local knowledge as well as solving social conflicts within a community. It does not interfere with Islam, which is a matter of faith and of metaphysical issues. He therefore found it sad when *adat* institutions were sidelined in the name of Islam.

Bung Nur sometimes accompanied me to communities that had successfully applied for recognition as Indigenous or were in the process of doing so. One of the latter communities at that time was Uru, in the far eastern part of the Duri territory. Located at an elevation of about eleven hundred meters, Uru consists of several settlements and four administrative villages but forms one single *adat* unit. About a year earlier, a concrete road had been built that improved access to the villages. The road is narrow, however, and accessing the villages by car remains challenging. Although Uru is located in a remote part of Enrekang, its customary forests were quite well protected by officers of the Ministry of Environment and Forestry. The community claims that about two thousand hectares are customary forest, which is significantly more than the area of forest acknowledged in Orong and Marena. In the past, people from the villages occasionally entered the area to harvest forest products, such as fruits, rattan, and resin. Some even planted coffee trees, but harvesting was a risky endeavor because people were sometimes caught and had to pay fines. Pak Hassan, the *adat* chef with whom I was able to stay during my visits to Uru, told me about the community's plans for when their forest is no longer a state forest: Not only would the community be able to extract natural resources, such as rattan and resin, but the communities' aim was also to plant coffee and durian trees. As another goal, Pak Hassan said that the community wanted to open the forest to tourists. He stressed in our conversations that although the state restricted access to the forest because of its status as a protected forest, the forest was not managed at all and much economic potential was being lost because of this.

To apply to the Ministry of Environment and Forestry for recognition of the customary forest, the community first had to be recognized as an *adat* community. AMAN carried out investigations in Uru in 2016. The community became a member of AMAN and AMAN activists collected data to prove its status as an Indigenous community. In 2017, only a year after the local regulation was issued in Enrekang, Hassan submitted the required documents. According to him, the most important criteria for being Indigenous are the history of origin and the mapping of customary territory. In many of our discussions, he talked about the history of the community, which turned out to be mostly a history of his ancestors. Together with AMAN, he developed a diagram of ancestry that covered eleven generations. The first generation, which is said to be people from Kaloppini (another Indigenous community near the town of Enrekang), established the settlements by cutting a large Uru tree, which also gave the village its name.

In contrast, mystical elements were more prevalent in Nur's narratives on the establishment of Uru. He told me about an ancient time when Uru was at the seashore (because the sea level was much higher at that time) and people went there to build large boats. This story was also common among farmers in Uru, as I mentioned in chapter 5. Pak Hassan did not say that this was not true, but for him, ancestry is what counts and what proves the continuous history of the village: All families there, he told me, were descended from common ancestors. The genealogy of *adat* chiefs as proof of an Indigenous history became a common method among Duri communities applying for Indigenous community status. *Adat* chiefs also showed me with pride such diagrams of ancestry in other villages, such as Marena and Orong. Organizations such as AMAN or the Customary Area Registration Agency (*Badan Registrasi Wilayah Adat*, BRWA) adopted this approach because it seemed to convince the local state institutions of their ancestry and thus their indigeneity. Only occasionally did AMAN's data on Indigenous communities provide more detailed insight into history. In the account of the history of the Angge Buntu community, for instance, the Darul Islam rebellion is mentioned more prominently. Darul Islam is said to have had rebellious gangs that imposed Islamic teachings by destroying ancestral values. In the field, however, I never heard such arguments. As explained previously, the Darul Islam rebellion was usually not mentioned in a negative light, although it had a huge impact on the disappearance of *adat* structures. Simply stressing the ancestry of the *adat* heads became an effective way of sideling other aspects of local history, especially when Indigenous narratives were at risk of appearing to be contradictory to Islam.

According to Pak Hassan, the inhabitants of Uru actively asked for Islamic teaching from the sultanate of Bone—they went to Bone to ask for Islamic lore—but he could not tell at what time the people in Uru converted to Islam. When he spoke of ancient tombs, he emphasized Indigenous culture, such as the tradition of burying people in caves on cliffs, similar to traditions in Toraja. Anything related to pre-Islamic worldviews is unclear in cosmological terms. On several occasions, Hassan also mentioned a place within the Uru *adat* territory that is considered to be especially dangerous; people should not mention the names of their ancestors there and it is better to avoid the place altogether. Every time I asked why it is so dangerous, whether spirits might be dwelling in that place, he just answered that he did not know. Spirits, for him and for other people in Uru, are a vague threat, as they have learned from modernist Islam that interaction with spirits should be avoided. This means, however, that the spirits are not controlled in rituals. Pak Hassan stressed that all *adat* rituals are always carried out alongside giving thanks and praise to Allah.

Despite lacking an Indigenous worldview in terms of religion, Uru is a community very much in line with what Indigenous activists in the local context imagine to be Indigenous: a community with a long ancestral history, *adat* institutions, and rituals. It is not an issue that the *adat* institutions and rituals are largely incorporated into Islamic contexts. For activists as well as for government officials, it is more important that *adat* institutions are intact and acknowledged in the community and that the rituals, as well as traditional worldviews, do not have any "un-Islamic" content. Uru also represents a community with a rather egalitarian social order, especially if one compares it with the nearby Toraja communities. Uru has no history as a sultanate and during my stay there in 2019 I found that social inequality is not prevalent. It does exist, though. Pak Hassan's children, for example, occupy some of the rare and desirable positions outside the agrarian sector, for instance, as teachers in the village school. His family also possesses a bit more land than the others. At the time of one of my visits, the price of cloves was quite low, and the people in the villages decided to store their cloves and wait to sell when prices were higher. Pak Hassan stored twelve sacks in his house, the highest number I have seen in any household. Most had about half that number. In addition, his family has a car, a luxury not all households in Uru can afford. But overall, the community fits well into the activist's imagination of a rather egalitarian, marginal Indigenous community with *adat* institutions, laws, and a history of residing in the same place for many generations.

As suggested in the discussion on the local regulation and experiences in Uru, the state and AMAN are both crucial actors in the process of recognition. The local state institutions grant recognition but this process is, in practice, impossible without the assistance of AMAN activists. AMAN activists collect data to prove that indigeneity exists. In fact, they create indigeneity through that process and in cooperation with the state. The data they collect depicts, to them, an objective reality they find in the field, but the existence of indigeneity is the result of a process of producing data in the field and selecting the relevant elements. In this sense, it is telling that Nur and other local AMAN activists call their collected, written data *etnografi*. Just like other ethnographies (this book included) the *etnografi* of the Indigenous activists is something constructed. Rather than simply describing an objective truth, the Indigenous ethnographers engage in a process of creating a specific history, *adat*, and indigeneity through their work. The outcome, however, is not simply a mere construction; it is rooted in reality insofar as the narratives of the people in the villages and *adat* authorities do exist in the minds of the people in question and, once written down, they become official and part of the political reality.

The first step in this process is the collection of the data in the field. Activists like Bang Nur attend workshops in Makassar or Jakarta to learn what they are looking for. Their goal is, of course, to find indigeneity as outlined in both international discourses and local regulations. The dominant factor, however, is the local regulation, which specifies in paragraph 8 that an Indigenous community has to have a history, a territory, *adat* law, Indigenous artifacts, and Indigenous institutions. The first two criteria clearly stem from international discourses on indigeneity. They represent the principle of having a long history on and relation to the land on which people live. The criterion of *adat* law is specific to the Indonesian context as *adat* in general, and specifically as law, became a marker of cultural distinctiveness during late colonialism (see chapter 1). *Adat* artifacts are an Indonesian criterion that reminds one of the domestication of cultural diversity in New Order Indonesia when cultural diversity was expressed primarily in terms of material culture (and was otherwise depoliticized). The customary institutions also serve as a proof that indigeneity in its distinct and "original" form still exists. As we read in chapter 1 in the part on the New Order, for the Indonesian state, indigeneity cannot be revived once it has disappeared.

After AMAN activists collect data on the existence of indigeneity, they write an *etnografi* and then a report based on the *etnografi*, called "baseline data." These baseline data are then submitted to the government for verification and therefore are crucial to the process of creating indigeneity. The baseline data on Orong, like other such documents, emphasize their history. As in other Indigenous Duri communities, history is narrated along the genealogy of *adat* leaders. According to the document, the founder of Orong, Tau Malangke, descended from Luwu nobles who came to the area in 1566. The history begins with the establishment of permanent settlements. Even though Indigenous activists in Jakarta often stress that kingdoms and sultanates are not *masyarakat adat*, the document refers to the early leaders as kings (*raja*). In the early times, *adat* customary law (as the community's internal order) was the domain of women, whereas kings (in the domain of the political) were men. Men made the rules, but women oversaw *adat*. Throughout the narrative of Orong's history, a genealogy of *adat* leaders (*pemangku adat*) is the leitmotif, but gender is not mentioned. Instead of referring to kings, the document adopts the term *pemangku adat*, and the king and his noble heritage appear only at the very beginning of the narrative. Through this strategy, a strong emphasis on the importance of descent and a notion of an Indigenous, rather egalitarian community is evoked. This approach is crucial as the document makes the community fit into AMAN's image of less hierarchical communities.

Historical narratives in written documents have had an outstanding role in South Sulawesi since the introduction of written language. William Cummings (2002) has demonstrated how social stratification was evoked through the writing (and making) of history in early Makassarese documents. These documents were not just representations of the past but preservations of a history still alive and present. This helped to create an increasingly stratified society through the distinction between white-blooded (noble) and red-blooded (commoner) people. Although the idea of red and white blood is also known among the Duri, the baseline data do not mention it. These data are a means to indicate the presence of the past (because indigeneity is the continuity of an "authentic" past present in rituals and law) just like the early Makassarese documents, but their emphasis does not lay on social hierarchy, except for the gender distinction. This is indeed typical of Duri history. Their encounter with other, hegemonic kingdoms and their relatively marginal position, the Darul Islam movement, and modernist currents of Islam have made society in general more egalitarian while at the same time introducing stronger hierarchies between men and women.

During my stay in 2019 I found that *pemangku adat* are all men. The baseline data mention nine *pemangku adat* in Orong's history. It was Tuttu II, the second mentioned, who introduced Islam. This *pemangku adat* was probably a woman because the name Tuttu is the same as the first female child of the founder Tau Malangke. The document also says, however, that even though the people converted to Islam, *adat* life was still rooted in an animist paradigm. An important change occurred during the time of Pese', the fourth *pemangku adat* mentioned in the list: The people started to establish paddy fields through mutual help. The sixth and seventh *pemangku adat* are said to have been close to the government. They lived in the late colonial era, but "government" in this case means the precursor of the Indonesian government. The seventh *pemangku adat*, Nene' Sundari, is said to have engaged in the war against the Dutch colonizers. As discussed in chapter 3 on South Sulawesi, traditional authorities usually cooperated with the colonial authorities, and the notion of aligning with republican forces can be doubted. This narrative, however, is important because it underpins the argument that customary communities were an integral part of the Indonesian nation from the very beginning and support the ideology of nationalism.

After Nene' Sundari, only two more *pemangku adat* are mentioned. The next on the list, Nubuning, is said to be the predecessor of the most recent *pemangku adat*, Dr. H. Safaruddin. It can be assumed, therefore, that there was a gap between the late colonial–early independent period of Nene' Sundari and the time of Nurbuning, in the New Order era, probably because of the intervention of the Darul Islam movement. This gap, however, is not explicitly mentioned in the chronology; indigeneity disappeared, but this disappearance is also removed from the narrative of Orong's history (figure 6.1). To summarize, the history of the customary community of Orong appears to be a continuity of the history of *adat* leaders. This history of indigeneity is in line with the Indonesian nation.

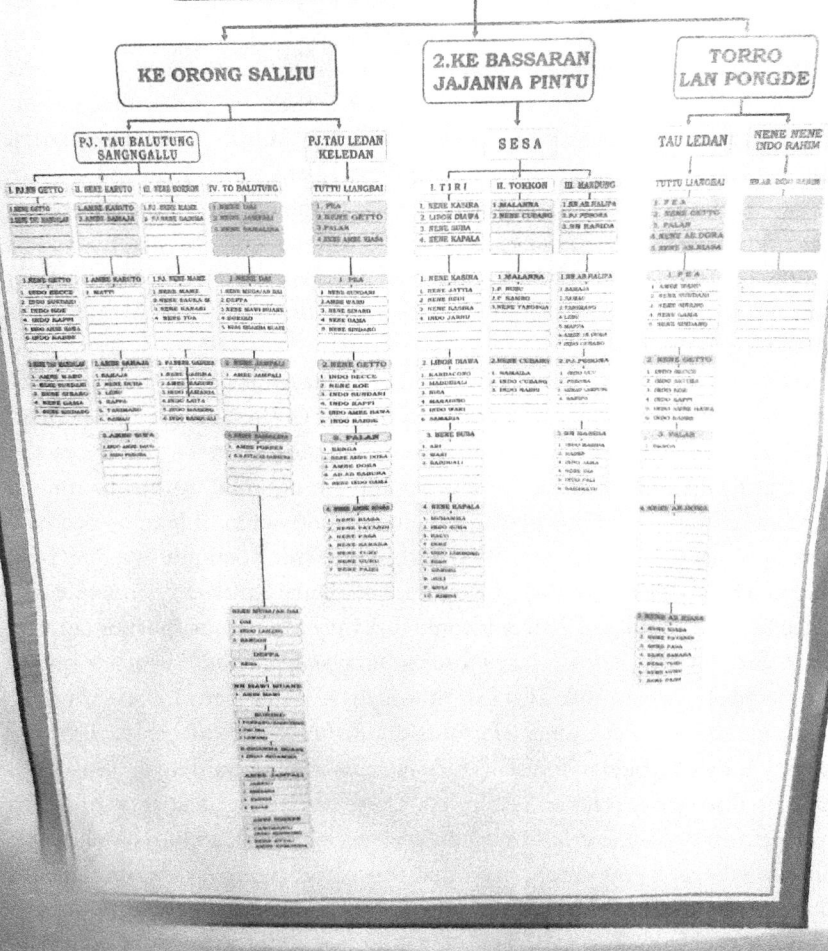

FIGURE 6.1. Acknowledged proof of being Indigenous: genealogical table of Orong

Another important feature of Indigenous identity is the existence of distinct cultural features. The baseline data describe several Indigenous rituals, namely *Mano'tok*, *Pata'pa*, and *Magrundun*, which are agrarian rituals conducted in the context of paddy irrigation and harvesting; *Rara' Bulu*, which is a ritual carried out when a forest is cleared to establish a garden; and *Manganta'*, which is a blessing ritual for children. In the descriptions of the rituals, which are meant to portray the cultural difference of the Indigenous community, references to the hegemonic sameness of religion are frequent. The Mano'tok ritual is portrayed in rather technical terms, the only indication of spirituality is the common prayer for safe irrigation. The *Magrundun*, *Manganta'*, and *Rara' Bulu* rituals require the offering of chickens. It is not mentioned, however, that the chickens are offerings for ancestors or spirits. For the *Rara' Bulu* ritual, a common prayer is mentioned, and it is written that the *Manganta'* ritual is a sign of gratitude to the almighty God. The notion of *Tuhan yang Maha Esa* used in this case is clearly a reference to the first pillar of the national ideology of *Pancasila* (*Ketuhanan yang Maha Esa*), and it integrates cultural distinctiveness (and the community's indigeneity) into the national framework. The abstract *ke-an* noun, which indicates a divine entity, is more concretely mentioned as God, which in this case refers to the Islamic God.

Another feature of indigeneity outlined in the baseline data is the ownership system and inherent pattern of natural resources. Coffee and durian are mentioned as plants whose cultivation inheres the tradition of the ancestors. Different forms of Indigenous landownership are outlined in this document, including individual landownership; changing cultivation of land owned by a group or social unit (Duri: *batu ariri*) within the Orong community; *adat* land cultivated by the *pemangku adat*; "youth land" (Duri: *barabba pea muane*) cultivated by *adat* youth to generate income that they can use for sport or cultural events; and, finally, the customary forest (Duri: *pangala ada'*), which is said to be collectively owned, but the use of which requires permission from the *pemangku adat*. The customary forest is divided into two categories: The first category is the "forbidden forest" (Duri: *pangala' eda na wa'ding di bela'*) from which no resource extraction is allowed. These forests are located on hillsides, at springs, and in cemeteries. In my interviews with both activists and people from the village, it was emphasized that this category proves that Indigenous management systems are sustainable—a discourse and a categorization similar to those of the Ammatoa Kajang (Maarif 2012, 36). Only during long conversations was it occasionally mentioned by some that dangerous spirits dwell in these parts of the forest. These spirits were not mentioned in the official baseline data, probably because this could be seen as animist belief. The second category is forest for use (Duri: *pangala' wa' ding di bela'*), which is located far from the springs and has no hills. The document also describes where the customary forest is located to avoid any conflicts with other customary communities that might claim the same forest. Protected plants and animals are listed in the document as well. Finally, the document confirms that there are no potential conflicts regarding the borders of the customary forest.

The section on *adat* law is interesting. In Orong, two categories of restrictions exist: prohibitions (Duri: *pemali*) and taboo (Duri: *pantangan*). *Pemali* restrictions do not fall into the Islamic category of *haram*, and they are usually subject to discussion and consensus-finding. Taboos, such as incest, require the death penalty by strangling. The baseline data also say that in cases of such violations there can be discussion and consensus-finding to identify the best solution. Because both categories are subject to consensus-finding, the compatibility of *adat* law and Islamic law is outlined, as *haram* and *pantangan* seem to be equivalent. In fact, both categories of restrictions mention discussion and consensus-finding, and as such, they are equal. To integrate Islamic law principles into *adat*, they are nonetheless mentioned as distinct categories. It is also surprising that capital punishment is mentioned. Capital punishment is subject to the national penalty law and thus cannot fall into the domain of *adat* authority. In practice, the death penalty is not applied, and neither the *pemangku adat* nor *adat* activists could remember such a case. The fact that the death penalty is mentioned as part of *adat* law, however, emphasizes the fact that *adat* law matters, at least in theory. This symbolically strong claim has not been challenged by local state institutions. What is relevant for the process on the local scale is simply the fact that *adat* law still exists and not the fact that it might conflict with national law (at least as long as this conflict does not become manifest).

Another customary community that gained recognition in 2018 was Marena, which also is located in the northern part of the regency. Marena's baseline data, as collected by AMAN activists, share some structural similarities to those of Orong as well as some differences. For instance, the section on history does not contain a chronology of *pemangku adat*. Instead, it stresses mystical origins: The founder of Marena, *pangunturan*, is said to have suddenly appeared. *Pangunturan* is a described as a supernatural human being who emerged from a bamboo grove. Such myths are indeed common throughout the Duri area, and often these suddenly emerging supernatural beings are described in myths as cultural heroes introducing cultural techniques, such as rice farming or fire. Given that the *pangunturan* emerged from a bamboo grove, bamboo has become an important plant for the people of Marena; it is only used for coffins. Bamboo groves are not cleared to establish new fields as such an act would damage the house of the *pangunturan*. It is common in many places in Southeast

Asia for natural features, such as bamboo groves, to be connoted with the dwellings of spirits. Århem (2016, 296) calls these spirits "owner sprits," because they dwell in a certain place before it is occupied by humans. In the case of *pangunturan*, the category of owner spirits seems to merge with that of ancestor spirits, another feature that is common in Southeast Asian animism (Århem 2016, 291). Generally, references to Islam are less frequent in Marena's baseline data compared with those of Orong. The only thing that is mentioned is that a religious teacher leads prayer during *adat* rituals, but the rituals are not explained any further. The data thus outline the existence of customary institutions and customary law. In this case, the same categories are mentioned as in Orong (*pemali* and taboos, called *sapah*). The capital punishment for *sapah* violation is also stressed, but as in the case of Orong, deliberation is crucial and can avert the death penalty. Like in Orong, a crucial part can be found at the very end of the baseline data document where it is stated that no potential exists for conflicts over the borders of the customary forest as they are documented in the report.

The customary law communities gain their recognition with the decision letter from the regency's head (*SK bupati*). In February 2018, Marena, Orong, Baringin, Pana, Patongloan, and Tangsa received their *SK bupati*, with all of the documents being quite similar in their wording. These documents specify that the decision is based on the verification conducted by the committee on customary law societies. Thus, the documents refer to all laws and regulations that the recognition of customary law communities relies on. The final parts of the documents outline the borders of the customary territory, both with regard to natural boarders and administrative borders, and establish some conditions for *adat*. Management of customary territories and the settlement of disputes that occur between members of the community should be carried out by taking into account the principles of social justice, gender equality, human rights, and environmental sustainability. Compatibility with Indonesian laws is not mentioned. References to the principles of gender equality, social justice, and sustainability are progressive, and it is notable that the state brings in these progressive issues. They are quite vague, however, in the *SK bupati*. The final part of the *SK bupati* also mentions that the *lembaga adat* represents the customary society in juridical issues, but this representation must be based first on discussion within the whole community.

On July 10, 2018, the *adat* community of Marena received 155 hectares of customary forest in an official ceremony at the state palace in Jakarta. The government celebrated the acknowledgment of Indigenous land titles in Jakarta to demonstrate for the Indigenous peoples' movement that it took the issue seriously. Receiving the land titles in a ceremony in Jakarta also emphasized the crucial role of the central government and the state. Marena was among the first Indigenous communities in Indonesia to receive their certificate. AMAN activists as well as *adat* leaders of the respective communities joined the ceremony, for which they were dressed in traditional clothes. This staged authenticity of Indigenous identity in the very heart of the state apparatus brought together the activists' struggle, the state's efforts to incorporate Indigenous peoples as part of the nation, and the will to develop Indonesia's margins along with Indigenous communities. Although the activists always stressed that this was only the beginning of a large program of land redistribution, the government was much more careful, and indeed, not much progress was made afterward. For the respective customary communities, however, this day of pride made them feel part of the nation. When I met the *kepala adat* of Marena for the first time in early 2019, he proudly showed me the photographs of the ceremony as well as a recording of the event on his television. The document he received that day from the president was a treasured object. It states that 155 hectares had been given to the *adat* community of Marena. The largest part (about 150 hectares) is limited production forest (*hutan produksi terbatas*). Furthermore, the document reminds the customary community to manage the forest based on the existing laws and notes that the community is obligated to maintain the function of the forest. The forest cannot be sold, not now nor in the future.

The *adat* community of Orong also received their land certificate from the Ministry of Environment and Forestry in 2018, but their customary forest is smaller. It covers thirty-three hectares of protected forest (*hutan lindung*) and forty-eight hectares of other forest categories. There is also production forest within their customary forest because a company produces resin in the *adat* forest. Not much changed for the company, however, after the forest became *adat* forest: Contracts were agreed on between the company and the *adat* community. In my conversations with *adat* functionaries in Orong, they stressed that the company was obligated to use the forest in accordance with customary land tenure rules. This basically limited the amount of resin that the company is allowed to extract from each tree according to the diameter of the respective tree; extraction from small trees is forbidden. For the company, these restrictions were not too stringent, and the Orong community was eager to ensure a constant flow of earnings from the company.

The process of Indigenous recognition and the acknowledgment of Indigenous land was quite successful in Enrekang, especially when one contrasts it with the slow political process on the national level. By early 2023, AMAN Enrekang had twenty-three members and ten had already been recognized by the government of the regency. Seven communities (Orong, Marena, Uru, Pasang, Tangsa, Tondon, and Andulang) had received land titles, creating new economic opportunities for these communities. By mid-2024, there were no new recognized communities or land titles, which indicated that the process of recognition both in the regency and on the national level for land titles had slowed down.

In Search of an Indigenous Economy

The history of the recognition of Indigenous communities in Enrekang shows how Indigenous activists have successfully played along with state institutions and hegemonic discourses on religion and entrepreneurship. AMAN, however, has promised change. AMAN activists have always stressed that their struggle for economic independence would make a difference. I next explore in what regard the recognition of Indigenous communities and their *adat* forest offers opportunities for new economies that might challenge predominant notions of individual ownership and traditional hierarchies.

When I stayed in Orong in October and November 2019, the *adat* forest was back in the hands of the community, and people had begun to use it with support of the regency government. According to Pak Abdul, the *kepala adat*, Orong became an AMAN member in 2012 after activists came to Orong and talked about AMAN's goals, eventually persuading the villagers. I asked Pak Abdul how the people of Orong decided to join the Indigenous movement. He said that the activists talked about AMAN's agenda, namely about their goals that Indigenous peoples should be "economically independent" (*mandiri secara ekonomi*), "sovereign in political matters" (*berdaulat secara politik*), and "culturally dignified" (*bermartabat secara budaya*). Without doubt, he added, for the people in Orong, the most important goal was becoming economically independent and the chance of getting their customary forest back was an important step. Becoming economically independent incorporated the promise of improvement, a promise so long given by the state and its development ideology, but so slowly implemented in the Duri highlands. The other important point, according to Abdul, was the desire to be culturally dignified. People in Orong were tired of being judged as uneducated savages by technocrats and pious Muslims in Enrekang town, as well as by people in the lowlands and Makassar. Interestingly, being sovereign in political matters was not really a motivation for the people in Orong. This might indicate that the issue was too abstract for them. The state was inchoate in Orong. A small office building was provided for the village government, but the offices were inhabited by people from Orong, and they never saw it as something alien invading their village. The fact that entry to the customary forest was forbidden by the government was a more serious concern. Most of the time, people used the forest knowing that it was forbidden but also knowing that the risk of being caught was low. For the people in Orong, this issue appeared to be more an economic than a political one.

In 2016, the customary territory was mapped and registered. Because no conflicts concerning the borders of the territory occurred, the *adat* council applied for recognition shortly after the *perda* was issued, and since then, the relation between the *adat* community and the regency government has been good. After the recognition of the customary forest, the local government gave one thousand durian and one thousand nutmeg seedlings to the Indigenous community, which they planted in the customary forest. That was, however, at the beginning of the dry season, and by October 2019, many seedlings had not survived. There were plans to build a road into the forest to bring heavy tools. Some people argued for an irrigation system because some seedlings needed additional water; others suggested establishing an ecotourism site in the customary forest, hoping to attract tourists on their way to Toraja as the community is located just thirty minutes off the main road to Tana Toraja. Many villagers were quite excited and presented their ideas, but others called for caution.

Pak Denny, at that time the *kepala desa* of one of the two villages of the Orong community, reminded the people not to overexploit the forest and to care for its ecology, by which he meant that something must always be covering the soil, such as shrubs or leaves: Some parts of the customary forest are quite steep, and he was afraid of landslides. Pak Denny was the first to admit to me that that the forest had actually already been used by the local people long before it was "liberated" (*dibebaskan*) with the help of AMAN in 2018. He became *kepala desa* in 2008 and said that people went into the forest all the time, planting cloves, durian, mango, pepper, coffee, and even dragon fruit in forest glades. Some of these plants (e.g., pepper and coffee) need rather intensive care outside harvesting season. Dragon fruit need supporting frames for the long cacti to climb on. It was therefore not uncommon to enter the forbidden state forest. The people were already farming inside the forest but were risking a cat-and-mouse game with the Ministry of Forestry staff. During his time in office, surveillance was infrequent, and nobody was arrested. Local authorities had little interest in preventing people from entering the state forest. In this sense, the acknowledgment of customary forest was an acknowledgment of the de facto practice of the customary community. The recognition of the community's right to their forest took away people's fear. It is crucial in this situation, Pak Denny told me, that people understand the limits of exploitation and the importance of maintaining the function of the forest. AMAN plays a crucial role as the nongovernmental organization (NGO) has conducted workshops with the community and has developed methods of making sustainable use of the forest. From AMAN's point of view, the goals of these workshops are to strengthen Indigenous knowledge that already exists in the community. It is also true that new concepts of sustainability have been introduced and thus have become part of Indigenous knowledge.

Note that all the interlocutors I have written about thus far are male. Duri societies are indeed male dominated outside the households. In politics and academia, for instance, men far outnumber women. Some women are involved in the *adat* movement, however, and in their activism, they pay particular attention to women's situations. One female AMAN activist is Mbak Novi. Novi is one of the very few female Indigenous activists not only in Enrekang but also in South Sulawesi in general. Only in Toraja did I find a significant level of female activism. For Novi, strengthening *adat* also provides an opportunity to strengthen women's rights and participation: *Adat*, to her, is not inherently a patriarchal system. Like Rukka Sombolinggi, Mbak Novi does not accept claims that patriarchal structures are integral parts of *adat*. This is especially true when it comes to the economy. In Indigenous enterprises, women should play a crucial role, Novi explained, given that they are known for better economic management. She is convinced that the establishment of enterprises owned by Indigenous communities (*Badan Usaha Milik Masyarakat Adat*, BUMMA) would provide new opportunities for women. Novi is one of the most pious, religious AMAN activists I have come to know. Regular prayers and wearing a headscarf are obligatory for her. Her relations with state institutions are far from conflictual. When I met Novi for the first time in 2018, I visited her in the office of the general election committee in Kalosi, where she worked to organize the 2019 election in Enrekang's northernmost subdistrict. From that time on, she became a great help to my research. Mbak Novi showed me machines for roasting coffee, explained the communities' plans to me, and introduced me to *adat* elders and ordinary villagers. She is a grassroots activist, yet she perfectly represents an activist not in conflict with the state or its institutions.

Her concern, however, is not so much the processes of acknowledgment by the regency but the establishment of Indigenous enterprises and groups within AMAN member communities. In 2019, *kelompok ekonomi* (economy or business groups) were established in some Indigenous communities. Mbak Novi explained that there are two kinds of *kelompok ekonomi*, the first of which are general groups open to all members of the community. In Duri communities, these groups are called *pammesatan*, which means "unity" in Duri. Unusually, a household represented by the household head becomes a member, but all members of the household can engage. In early 2021, forty households in Orong and thirty-two households in Marena had joined the groups in their communities.

In some meetings of these economic groups, it was obvious that women were less engaged in discussions, and Novi became aware of that problem.

To address this issue, some communities founded a second economic group, namely *kelompok ekonomi perempuan adat* (business groups of Indigenous women). These groups had already started to operate in some communities, but most of the *kelompok ekonomi* were just in the process of consolidating. In Uru, the nucleus of such a group for the production of coffee existed, but Bang Nur pointed out that many still felt safer selling their coffee directly to the merchants in Barakka, Enrekang, or the towns in the Bugis lowlands. This feeling of safety is the result of stable and trustful relationships with the traders, who sometimes are seen as patrons to the coffee farmers. These relations provide security for the coffee farmers: In times of shortage and low production, credit can be given, but they also establish dependencies between the buyers and the farmers. If the *adat* forest of Uru is eventually acknowledged, then Novi and Nur will argue for planting coffee and for organizing coffee production in a *kelompok ekonomi*. For them, the economic groups of *adat* women in the customary community of Kaluppini are an ideal model case because they deliver the goods directly to local markets in the nearby towns and even sell their products online, notably ginger. Both the regular *kelompok ekonomi* as well as the *kelompok ekonomi perempuan adat* distribute their products though the BUMMA. Some goods, such as ginger and coffee, are sold on traditional markets as well as directly to local customers in Enrekang, but they also aim to bring their products to national and international markets. The latter plan mostly concerns coffee. Workshops have been carried out with NGOs in recent years to create Indigenous labels. AMAN Enrekang established a coffee storage room at the AMAN office north of Enrekang town (which was, however, empty every time I visited it, indicating that the process was still in its early stages). Some communities also purchased roasting machines for coffee.

When I asked AMAN activists and people in the villages why they engaged in or became members of the *kelompok ekonomi*, they often answered that they liked the idea of *gotong royong* (mutual help) and *kebersamaan* (togetherness) as the foundations of these groups. Several stressed that the communities have a strong culture of mutual help. They depicted *gotong royong* as an original feature of the Indigenous communities as well as a genuinely Indonesian notion of cooperation. Using this term means also using the very language peasants in these communities possess to express their ideas of a solidarity economy. Despite their emphasis that a culture of mutual help is prevalent in the villages, that culture has never existed in an organized economic group. When asked about the aims of these groups, people referred to notions such as capacity building, living in well-being, and self-development. Although these concepts derive from mainstream discourses popular among NGOs, the last notion also reveals their wish to develop independently as individuals.

The question that puzzled me was the following: If *gotong royong* was always an original feature of the communities, as my informants stressed, why do they think that the *kelompok ekonomi* are useful or necessary? What should change with the introduction of an Indigenous economy? When I directly asked about that, I did not get clear answers. It was as if the *kelompok ekonomi* only expressed a cultural feature of original village life. In this regard, it is crucial to consider how cooperation in South Sulawesi (and indeed in many parts of the archipelago) was historically organized. A prevailing form of social relations in which cooperation in South Sulawesi is embedded in is evident in patron-client relations. In his account of patron-client relations in South Sulawesi, Christian Pelras (2000, 394) defines this relation as follows:

> Generally (. . .) an unequal (but theoretically nonbinding) relationship between a superior (a patron or leader) and a number of inferiors (clients, retainers, or followers), based on an asymmetrical exchange of services, where the de facto dependence on the patron of the clients, whose unpaid services may include economic obligations, paid or unpaid work, armed service, political support and other services, is counterbalanced by the role the patron plays as a leading figure for all the clients and by the assistance, including monetary loans and protection, he or she provides when necessary.

Pelras also explains the persistence of these relations across the eras of Indigenous kingdoms, colonial rule, and independent Indonesia. Despite the fact that these relations are theoretically voluntary, Pelras also stresses that they often limit freedom of choice through the economic dependency of the client. Most important, he emphasizes that the system of patronage and clientship allows for cooperation between members of different social strata (Pelras 2000, 397–401). In other words, it is only though social stratification that cooperation becomes possible. I have argued that Darul-Islam rule had a great impact on Duri societies as it weakened traditional authorities. That does not mean that patron-client relations are now uncommon among the Duri. On the contrary, they not only occur within communities but also reach beyond the community border, for instance when a client living in a village has a patron in the towns of Kalosi, Cakke, or Enrekang. These relations become clearly visible during election campaigns. Patrons seeking votes visit the villages and persuade their clients to campaign for them.

Another question is whether *adat* authorities also have patron qualities. In Duri *adat* communities, the *pemangku adat* has the right to *adat* land and utilization of the *adat* forest requires his permission, as I outlined in the section about the Indigenous activists' baseline data. In theory, the *pemangku adat* has authority over the means of production and resources, which makes him quite powerful. It is, however, precisely through the *pemangku adat* that cooperation within the community is made possible. His permission provides guidelines for the whole community. This outstanding position is subject to change when *kelompok ekonomi* emerge as new institutions, or at least there is the possibility of change. The economic groups stress that all decisions are made collectively through mutual deliberation. Indeed, in discussions, the *adat* elders mostly just listened to what the members suggested and later agreed with their decisions about how the *adat* forest should be used, and which economic activities the groups would carry out in the future. The management of resources thereby shifts from the *pemangku adat* to the *kelompok ekonomi*. A part of the value they create is used for *adat* ceremonies but not for the accumulation of wealth for a patron. Therefore, at least in theory, the *kelompok ekonomi* are an important step toward the self-administration of the peasants. In other words, *gotong royong* is part of the traditional culture and, as such, is often embedded in patron-client relations. The *kelompok ekonomi* represent a new form of economic organization, but it is drawn on an "authentic" traditional culture of cooperation.

The norm of reciprocity structured by patron-client relations is thus subject to negotiation and change. James Scott (1976, 157–192) has argued in his classic work that the Southeast Asian peasants' notion of social justice derived from the norm of reciprocity and their right to subsistence. In post-*reformasi* Indonesia, that right to subsistence has, in entrepreneurial ideologies, increasingly been replaced by the "right to self-development," as Indigenous activists and villagers put it. Subsistence is still an important pillar for the majority of households in Duri communities, but the norm of reciprocity now also factors in the right to self-development of the individuals and households. This means that the norms of reciprocity are also affected by what Tania Li (2007) has termed the will to improve, which is now expressed in terms of capacity building, living in well-being, and self-development. *Adat* elders still hold important symbolic positions in the *kelompok ekonomi masyarakat adat*, but management is an internal issue for the group and its members.

In my observations, decisions were made through mutual deliberation (*musyawarah*), and *adat* elders did not interfere much (at least not directly) in decision-making; decisions made by the members were instead approved by the *pemangku adat*. It is too early to say, however, whether the *kelompok ekonomi* and the BUMMA will really change the local economy. It is still possible that these networks will become embedded in patron-client relations both within the Indigenous communities and in networks reaching far beyond them. It is also possible that state institutions will not only provide support for solidarity economies in the Indigenous communities but also demand a say in their internal decisions.

At the time this account was written in 2022, the *masyarakat adat* economy was at a fledgling stage. The possibilities I have outlined, however, demonstrate how indigeneity as an ideology functions at the local level: The ideology attaches itself to familiar concepts like *gotong royong*, claiming to express these "original" features of the local society while also representing the possibility of new relations between the peasants and the relations of production and the sociopolitical relations deriving from them. As a result, the relations of production are subject to change: The state acknowledges Indigenous landownership, which then falls under the self-administration of the group. This self-administration is conducted by all members of the *kelompok ekonomi*, acknowledging a rather symbolic position for *adat* functionaries. This is akin to *adat* punishments mentioned in the baseline data, such as the death penalty for adulterers, which are rather symbolic as they make a claim for *adat* being an independent law that is, however, not executed. The ideology of indigeneity could potentially do no more than sell old wine in new bottles, but it might also bring some profound changes in the local economy. Another observation supports the thesis of a new economy in the Indigenous communities. In rural Indonesia, movable collective property has usually been restricted to kinship groups. Collective credit institutions have also traditionally been rare in villages in Southeast Asia (Henley 2007, 101). The *kelompok ekonomi* as well as the BUMMA, however, represent collective institutions that can acquire capital for investment. The means of production, other than land, are then owned collectively. This is indeed a novelty in these communities and might be an important step toward peasants' self-administration. Only time will tell whether these experiments will lead to a new local economy.

Hopes of improvement as a result of economic change are widespread among activists, *adat* functionaries, and common people in Duri villages. In pursuing this goal, activists and *adat* communities meet with the government. One day, I asked Mbak Novi and Pak Budi if they could help me interview some government officials. The very next day, they took me to the *bupati* office where we met with Pak Tamma, who was an assistant to the *bupati*. Later I learned that it was, to a considerable degree, through Pak Tamma that AMAN was able to influence the government and persuade the *bupati* to acknowledge Indigenous communities. Pak Tamma was neither a member of a specific *adat* community nor an institutional activist. He was a government official, often representing the *bupati* and the government at various events. Tamma stressed that the relationship and the collaboration between all stakeholders, that is, the communities, AMAN, village-, district-, and regency-governments worked well in Enrekang. Interviews and field trips to communities that applied for recognition were usually conducted in collaboration between government and activists. He stressed that it is now the government's goal to respond to the demands of the *adat* communities: When the customary communities have formulated their plans, the government will come and provide support. The overarching goal, according to Pak Tamma, is the development of the economy. Pak Tamma made that clear several times when he talked about the government's effort to push the economies of the customary societies and about the economic potentials that lie in the territories of the customary law societies. The aim of the process of recognition, he concluded, is to support the communities economically. Without doubt, a vague idea of boosting the economy and, more generally, of development serves in this case as an ideological conjuncture between local government institutions and Indigenous communities. AMAN serves as a kind of transmission between these two groups, and it is within this process of transmission between state interests and goals, on the one hand, and the interests of peasants, on the other, that indigeneity constitutes itself.

The interests of the *komunitas masyarakat adat* appear to be universal, seemingly an instrument to boost the local economy. *Adat* comes into being through this process; however, as the examples in this and previous chapters have shown, *adat* is rather a container, or an empty signifier, and different actors, such as state officials, *adat* heads, activists, or traditional elites, are eager to contribute their meaning to that signifier. In the example of Enrekang, where only petty kingdoms existed and the Darul Islam rebellion in the 1950s and 1960s leveled some of the traditional hierarchies, indigeneity has emerged as an ideology of small, rather egalitarian groups seeking acknowledgment from mostly well-disposed local state institutions. Their unifying ideology, on closer examination, is not really radical: Rather than aiming at large-scale redistribution, the acknowledgment of customary forests in Enrekang is, to a large extent, the recognition of de facto usage by local communities. Indigeneity thus appears to be a part of the state as well as part of the nation.

Conflicts

When talking to both *adat* officials in Orong, Marena, and Uru and to AMAN activists in Enrekang, the relationship between *adat* and other forces in society, such as the government or religious groups, was always depicted as harmonious. Conflicts such as the dispute between Islamic groups in Enrekang and *adat* were downplayed, although they had led to some serious disturbances.

The *peraturan daerah* on the acknowledgment of customary law societies was probably one of the more controversial in recent years in the regency.

When asking about current developments, *adat* functionaries emphasized the benefits of the process and seldom mentioned any conflict or potential for conflict. I only came to know about these conflicts when talking directly to ordinary people in the communities. My friends from AMAN often accompanied me on these occasions, and I even took some information from interviews that they conducted for me during the time I could not visit Enrekang because of the COVID-19 pandemic. In other words, common people were not hesitant to talk about conflicts in front of and directly with AMAN activists. The activists therefore know well what villagers thought. For instance, *adat* officials said that the relationship between the companies extracting resin from pine trees in the *adat* forest of Marena was fine. I eventually learned from Pak Rahman, a farmer, that the community decided to break the contract unilaterally for the sake of the recovery of the trees. In contrast, the *adat* elders never used the term of *putus kontrak* but instead emphasized a trustful relation with the company. Although the company seemed to accept that step, this situation revealed a potential conflict between the company and the community. For Pak Rahman, however, withdrawing the permission for extracting resin was an important step because it emphasized the independence of the *masyarakat adat* community.

Conflicts, however, did not arise only between *adat* communities and outsiders (religious groups or companies). Internal conflicts within *adat* communities, of course, were not uncommon, and these conflicts seemed to contradict the cultivated image of harmonious Indigenous village life. A case in point is the iconic Kajang community in Bulukumba. Fisher and van der Muur (2019, 55) conclude that the "communal territory in Kajang is a site of contestation, entangled in conflict over who can claim cultivation rights" and that "representation[s] of Kajang as harmonious forest communities governed by communal tenure [are] misleading." I did not see such long-lasting, persistent conflicts in the Duri area, but internal conflicts were not unusual. In Uru, for instance, some hamlets (*dusun*) felt that they were not represented in negotiations over the community's economic activities. Ibu Ani, for instance, told Bang Nur and me:

> I have heard that there are meetings in the village, also meetings concerning the economy, but there should be at least one person representing every *dusun* in the *adat* territory, and the meetings should not be dominated by representatives of only one *dusun*. At the beginning of the process of acknowledgment, many of us were involved, but now not all *dusun* representatives are invited to the meetings.

It is interesting that conflicts rose among *dusun*. The *dusun* is a social unit and is distinct from traditional *adat* units. Ibu Ani both pointed to the distinct interests of each *dusun* and stressed *adat*'s potential to solve social conflicts. According to her account, it is only in her *dusun* Dante Malua that people dedicate themselves to *adat*; *adat* is still strong there, whereas in other *dusun*, *adat* is fading. In other words, the problem, in her view, is not *adat*, but rather the particular power relations between parts of the *adat* community. This is a typical view: Among people in Duri villages, *adat* is usually regarded as something entirely positive. Like Ibu Ani, Pak Tony in Marena, for instance, stressed the conflict-solving potential of *adat*. Strong *adat* means unity among the people—mutual help as well as a safe and peaceful life.

In Orong, there had been some debate within the Indigenous community as well as between the community and AMAN about the use of the Indigenous forest. Initially, some argued that only certain people in Orong are entitled to extract resources, and this should be determined by social status and kinship. AMAN activists thus argued for an egalitarian approach. Arif, a student from Hasanuddin University with whom I talked about this issue, called this attempt to restrict access to certain people a privatization of the Indigenous forest. In AMAN's view, this could well be taken as attempted feudalization. Although the community eventually agreed to communal use open to all community members, it is too soon to tell whether this is working in practice. According to Arif, despite AMAN's intervention, the local population may later adhere to the restriction advocated by the elite. In Marena, this problem did not occur, perhaps because of the former use of the forest which, from the 1970s onward, was used as a production forest by the forestry department. Before that time, the areas were gardens and forest gardens. In the course of the transformation to production forest, former landownership sunk into oblivion such that the area is now perceived as a common forest of the community.

There are many of these testimonies about *adat* and harmony from both activists and ordinary people in *adat* communities. *Adat* is seen as a legal context in which disputes are solved by deliberation and compromise rather than by declaring one side to be the winner and the other the loser, as Pak Budi, the Enrekang AMAN head, stressed. He contrasted this notion of compromise with state law. Even though he knew that conflicts frequently occurred within Indigenous communities in Enrekang, he argued in favor of *adat* law. This is similar to what Laura Nader (1990) has called the "harmony ideology" of Indigenous groups: Confining a dispute or a conflict and its resolution to within the community also has the function of ensuring the survival of the community's autonomy and of the associated Indigenous culture. The community thus appears to be harmonious as long as its autonomy is preserved through its distinct law and customs. In this sense, the harmony ideology serves as a means of distinction from the state, the state legal apparatus, and state law. Harmony ideology also plays a crucial role within the Indigenous communities: It downplays conflict and also serves as a tool for particular claims. When Ibu Ani, for instance, complained about the lack of representation of her *dusun* in community negotiations, she did not blame *adat*. On the contrary, she complained on behalf of *adat*. Even though activists and villagers use a language of harmony when talking about *adat*, this should not be confused with actual harmony within the community or between the state and companies, on the one hand, and acknowledged Indigenous communities, on the other. Notions of harmony express notions of autonomy. In this regard, indigeneity as harmony is an ideological feature: It represents the people's imaginary relationship with the relations of production and the relations deriving from that production (cf. Althusser 2014, 183), such as state authority over forests. Harmony ideology and thus autonomy, whether actual or imagined, express a stance on social and economic relations, whether they are within a community or between a community and outsiders, such as state institutions or companies.

THE AMAN COUNCIL OF SINJAI

In this chapter, I outline the ways different types of Indigenous activists and state representatives interacted at a regional *Aliansi Masyarakat Adat Nusantara* (AMAN) council. I shed light on how activists approach indigeneity in different ways and how these relate to the state. In this analysis, I show that the discourses and practices of the council point toward a dialectical notion of indigeneity as an ideology that simultaneously reproduces and contradicts given political and economic structures. Thus, in this chapter, I summarize some of the general features of Indigenous dialectics discussed so far.

In November 2019, the regional council, or convention (*musyawarah wilayah*, *muswil*), of the South and West Sulawesi AMAN branch took place in Karampuang, an Indigenous village in the regency of Sinjai (figure 7.1). AMAN activists came from all over South Sulawesi, except from the Luwu area because Luwu constitutes a separate region in AMAN's territorial organization. In addition to local AMAN activists, others, including AMAN's chair, Rukka Sombolinggi, came from Jakarta. Ordinary people from Karampuang and local politicians joined the four-day event as well. Therefore, the *musyawarah wilayah* provided an excellent opportunity to meet all kinds of actors involved in the process of making indigeneity and to observe how AMAN activists from Enrekang engaged with these other actors.

Karampuang is an iconic customary village because it has two large, traditional *adat* houses. These houses are frequently used for ceremonies and other community events, such as *adat* rituals or marriages. I arrived in Karampuang together with Pak Ari and other activists working in AMAN's Makassar office

FIGURE 7.1. *Rumah adat* in Karampuang

in the evening before the first day of the convention. I met Bung Nur, Pak Budi, and Mbak Novi as well as other activists and Indigenous leaders from Enrekang. Guests stayed in the villagers' houses as well as in the guesthouse the community had built for tourists. On the first morning, I visited the *adat* house with Nur and other friends from Enrekang, and locals proudly explained about their Indigenous houses. A large tent was erected in the center of the village and a banner sponsored by the *bupati* of Sinjai was displayed, reading "the *bupati* and vice *bupati* wish a successful council."

Indeed the vice *bupati*, who had closely cooperated with AMAN for the *perda* in Sinjai, also paid a visit the next day. Despite their iconic traditional *adat* houses, indigeneity in the village was not always in line with what the activists from Jakarta expected. Mary, an activist originally from Kalimantan who had worked for several years in AMAN's Jakarta office, took action against the "unindigenous" habit of littering. She taught the village children to became rubbish patrols, reminding adults to throw rubbish in trash bins. The Jakarta activists also organized collective cleaning. Locals took part, but just two days later, the village was full of plastic garbage again.

The convention was inaugurated with a Karampuang *adat* ceremony, but in addition, Islamic greetings and the Indonesian national anthem, as well as

AMAN's anthem, were played. In total, 140 delegates from almost all of the regencies of South Sulawesi joined the event. In the opening speeches by Rukka and others, *adat* was portrayed as part of the nation: Indonesia was, according to Pak Ari from the Makassar office, born from the *adat* villages. Therefore, destroying the traditional villages would mean no less than destroying the nation. He went on to say that destroying history, the proof of the existence of *adat*, and cutting connections with ancestors would mean destroying the nation. *Adat* and the nation were distinct in his remarks, but *adat* appeared as the sine qua non for the existence of the Indonesian nation. Rukka followed with her speech, starting with AMAN's greeting of *Salam Nusantara*. The speech was fierce, but she also expressed her thanks to the state apparatuses of the military and the police that accompanied the event (after the second day, however, they went home), inviting the delegates to applaud them. She said that all felt safe with them at the village and contrasted this feeling with previous intimidatory actions by the security apparatus. Later in her speech, she talked about the intimidation around the 1994 Indonesian Forum of the Environment (*Wahana Lingkungan Hidup Indonesia*, WALHI) congress that had been intended to take place in Makassar; however, because of intimidation by the security apparatus, it had been relocated to Tanah Toraja, where it was held with the support of Indigenous peoples. It was on this occasion that the term *masyarakat adat* was chosen as the Indonesian translation for "Indigenous peoples."

At the same time, Rukka also criticized the term *masyarakat hukum adat*, because *adat* is more than codified law. After this, she discussed another topic of concern, namely the differences between *masyarakat adat* and kingdoms (*kerajaan*): kingdoms had suppressed *adat* communities in the past. Rukka said that kingdoms also have the right to organize and revitalize their tradition, but that it should not be done under the banner of *adat*. Finally, Rukka criticized the New Order regime heavily. Overall, she stressed the struggle against the state and thus the fact that Indigenous communities are different from that state. At the same time, her speech emphasized that this difference was largely a matter of the past. Now, in the Jokowi era, even state institutions such as the police and military cooperate. Representatives of state institutions delivered speeches on the first day as well. The vice *bupati* of Sinjai, for instance, talked about the economic potential of Indigenous tourism. The governor of South Sulsawesi was invited, but only a representative came. He adopted Rukka's *Salam Nusantara* greeting at the beginning of his speech, read a short welcoming statement, and quoted from legal documents the definition of *masyarakat hukum adat*, emphasizing that this was already a legal term. Workshops followed, and I took part in one on Indigenous communities' recognition through *peraturan dearah*. These *peraturan dearah* were said to be a nonnegotiable issue for the Indigenous movement. This first day of the council was representative

FIGURE 7.2.   The *bupati* and his deputy welcomed the participants on a banner

of AMAN's current relation to the state: Whereas government institutions, especially those among the lower ranks, stressed cooperation, economic growth, and potential as common goals, others were more reluctant. AMAN representatives were eager to stress their good relations with the state and the nation, even suggesting that the Indonesian nation relies on *adat* for its very identity. They, however, also adopted a language of struggle against intimidation by state forces.

A conciliatory moment came on the next day. Pak Tamma, an assistant to Enrekang's *bupati*, came to hand over the certificates of the *bupati*'s decision to acknowledge three Indigenous communities in Enrekang (figure 7.2). Uru was among them and Pak Hassan, the *kepala adat* of Uru, came to the convention for this occasion. For him, this was a great day, and he told me that he expected that the customary forest would also be acknowledged soon.

During the council, separate workshops were held. I attended a workshop on Indigenous economies. Participants from Toraja and Enrekang talked about Indigenous coffee production and the process of establishing an Indigenous label. This label should ensure a certain quality standard, but the important point was that this standard should not be brought in from outside but instead

FIGURE 7.3.   The assistant of the *bupati* hands over the recognition letter to the *kepala adat* of Uru (right)

should be developed by Indigenous farmers together with other stakeholders, such as the nongovernmental organization (NGO) Hivos and potential buyers. This process was underway in Enrekang and Toraja, and the Torajan delegation stressed that it was important to bring the certified products to market as close as possible to ready-for-use condition to ensure that as much value as possible was generated from within the community, for example, by roasting the coffee beans. Novi and Pak Budi proudly showed me the small coffee-roasting machine in Benteng Alla Utara, but recalling how long it took to roast only a small amount of coffee, coffee roasting still had a long way to go in Enrekang. Without the means of production, that is, roasting machines, there will not be much progress. An interesting contribution came from an activist explaining cooperatives as a means to organize production. This organizational approach fit with the cooperative structures in Indigenous society, but, more important, he stressed, it was a means to become more resilient against big corporations. He identified social inequality as the root problem of rural development in Indonesia. Indigenous cooperatives therefore had to work against this structural inequality. His input was surprisingly political, and it transpired that he was not the only one to stress economic issues.

In the evening, I noticed a group of about ten young people, most of them from nearby villages. One was wearing a Haji Misbach shirt, the Islamic preacher who had argued in the late colonial period that communism and Islam were compatible. The shirt read "When I give food to a starving person, I am called a saint. But when I ask why this person is starving, I am said to be a communist" (*ketika aku memberi makanan kepada orang lapar, aku disebut orang suci. Numun ketika aku bertanya kenapa orang itu lapar, aku disebut komunis*). Even though communism is a controversial issue in Indonesia, nobody was bothered by the shirt; even the military and the police ignored it. The young people were between fifteen and twenty-five years old, but when we engaged in political conversation, I was surprised by their profound knowledge of Marxism. They told me that they supported AMAN because it was the only reasonable progressive organization in rural Sinjai. Their aim was to organize peasants—if this happened under the banner of *adat* that was fine as long as *adat* was interpreted progressively. These radical youths, however, engaged rather carefully in activities during the convention. I suspected that they wanted to find out what opportunities AMAN could offer for their agenda. In some respects, these radical youths represented a contrast to older activists from both the grassroots level and from the Jakarta office. Although they all shared a certain degree of skepticism toward official politics, established activists from Jakarta, as well as from the regencies in South Sulawesi, also have some trust in certain politicians that they know personally. The radical youths, in contrast, argued that profound change was not possible within the oligarchic system. *Adat*, to them, was a means for a larger agenda of social change, and they hoped that *adat* activists could be mobilized for their purposes. They were certainly right when they told me that *adat* could mean a lot, which included the possibility of a leftist force. Not surprisingly, they assessed institutional activism rather critically. Although they did not deny some positive effects, they also said that this would not make large-scale land reform possible. After all, large land reform as a means to radically change ownership structures in Indonesia was their aim.

I discovered another group of activists on the penultimate day of the convention when more activists arrived from Jakarta. They were heading to Luwu to discuss some research findings with local activists, but they stopped in Sinjai to participate in the South Sulawesi convention. These activists did not engage in debates and speeches; instead, they were observers. When I spoke with them, I got an idea of why that was the case. They were intellectuals, interested in political theories. They had a profound understanding of the political processes of Indigenous recognition, both on the local and national scales. Moreover, they were also able to discuss these processes with regard to various political theories. The way they talked was not the way of the grassroots organizations, but I found conversations with them very interesting both at this time and during later meetings when I visited them in AMAN's Jakarta office. Like the radical youths applying Marxist ways of looking at indigeneity, the intellectual activists were knowledgeable about various theories. They believed in the *adat* movement, but they also emphasized that indigeneity is always something in the making and is ever-changing. Their anti-essentialist notion stood in contrast to the (at least strategic) essentialism of many grassroots activists.

The Sinjai convention provided further interesting insight into the diversity of the Indigenous movement in Indonesia. Thinking of all the activists I was able to meet in Jakarta, Bogor, Makassar, Sinjai, and Enrekang, I regarded these groups as ideal types of Indigenous activists. First, they included established, high-ranking activists, such as Rukka Sombolinggi, as well as others who had been active in the movement for many years. Because they knew the grassroots movement and keep in constant exchange with it, these high-ranking activists place was the organization's offices in Jakarta and Bogor where they also keep in touch with politicians and other important stakeholders. Although they constructed indigeneity in contrast to the state, namely to the New Order regime, they nonetheless stressed that *adat* was a constitutional part of the nation and that Indigenous recognition was possible within this political framework—which was nonetheless a difficult and often frustrating task, especially at the national level. Their rhetoric, therefore, oscillated between hegemonic language stressing economic growth as a common goal and indigeneity as essentially Indonesian, on the one hand, and a language of struggle against oppressive state institutions, on the other. The critique they offered from their Indigenous perspective was not a fundamental one, and in principle, they argued that *adat* and the state could be reconciled if politicians and activists were willing to cooperate.

Another group included those I have called intellectual activists. They were more skeptical because they were more aware of the oligarchic structure of Indonesian politics because of their knowledge of critical political theory. Their image of *adat* was even less essentialist than that of the established activists. The intellectuals were usually younger than the established activists in the top ranks (who often had experiences since the *reformasi* struggle) and thus they did not remember the New Order. This may explain why they did not construct indigeneity in contrast to the New Order but in contrast to existing oligarchic patterns in Indonesian politics. Furthermore, some activists in the Jakarta and Bogor offices as well as at the grassroots level could be described as traditionalist activists. To them, *adat* was a rather fixed identity. Instead of dealing with political theories, they enjoyed traditional music and dresses and dreamed of a diverse Indonesia in cultural harmony and mutual respect.

Finally, the group I have called "radical youth" was rather loosely associated with AMAN (some were members, but most were just sympathizers). In sharp contrast to traditionalist activists, these young people wanted profound political change. *Adat* and tradition were not their final goal. They shared their interest in politics with the intellectual activists, but the radical youth were solely Marxist in their approaches.

In practice, most activists shared characteristics of more than one of these ideal types. Nur, for instance, sometimes showed characteristics of traditionalist activists when he talked about the good old times before the Darul Islam rebellion and the New Order, when the Duri highlands were still "traditional." On other occasions, he used a radical language of struggle and pointed to structural injustice in Indonesian politics. My aim, however, is to show how different the activists I met in Sinjai and in other places in Indonesia were. They all struggled in the name of *adat*, but the political ideas behind their engagement differed considerably.

The issue of ideology comes into play once again. I have argued in keeping with Althusser that ideology represents people's imaginary relations to the existing relations of production and the relations deriving from them, such as political processes and ownership structures. The process of acknowledgment provides the frame of indigeneity as an ideology that is, at most, an ideology of gradual reform within the existing political system. The relationship to the relations of production is one of gradual change: Although Indigenous communities should own their land and organize their economy seemingly independently, there is no outlook for a larger change in the economic processes within society. AMAN's slogan of being independent in economic issues (*mandiri secara ekonomi*) shows this ideology quite clearly. The Indigenous society is portrayed as a closed group that should organize its own economy. They have to interact with the outside world, however, and in this regard, market mechanisms are still the rule of the game. To become a successful player in this game, they must seek to maximize the market value of their products, for example, by introducing Indigenous labels for their products or by creating value in their domain, such as by roasting coffee within their Indigenous enterprise.

Some of the groups I have mentioned, in particular the radical rural youth, go beyond that approach. Although rather radical activists have argued that AMAN's aims of introducing Indigenous enterprises and acquiring land for Indigenous purposes is a first step, this has to be seen within the wider context of market mechanisms that still structurally disadvantage peasants. Unequal landownership is a core issue, and Indigenous land can be a solution. But the problem is larger, according to radical activists, and general land reform is still needed. In addition, the free market has continually put peasants at risk. The state should step in and guarantee, at the least, minimum prices.

Indigeneity, I argue, is not a single and coherent ideology. It can take on elements of distinct ideologies, and the Sinjai convention made that obvious. These distinct ideological frames have never resulted in disputes among the Indigenous activists. Similarly, I have never observed ideological disputes among the activists in the AMAN offices in Bogor, Jakarta, Makassar, or Enrekang. Most discussions were about technical details and strategies, but they had reached consensus about the chief aims. These aims were pragmatic and the activists were working on concrete projects, for example, the *peraturan daerah*, the gathering of data from the communities, or the mapping of Indigenous forest to make land claims. How is such a consensus reached? Again, the Sinjai convention, offers an interesting case in point. On the last day, a resolution was presented. Several groups had worked on this resolution during the convention, and in ideological terms, the resolution represented a consensus of ideological currents within the organization.

This resolution defines "we"—that is, the *masyarakat adat* in South and West Sulawesi—a social entity that inherits the right to own, regulate, and manage itself, and the right to administer a system of government, customs, religions, and ancestral beliefs. The issue of sovereignty echoes in this self-definition and therefore this definition can also be read as an oppositional stance toward the state. Other markers of difference are mentioned, such as cultural identity, ancestral values, and original or traditional knowledge. The resolution also complains about the absence of the state in the process of completing the administration of recognition of the constitutional rights of Indigenous peoples—a right that is obviously conferred by a state body. Consequently, the resolution calls on state institutions at all levels to cooperate with Indigenous peoples and to acknowledge their rights. For AMAN in South and West Sulawesi, the resolution calls for sending the best members as political representatives to seize strategic political positions on several levels. This call to action suggests a strategy of institutional activism and an entanglement with the state.

It is obvious that radical positions are less prominent in the thrust of the resolution. The state and Indigenous communities appear as two distinct entities that nonetheless strive for reconciliation. The Indigenous paradox, the crucial contradiction of indigeneity, appears in the resolution: Indigenous peoples are first of all introduced as seemingly independent entities claiming sovereignty. The majority of the resolution then deals with the relationship between Indigenous peoples and state institutions. By claiming constitutional rights, indigeneity is introduced as an identity present in the state, which also means that the state is acknowledged as the very frame of indigeneity. To become political subjects, recognition is needed and desired, and this is nothing less than the desire to be interpellated by the state. In fact, one can argue that AMAN's general efforts at recognition represent the very desire for interpellation by the state. As such, this desire might represent an ideological illusion as it is based on the premise that Indigenous communities can freely organize themselves and thus interact with the outside world; it does not indicate a genuine aim to change the state and its economic foundations. Indigenous peoples' struggle, in this sense, is largely a particular struggle that does not include other economically marginalized identities. Unsurprisingly, radical notions did not appear in the resolution. The resolution is primarily a consensus document of traditionalist activists, established activists, and grassroots activists as well as *adat* village representatives.

This pragmatic approach deriving from the dynamics of recognition has led to some success in South Sulawesi. Although the resolution outlines several problems and calls for more state efforts to be made toward Indigenous recondition, the *Muswil* in Karampuang clearly shows how AMAN and state institutions are interwoven and have engaged in political processes. This is also true in Enrekang, as outlined in chapter 5. This form of identity politics, however, limits opportunities for engaging in larger struggles. But what would the alternatives be? In rural South Sulawesi, other potential political identities that peasants could rely on are weak. The emergence and relative success of Indigenous identity politics have been possible because of the weakness of the rural left, but Indigenous identity politics can also facilitate leftist demands for redistribution.

The declaration and the speeches mentioned in this chapter suggest once more that Indigenous activists play along with state institutions and the given ideological and economic conditions. It would be wrong, however, to simply dismiss the movement as a conservative or reactionary one. When we remember the arguments delivered in the opening speeches of the council, we can investigate how this playing along with given conditions holds the potential for change: *Adat* communities are said to be the origin of the Indonesian state, and Rukka argued that *masyarakat adat* is different from kingdoms because the latter have always subordinated the former. The spirit of Indonesian-ness that the Indigenous activists evoke is a spirit against domination and hierarchy. As I argued in chapter 1, this was indeed the thrust of a large part of the struggle for independence and was a common ideological factor during the Sukarno era. *Adat*, at that time, was often considered as old traditions and hierarchies that had to be overcome. Ironically, *adat*, in the sense the activists apply it, is what expresses egalitarian and genuine Indonesian efforts. In other words, the activists portray themselves as defenders of Indonesian values by recalling the egalitarian promises of the Indonesian revolutionary struggle against feudal kingdoms and colonialism. They aim to achieve the progressive potential that Indonesian identity can still express, a potential that comes into existence through cooperatives and other forms of solidarity economies. As David Henley (2007, 107–108) has argued, the spirit of cooperation and community, a crucial part of economic ideas linked to Indonesian nationalism, is an Indigenous ideal and not just a piece of ideology borrowed from Western scholars. Note, however, that they are ideals. It is an idealization that people in Indonesia perform because they often lack it. *Gotong royong* and economic cooperation, and thus egalitarian forms of politics and economics, persist as cornerstones of Indonesian ideals precisely because they are so often absent. By referring to these ideals, the Indigenous movement points toward a crucial contradiction of Indonesian-ness. The actual achievement of such forms of cooperation and alternative economies, although they might only be local in character, is thus nothing less than an actual change. Being Indigenous means being Indonesian in the sense of respecting and recognizing the state and its institutions, but also in reminding them of the unfulfilled promises of the Indonesian struggle. This is also why the Indigenous movement can appear to be both a force just playing along with the given political-economic structure and a movement capable of economic change. Indigeneity, in a dialectical sense, emerges precisely within this contradiction.

Indigeneity as Ideology and Interpellation in South Sulawesi

Thus far, I have detailed the forms of indigeneity in local contexts in South Sulawesi, especially among the Duri in Enrekang. I next summarize some of my main findings about indigeneity as a dialectical ideology and how it relates to new practices in projects that are now common in rural Indonesia.

When discussing the relationship between the state and indigeneity in South Sulawesi, it is important to remember that the state is intelligible specifically as a function of state power, that is, in its existence as the state apparatus. Althusser reminds us that the "whole political class struggle revolves around the state: around the possession, that is, the seizure or conservation of state power by a certain class or 'power bloc'" (Althusser 2014, 73). AMAN engages with state apparatuses to reach this goal. Because establishing a political party is not a promising endeavor, they directly engage with the structures they find within the state. Therefore, AMAN cannot be independent from the state, although the autonomy of Indigenous communities is crucial for their very subjectivity. In the *muswil* of Sinjai, state power was exercised by handing out certificates of acknowledgment, in speeches by state officials, through the presence of the police, or by applying the symbolism and language of Indonesian nationalism. AMAN thus emerged as part of the local power bloc. In terms of the Indigenous paradox, it is obvious that AMAN, on the local scale, is not so much against the state as a part of it. Indigenous communities, for AMAN, are given social entities to be represented within the state, and therefore they cooperate with state power. Difference as a crucial means for Indigenous identity emerges through the harmony ideology of *adat* (as I have argued) and in narratives of the repressive nature of the New Order era, when dispossession was conducted by the state apparatus.

Concerning the local regulations, it has been shown that acknowledged Indigenous communities—and thus the individuals in them as Indigenous individuals—were simultaneously interpellated as both Indonesian citizens and Indigenous people. The local regulation is therefore a constitutive means for the ideology of indigeneity. In other words, a process of interpellating or hailing (Althusser 2014, 190) is executed in these regulations and thus in the "project system" (Li 2016, 79) in which state representatives, bureaucracies, academics, and NGOs meet with people now interpellated as Indigenous. This interpellation is thus reproduced by AMAN, for example, in the way that AMAN activists address the state, namely as the legitimate political entity that must address and interpellate Indigenous communities.

Unlike the notion of *masyarakat terasing* (estranged societies) in use especially in the New Order era, however, this interpellation as *masyarakat hukum adat* is more exclusive. In the discursive regime of the New Order, denomination as being marginalized was an effect of authoritarian developmentalism, as I argued in chapter 1. The notion of indigeneity derives from that discursive formation as indigeneity is marginal, yet it is also, as we have seen in the context of Enrekang and the Sinjai council, well embedded in nationalist discourses. Indigeneity is inscribed into the juridical regime. Peasants without distinctive political identities can thus emerge as Indigenous. As this process incorporates them into the state and its political-economic order, it also offers control over the resource of land. Interpellation as Indigenous is, therefore, a double-edged sword: It subordinates subjects as objects of state legislation *and* enables them to organize their local economies.

Adat and the Project System

In critical academic discourses, rural governance in Indonesia has been described as a project system. Instead of rethinking the mechanisms reproducing rural inequality and poverty and struggling for profound economic-political alternatives, projects usually carry out funded, short-term, and rather technical interventions concerned with a particular problem for a rural community (Li 2016). Van der Muur et al. (2019, 385–390) have noted that the *adat* movement in Indonesia has become increasingly concerned with these kinds of projects as the "main ideas about indigeneity as countless small communities fragmented across the archipelago suit the project system well" (386): Each community has its own particular problems, which are then addressed in an assemblage of activists, state representatives, *adat* elites and ordinary villagers, academics, transnational NGOs, discourses, and policies. As we have seen, this is also the case among the Indigenous Duri communities: Engaging in cooperation with a resin company to extract the resource from the *adat* forest, receiving fruit tree seedlings from the local government, or establishing Indigenous coffee labels and community production with the help of NGOs are indeed fragmented projects. The critique by van der Muur et al. (2019, 387) that these projects are carried out instead of an "adoption of society-wide policy," however, tends to overlook the fact that a nationwide policy of redistribution is already the necessary condition for these projects. They would be impossible if no land were redistributed. One can argue that these projects unfold within the neoliberal premises of Indigenous entrepreneurship, strategies of increasing market value and intensifying resource extraction from land that was previously not used efficiently. That is certainly true, but at the same time, these seemingly inconspicuous projects provide an opportunity for a more egalitarian local economy as well. An egalitarian local community is, however, not desired by all *adat* representatives because *adat* has often been a resource almost exclusively for *adat* elites (e.g., see Klenke 2013; Vel and Makambombu 2019).

The Duri cases are complex because *adat* elites often have close connections to AMAN, the state bureaucracy, and NGOs. As I argued in regard to Duri history, however, the communities are rather egalitarian, for example, when compared with nearby Toraja or with the traditional Bugis or Makassarese kingdoms. In particular, the Darul Islam rebellion's rule in the region introduced a greater level of equality within the communities: To survive, *adat* institutions had to adapt to the requirements of the Islamic socialism of Darul Islam. The abolishment of animism and some traditional hierarchies continue to shape Duri indigeneity. In addition, the notion of Indigenous communities as egalitarian has been introduced by Indigenous activists and further shapes Duri indigeneity. This is critical for the way the project system unfolds among Duri communities. Because it relies on patron-client relations and may even introduce new power inequalities, for example, on the subcommunity level, a project can also be an economic-political practice of an alternative political economy, even though this local political economy is embedded in wider capitalist market relations. When asked about their concept of Indigenous economies, activists often opposed it to some vague notion of "capitalism," which also played an important role at the AMAN convention in Sinjai. In the workshops at the Sinjai convention, activists suggested cooperative economies as the basis for Indigenous communities. The common villagers in Orong and Uru were eager to participate in mutual help and community work on *adat* land for the benefit of the whole community. The nature of *adat* land as land not to be sold and not to be possessed individually also underpins the efforts to establish communitarian economy. In this way, these projects are embedded in alternative economic practices, albeit on a limited and local level. They thus have the potential to create cracks in the very foundations of rural economies in Indonesia.

CONCLUSION
Toward a Dialectics of Indigeneity

As I have argued in regard to the process of recognition in the Duri highlands, indigeneity is not simply a force that has always been there. It emerges as such a force only in retrospect through the very process of its recognition. Indigeneity emerges as a cultural identity, but it clearly has a material goal. At stake is access to land and land rights as the basic means of production. Through that process of economic struggle, the Indigenous Alliance of the Archipelago (*Aliansi Masyarakat Adat Nusantara*, AMAN) activists found in the Duri communities something they recognized as indigeneity, but to be acknowledged, this indigeneity had to engage with its other, namely the state, which had prevented the communities from using their land by declaring it state forest. What AMAN activists found and categorized as indigeneity was, I have argued, social formations that had been subject to rapid social change, communities that had passed through the feudalism of petty kingdoms, colonialism, Islamic socialism, and authoritarian developmentalism in only a century. Duri indigeneity is a product of this history.

In the Duri highlands, it is clear that indigeneity is part of the state: Indigeneity comes into existence through state recognition. In the wake of institutional activism, it is indeed sometimes difficult to tell the Indigenous movement and the state apart. AMAN and the local state apparatus are both integral parts of the process of Indigenous recognition. Indigeneity recognizes itself through and in the state. It is also the opposite, however, of the state and hegemonic society. This became clear when conservative political parties and Islamic groups initially rejected the local regulation on Indigenous recognition. Most of all, it is the antithesis to the state in terms of land tenure because the state loses direct control over land. This loss, however, has been sublated as Indigenous communities acknowledge their submission to the state and the nation.

Indigeneity is not a monolithic force but consists of contradictions. In chapter 7 on the AMAN council in Karampuang, I outlined some of these contradictions: Although they criticized the state as an oppressive force, they welcomed the police and representatives from local state institutions. Although they debated about how they could best engage in markets and become competitive, some rejected the idea of the market and capitalism as the best institution and system for economic distribution. Although they stressed the importance of tradition, they emphasized that *adat* is a force for social change, also within the respective communities. In these contradictions, indigeneity always strives toward its other, the state and the capitalist market, to both gain recognition and sustain ideological cohesion, only to then realize that it has to reject them to exist.

In chapters 4 and 5 on indigeneity in South Sulawesi and in Enrekang, I also argued that after the downfall of the authoritarian New Order regime and in the wake of decentralization, local state institutions began to engage with *adat* as a means to gain political legitimacy. It was in its local form that the state found itself also in *adat,* but in the early 2000s, these attempts differed greatly from what AMAN and other grassroots activists had in mind. As some regencies attempted to co-opt *adat* institutions and traditional elites began to engage with the state and political power (e.g., as was the case in Jeneponto and Toraja), indigeneity simultaneously engaged with the state and rejected it. Traditional elites were eager to become part of the state, for instance, as part of the *lembang* system in Toraja or as the example of the king of Gowa has shown. In contrast, Indigenous grassroots activism has struggled for another concept of *adat* that should not become a part of state institutions but aimed for recognition by the state. They demanded local sovereignty in terms of resource control and *adat* governance. Eventually, this very engagement with the state made it possible to establish such forms of local sovereignty. The embrace of *adat* by some local state institutions transformed the local state in some places into a more regional apparatus, borrowing from local traditions and local elite structures. It marked a shift away from a Java-centric Indonesia, but it did not change the political economy and local social hierarchies. By stressing the importance of local, supposedly original features, *adat* activists also gain legitimacy for their struggle, which contains a more critical component when it comes to the political economy.

We can see how the state and *adat* dialectically engage with each other. *Adat* and the state are never identified as two separate entities, they always refer to each other as their opposites *and* their conditions of existence, and within this process, they transform themselves. This is also why the relationship between the state and *adat* has remained anything but unequivocal. Indigenous communities and activists maintain the narrative that they demand sovereignty (in terms of land control) and engage heavily with local state institutions, even portraying themselves as a part of the state and the nation. It is, however, crucial to stress that the dialectical process is an open one; it does not predict the future, it can only outline some possible developments. Whether *adat* grassroots activism is incorporated into the state and capitalist economy through the project system and the ideology of entrepreneurship or whether *adat* grassroots activism can pave the way to alternative forms of local economies—in which solidarity among politically and economically equal subjects, equal value distribution, and common ownership of the means of production are the main pillars—has not yet been decided.

This assessment of indigeneity in the Indonesian context has shown how one can approach indigeneity dialectically as a concept. It is not necessary to decide between the alternatives of either criterial or relational definitions of indigeneity (Merlan 2009, 304–305), or to decide whether indigeneity has an ontologically independent essence—that is, indigeneity as an authentic expression of a culture—or whether it is merely an identity that can be applied strategically (on the strategic concept, see Zakaria 2024, 15–22). Both approaches have their problems. Although the assumption of a preassigned essence of indigeneity expressed in criterial definitions upholds a problematic view of a stable, unchangeable core of culture and of indigeneity as ontologically different, it is nonetheless obvious that even in strategic uses of indigeneity, this concept is usually "authenticated" to become politically applicable (Escárcega 2010). This authentication is the retroactive emergence of the essence, of indigeneity as a thing-in-itself after the concrete indigeneity as a phenomenon has, so to speak, fallen from that essentialist-criterial category of indigeneity. I have argued that indigeneity has no authentic core, but, simultaneously, creates such authenticity in its unfolding. As in Kantian transcendental idealism, where the thing-in-itself cannot be known because of the limits of reason, one might argue that indigeneity cannot be fully understood by the limits of Western or non-Indigenous reason. As I demonstrated in the discussion of the Duri highlands, however, indigeneity is something that emerges only through history and globalism. It is a traveling concepts that fall into the concrete. There is no Indigenous thing-in-itself, no essence (or "criterial definition," as Merlan (2009, 305) puts it that is barred from Western reason and can be expressed only through Indigenous scholars, knowledge, and epistemologies, as some approaches of critical Indigenous studies might suggest. Nor is indigeneity, like poststructuralist approaches might suggest, simply a mere signifier that can only be understood in its relation to other signifiers and, as such, is without any essence. Indigeneity, I argue, is essence in the local-contingent appearance (the way essence only emerges in and through appearance in Hegelian idealism). As soon as one wants to investigate indigeneity's true, global nature (indigeneity as the thing-in-itself), one will find nothing and will always come to the conclusion that the concept of indigeneity does not fully apply to all concrete cases. Indigeneity might not be of much use as an analytical or political concept given that it affirms radical conservativism. But as soon as one understands essence as emerging from its fall into appearance (i.e., its concrete application in and through a political-social context), one can understand indigeneity's nature. In this sense, to exist, indigeneity must every time fall from abstract, global concepts and criterial definitions into concrete, local reality.

The Promising Contradictions of Indigeneity

How do these insights from this case study and the analyses of indigeneity in Indonesia inform general debates on indigeneity? The Indigenous movement as a global force, Anna Tsing (2007, 33) writes, "is alive with promising contradictions. . . . It endorses authenticity and innovation, subsistence and wealth, traditional knowledge and new technologies." As I have demonstrated in this book, this is also the case in Indonesia. What appear to be contradictions, however, are often two sides of the same coin for Indigenous activists as well as for people in Indigenous communities: subsistence, Indigenous enterprises, and a solidarity economy are their cornerstones for wealth and their engagement in local, national, and international markets. Innovation is a means to protect authenticity—for example, technical innovations, such as coffee-roasting machines strengthen the communities' economies and their preservation, as does their reinvention of traditional knowledge, such as applying traditional ways of fertilizing coffee trees. Indigeneity can be alive only through these contradictions, as Anna Tsing points out. As a dialectical identity, it comes into existence through its contradictions.

In many cases, these contradictions boil down to the basic binary that might be grasped as cooperative, local economies, on the one hand, and engagement in capitalist markets, on the other, but they are often accompanied by noneconomic factors, such as religious issues or cultural discrimination. Through contradictions within the way the economy functions, indigeneity emerges as an original identity, but it does so only in retrospect: Indigeneity appears as the "original" and the other of the state, but it can do so only through the process of opposing an entity that came later (in the Indigenous ideology, indigeneity came before all states) and in cooperation with the state (to gain recognition). The same holds true for the economic realm. Land rights are thus the foundation of both solidarity economy on a local scale and Indigenous communities' engagement in capitalist markets. This also includes another crucial contradiction, namely state subjects versus Indigenous sovereignty. Appearing as original and being "before all state," the Indigenous movement in Indonesia engages heavily with the state and emerges as a part of the nation, as I have argued throughout the book. I have discussed this entanglement on different scales, and I believe that this is a key factor to understanding the political economy of being Indigenous in Indonesia (and elsewhere).

The Indigenous movement is very much alive in Indonesia and arguably, despite all obstacles, more influential than ever before. After analyzing laws and the Indigenous movement's approaches, one can conclude that AMAN applies a cultural rather than a sovereignty approach to indigeneity (cf. Bens 2020, 187–191). AMAN argues that the state must protect the culture of its citizens, but in Indonesia, this is not just a matter of human rights or a right to culture. This protection is for the sake of the Indonesian nation as Indigenous Indonesia is the "original" Indonesia. AMAN also applies a sovereignty approach because it demands autonomy in economic and cultural terms. AMAN has seldom applied the idea that Indigenous communities in Indonesia are subjects of international law. In other words, the state is the one frame of reference for indigeneity. It is a sovereignty approach mostly limited to the very state with which AMAN engages.

At all levels within the state, however, Indigenous activists have experienced difficulties and sometimes harsh rejection. By 2025, the law on Indigenous peoples, which should serve as a legal framework for all laws concerning Indigenous communities by defining them and their rights, had not been put on the new government's agenda. In a conversation, scholar-activist Yando Zakaria even called the law a hopeless case. In the previous government, the Golkar Party, in particular, had rejected the draft, and Indigenous activists had started campaigning for people to boycott voting for Golkar in elections. Conversely, institutional activists had at least some symbolic success as the first lands were reallocated during Jokowi's first term in office. The situation on the regional level has been mixed as well. In South Sulawesi, activists hoped that a law on the provincial scale would boost Indigenous acknowledgment in the regencies, but such a law has not yet been passed, although some activists have established ties with politicians in Makassar. More important, however, is the regency level. I have outlined how success differed greatly between regencies across South Sulawesi, with Enrekang being an example of success. These opportunities derive from the legal framework explored in this book, a framework that allocates much power to the regencies as they are in charge of recognizing Indigenous communities in legal terms as a necessary precondition for making land claims. That legal framework is an outcome of the decentralization process started soon after the New Order era. As Duncan (2007, 728) concludes in his preliminary assessment of the impact of decentralization on minorities, the success of ethnic minorities (and this is also true for Indigenous communities) within the new framework depends heavily on their ability to maneuver in the political system of the regency and to engage with the constellations of political actors. AMAN has professionalized this maneuvering in recent years in many regencies, and AMAN's ties to politicians, respected religious authorities, academics, and others have made AMAN's success in Enrekang and elsewhere possible.

This local success, however, is embedded in the national legal framework and its history. In chapters 1 and 2, I explained how the process of *adat* came into being as a political force in Indonesian history, especially with regard to political economy. *Adat* as an ideology reflected economic and political questions prevalent in different eras and provided answers to the questions of how the Indonesian nation should organize land tenure and how to allocate resources. Sometimes *adat*'s answers have been heard by policymakers, but often that has not been the case. To conclude the findings of the discussion in the first two chapters, I suggest understanding indigeneity (as *adat*) as a preliminary outcome of a dialectical process of recognition and redistribution.

From the insight into the process of Indigenous struggles and identity formation, it can be concluded that indigeneity is not simply found in what people are (as essentialist notions of the term would imply), nor is indigeneity pure difference brought into existence through relations of separate discursively constructed units, such as the colonial state and native populations (as poststructuralist approaches would suggest). I have argued for a dialectical approach, which is one of relative difference. The state, the Indonesian nation, and indigeneity all dialectically contain their opposites and therefore their self-difference. This also explains why the Indigenous paradox is the very condition of Indigenous existence. Indigeneity contains the state as its other. In its recent manifestation, it contains capitalist approaches as well as their other. Indigeneity includes its self-difference and so do the state and the Indonesian nation. In such a dialectical approach of relative difference, indigeneity appears to be simultaneously within and outside the state. This is a dialectical reading of Jonas Bens's Indigenous paradox. As I have argued, this paradoxical (or, in other words, antithetical or contradictive) feature of indigeneity is not limited to the realm of recognition and law; it extends into, for example, the realms of economy and history. As a culturally underpinned identity, however, indigeneity always aims at recognition through law as its condition of existence.

Moreover, indigeneity already contains the conditions for its existence. Although critical scholars and activists suggest treating indigeneity, like all identities, as something that has no solid ground and thus exists only through its difference and relation to other notions (e.g., Merlan 2009), *adat* as a political tool nonetheless needs an essentialist concept for political struggle, because it makes political and economic struggles visible though its essentialism. Indigeneity has no a priori ontological status, and as such, it emerges as a strategic concept. When it becomes a strategic concept for activists (Zakaria 2024, 34), however, it is always already more than a strategy. It becomes a frame though which peasants, academicians, politicians, and activists evaluate social conditions. As such an ideological frame, it has an ontological status that cannot simply be reduced to a strategic concept, while it simultaneously and necessarily leaves its ontological core empty and develops around its contradictions.

Recognition of marginalized peoples or communities does not necessarily have to be in the form of recognizing indigeneity. The fact that this form seems to be common sense for many people reflects the political and economic struggles in Indonesian history. In the early years of Indonesia, peasant identity, organized under the banner of communism, was a tool used to seek recognition and redistribution. Like the modern Indigenous movement, these organizations were eager to appear to be an integral part of the Indonesian nation. The hegemonic nationalist-leftist ideology presented then just as much an opportunity as the entrepreneurial ideology now presents for the Indigenous movement. After 1965, peasants were dispossessed in two ways: ideologically, as anticommunism became a raison d'état, and, of course, economically, as the New Order state apparatus enforced land claims by the state, often on behalf of private capital (although it was argued that this was for the sake of the nation). This antithesis was thus sublated within the formation of Indigenous identity as an ideology of resistance: On the one hand, indigeneity did not go back to the economic identity of peasantry, but, on the other, it nonetheless opposed the very mechanisms that nullified peasant identity and its political-economic aspirations. During the late New Order era and at the beginning of Indonesia's new era of *reformasi*, this new political identity emerged as antistate in its purest form, threatening not to recognize the state if the state did not recognize Indigenous peoples. The antithesis of this original approach is, in some respects, the approach AMAN later followed to cooperate with state institutions and seek recognition within the state. Not only did AMAN activists argue in accordance with national law for their causes and appear to be ardent nationalists, but also they applied a language that aligned with capitalist-entrepreneurial notions prominent among certain politicians, in particular, those within Jokowi's camp. As a result, the Indigenous movement sometimes seemed tame and far less radical than it had been during its early years. The question, however, is whether it has the ability to transform crucial dispositions within the state's political economy—as a new synthesis of both an ideology of resistance *and* an ideology engaging with the state. Before we discuss this question in more detail, I want to conclude some aspects of the discussion about indigeneity as an ideology (as this is crucial when discussing indigeneity) and its relation to the state and (inevitably, as the state is the arena for economic struggles) the political economy. When talking about thesis, antithesis, and synthesis, however, it has to be repeated that these are not separate entities. Indigeneity does not come as an antithesis from outside of the state (the colonial state, independent Indonesia, the developmentalist New Order, or the post–New Order Indonesia). Instead, it is an integral part of the state and society—an integral part of their internal contradiction. When referring to thesis, antithesis, and synthesis, I want to emphasize the fact that state and indigeneity are in constant exchange and mutually constitutive that there is a process of exchange leading to change. *Adat*, as Imam Ardhianto (2022) has demonstrated in regard to *adat* and Christianity in Borneo, is subject to transformation. This is true also for *adat* among the Duri as well as on a larger national scale.

The observation of the constitutive character of the nation for indigeneity and vice versa contributes to our understanding of what the nation actually is. In a Levi-Straussian sense, it can be described as zero-institution, that is, an empty notion that functions only to demonstrate that social institutions are actual. The political struggle is thus the struggle over the way this zero-institution receives particular signification, which then is represented as the universal Indonesian. As a zero-institution, the nation is artificial in the sense that it is not grounded in old tradition and social bonds, but it has to at least appear to be natural—that is, as an entity with a pregiven content (on the notion of the nation as a zero-institution, see Žižek 2000, 113–114). This pregiven content of the essentialization of the nation is found in *adat*, although *adat* also shows what makes the nation not the nation, namely the premodern, traditional societies that were meant to be abolished in the project of an independent Indonesia.

I have suggested analyzing indigeneity as ideology in the Althusserian sense, that is, as a representation of people's relations to what Althusser (2014, 183) calls the "real conditions of existence"—that is, "the relations of production and the relations deriving from it." In other words, ownership structures, economic mechanisms, and contradictions as well as class struggles are all represented within indigeneity. Indigeneity, I argue, represents a relation to the state and resource access. The state organizes and legitimizes resource access (most of all to land), and much consensus has been reached among scholars that the struggle for land was and is one of the foremost concerns of the Indigenous movement in

Indonesia. Opposition to the state as well as cooperation with the state for recognition are therefore means to represent people's relation to their conditions. As such, it is not surprising that many Indigenous activists have emphasized equality, cooperation, and communal ownership as inherent features of indigeneity because indigeneity represents contradictions of the political-economic order organized by the state. On other occasions, indigeneity has been applied by local elites, as I explained in chapter 4 on indigeneity in South Sulawesi. This was especially evident in the case in Toraja when traditional elites emphasized hierarchies in political power struggles over the approaches of the Indigenous grassroots activists. In these cases, indigeneity as an ideology represented an affirmative relation to the current status and became instead a tool for traditional elites in their internal struggle over resources. The answer to the question of whether indigeneity is a reactionary or progressive ideology thus depends on *how* it represents *whose* relation to the "conditions of existence." Among the Duri community, I argue, an approach advocating for a rather egalitarian distribution of resources and communal ownership prevails, but at the same time, the ideology that represents these relations depends for its acknowledgment on the (local) state apparatus, which must not appear to be too radical. A common ground is what Tania Li (2007) has called the will to improve: Economic growth and entrepreneurship are also embedded into the ideology of indigeneity. Instead of stressing the will to improve as a form of governmentality, however, I have argued that indigeneity refers to unfulfilled promises of Indonesian ideas of a more equal and just society, in other words, to an internal contradiction of Indonesian society.

As Althusser has emphasized, ideologies have histories of their own, although they are, in the last instance, determined by economic contradictions and class struggles (Althusser 2014, 174). *Adat,* as an ideology, does indeed have its own history, and in chapter 1, I explained how it emerged as a response to, among others, economic questions (translating them into political and moral questions) during the late colonial order. *Adat,* as a notion of "the original," was thus applied by Indonesian nationalists, both populist-leftist and organicist-reactionary. As the latter camp finally prevailed over the former, indigeneity was acknowledged as a "traditional" foundation of a hierarchical society. As an identity of particular groups, *adat* was subjected to oppression. At this point in the history of the ideology of indigeneity, the state was somewhat Indigenous (as traditional-hierarchical), but indigeneity as it was understood in emerging transnational discourses was different from the state. Only through this history was it possible for indigeneity as an ideology to emerge in its current form against the New Order state and in reliance on the ideological foundations of late colonialism, notions of egalitarianism, and (neo-)liberal entrepreneurship. In this respect, chapters 1 and 2 outline the history of this ideology.

Althusser also argues, however, that ideology has no history in the sense that ideology appears as omni-historical—even though it is an effect of social relations, economic contradictions, and class struggles. As he puts it, a "particular feature of ideology is that it is endowed with a structure and functioning such as to make it a non-historical—that is, an omni-historical—reality" (Althusser 2014, 175). This is certainly the case for the New Order notion of the traditional, hierarchical Indonesian society, but this particular feature of ideology is also present in indigeneity as it has been applied by the Indigenous movement in post–New Order Indonesia. I argued in chapters 4 and 5 that that indigeneity among the Duri came into being through its history. In particular, the Darul Islam rebellion, which aimed to destroy anything feudal and traditional—accusing these of being *shirik*—set the foundation for rather equal communities that fit much better into popular images of indigeneity stressing social equality than, for example, nearby Toraja where indigeneity has often been a tool for the political elite. Islam seems to have increased gender differences, however, which are now visible to a higher degree among the Duri than in Toraja; even among Indigenous activists, many more women are involved in Toraja than in Enrekang. Althusser's argument that ideologies have a history of their own (as ideology develops and comes into existence in history) and, at the same time, have no history (as the seemingly omni-historical feature of ideology is a part of that very ideology) leads to the question of the critique of the ideology: When indigeneity has a history (in the sense that it comes into being in its current form as a result of struggles over resources, that is, class struggles in the widest sense) and it has no history (in the sense that indigeneity is not omni-historical, even though it claims to be), the question is how critical scholars can apply a critique that takes into account the fact that indigeneity expresses economic contradictions and, at the same time, is ideology in the sense of a false consciousness. I deal with that question later in this conclusion after discussing the relationship between indigeneity and political economy in more detail.

Indigenous Activism and the Political Economy

Having discussed the Indigenous movement on several scales (national, provincial, and local) and its entanglement with different actors, I next summarize some of my crucial findings and I theorize them by drawing on several theoretical frameworks. My fieldwork as well as the data I have collected represent a process in motion. Indigenous recognition in Indonesia is far from complete.

The struggle I have written about continues and my contribution is, therefore, an account of snapshots taken between 2015, when I visited Enrekang for the first time and the *peraturan dearah* was discussed, and 2022, when recognition in Enrekang was put into practice. Indigenous activists' efforts in other parts of the province or on the national scale, however, in many cases, still have not born fruit. Most important, the Law on Indigenous Communities on the national scale still have not been passed; it is considered a less important task for the government. Despite the unfinished process, however, I hope that some insight can contribute to the ongoing discussion about indigeneity in Indonesia and beyond.

A central topic of this book is the relationship between the state and Indigenous peoples. I have argued that the very notion of indigeneity needs the state, as the state emerges as the constitutive other as well as the regime that acknowledges indigeneity as an entity and all the rights that come with the construction of Indigenous identity. This relationship can also be analyzed in the local processes of recognition. Enrekang and the now Indigenous Duri communities are examples of a relatively successful process. That process of recognition confirms Tania Li's (2005) critique of James Scott: Scott (1998) argues in Seeing Like a State that states construct models of the realm they seek to control and that their schemes are simplified and prevent people from applying their local, everyday knowledge. Against this, Li noted that the state is not simply "up there." Li makes an excellent point when she argues that the state and its schemes also, and maybe primarily (especially in the neoliberal era during which ideological state apparatuses have gained in importance relative to the direct domination exercised by repressive forces), work "through the practices and desires of their target population" (Li 2005, 383). I have also argued that it is not only bureaucracies, repressive state apparatuses such as the military, the police, and courts that are proponents of the state but also nongovernmental organizations (NGOs) and even ordinary people. The ideology of indigeneity organizes these actors and interests. Indigeneity is a basis for cooperation just as it is a basis for struggle. It is a tool for progress, economic growth, and entanglement with the state—just as it is a means to seek autonomy in regaining control over land.

Tania Li has suggested analyzing improvement schemes through the Foucauldian concept of governmentality rather than through a vague notion of "the state" and high modernism, which suggests that society can be rationally organized and classified as the object of development. I suggest taking the state into account, however, because without the state, there is no indigeneity. The Foucauldian notion of governmentality is indeed a useful tool for dealing with the distinctive modes of power, but it is also hypercomplex because it takes into account virtually everything: humans and things, relations, links, resources, territory, climate, irrigation, and so on (Li 2005, 387). Of course, all of these play a role, but if we want to understand the process of recognition of indigeneity, a focus on the state and Indigenous peoples, both as activists and citizens, might be more useful than the elusive notion of governmentality (at least it strikes me as elusive when analyzing particular phenomena of Indigenous recognition).

But what is the state then? Li criticizes Scott for not defining that crucial term. The state, for him, seems to be something that demands oversight, to exercise as much as control as possible through centrally planned schemes (Li 2005, 385). Such a notion of the state is indeed simplistic: It is an ideal type of an authoritarian developmentalist state, such as New Order Indonesia, but it hardly grasps all of the crucial features of the state in post–New Order Indonesia, in which economic liberalization, decentralization, and the promotion of entrepreneurship are more prevalent. The state is also hardly a monolithic apparatus. The example of Enrekang demonstrates well that there *is* a state and that it matters: a parliament and a government that recognize Indigenous communities. But this state, in its local appearance, is far from what Scott has suggested. The state, he says, is an arena in which political and economic conflicts are staged. Indigenous activists, religious institutions, scholars, and policymakers are the state in Enrekang; they negotiate, struggle, and, most of all, cooperate; they are part of the state as an arena, and this also holds true for the provincial and national scales as well. On the national level, institutional activists engage directly with the state. AMAN engaged directly in politics when supporting Jokowi's candidacy in 2014 and criticized his government in the 2019 election. Institutional activists, as I argued in chapter 2, have become a major tool in AMAN's struggle. Moreover, as demonstrated in chapter 2 and in chapter 5 on indigeneity in Enrekang, a common language of improvement, progress, and growth has unified indigeneity and the state at times, whereas neoliberal policies, for example, as exercised in the omnibus law, have separated them ideologically on other occasions.

In his critique of Indigenous rights and aspirational politics, Mark Goodale argues that the struggle for Indigenous recognition often goes hand in hand with capitalist accumulation regimes. In his words,

> national Indigenous rights enforcement sets in motion a particular chain of events that brings together both collective identity formation and claims-making within the political and legal spheres of the state. The result is that peoples and communities under threat are both encouraged—indeed, in most cases, required—to pursue justice and

forms of (collective) self-representation by running on the political and bureaucratic treadmills that are meant to keep claimants in constant motion but going nowhere. In this way, Indigenous rights mobilization has become a *hyper-politics machine* that offers symbolic-political solutions to political-economic problems. (Goodale 2016, 442; emphasis in the original)

Is that also true for Indonesia? Some findings, indeed, suggest that Indigenous claim-making, especially in regard to land rights, might well fit into accumulation regimes. In their analysis of Indigenous land claims in central Kalimantan, for instance, Rini Astuti and Andrew McGregor (2017) argue that the emergence of a carbon economy has been strategically embraced by AMAN activists for their land claims. "Green" land grabs and land claims, the authors argue, overlap. Thus, no simple dichotomy exists between bad land grabs and good Indigenous land claims. In this book, I have shown that Indigenous activists also apply other problematic means, such as engagement with the state apparatus and political parties (which are largely in the hands of oligarchs) or capitalist discourses of entrepreneurship, resource extraction, and development. In other words, Indigenous activism has become a part of what it often opposes.

Astuti and McGregor (2017, 462) argue that there is a "largely unspoken consensus amongst critical scholars" that green land grabs by the state or corporations are bad, whereas land claims by Indigenous peoples are inherently good. Because critical interventions by, for example, Li problematize the relationship between capitalism, the state, green land grabs, and development regimes, on the one hand, and peasants and Indigenous peoples, on the other, this supposedly large consensus hardly exists. In fact, Indigenous activists who are knowledgeable about academic publications often expressed their dissatisfaction with academic knowledge production in conversations with me. They claimed that critical scholars have a lack of empathy for Indigenous peoples' struggles. Instead of talking about, as they put it, "large, abstract concepts," such as "governmentality," "assemblages," or "dialectics" and "ideology," Indigenous activists stressed that they must consider the everyday experiences and struggles of Indigenous communities and individuals who demand concrete improvement in their livelihoods. Otherwise, there would be no grassroots base for them. I have to confess that I felt guilty when accompanying my activist friends to their meetings and workshops or when living in Duri communities: Do I represent their struggle adequately in academic accounts? On the one hand, critical scholars need abstraction, concepts, and thus a certain distance from their objects of study, but on the other hand, it is necessary to express empathy with their struggle. It has been fashionable in academia to criticize

Indigenous movements for being essentialist, engaging with capitalism and the state, and so forth, and in this book, I expressed some of this critique as well. Is this critique a mere academic issue, or might it be helpful for Indigenous peoples in their struggles?

Another important aspect is that of indigeneity and class, and how they relate to each other. The main difference between any social position based on identity or authenticity, on the one hand (indigeneity is a prime example), and class as a social position within the process of production, on the other, is that the latter is a concept that dialectically aims to overcome itself. Class—at least in Marxist dialectics—is not an identity seeking a social space where it can assert itself, but instead is a social position within the process of production that aims to hegemonize itself in order to disappear. It does so by changing the very process of production from which it originally derived. Indigeneity, by contrast, is usually seen as an identity claiming a space of sovereignty to assert itself, a space where it can be the way it is as a cultural identity. This was prevalent in van Vollenhoven's concept of *adat* as a system that should be acknowledged and protected through legal pluralism—an essentially conservative approach, as Li (2010, 393) has argued. In the debates about the Indigenous movement, however, other scholars have stressed the aspect of class. Yando Zakaria (2024) has argued that the emancipatory aspect of the *adat* movement expresses a class-based approach, but to do so, it must be understood as a strategic, not as an essential, concept:

> However, the understanding of *adat* as essentialist must turn into a strategic one. Because, as has happened so often, customary land use does not escape despotic-feudalist aspects, which are of course contrary to the position of *adat* as a project of emancipation. Therefore, the despotic-feudalist aspects of land control must be excluded from the *adat* land tenure system. This has already been done by the Basic Agrarian Law 5/1960. (Zakaria 2024, 297, author's translation)

Understanding *adat* as a strategic approach might imply that people consciously hide their class-based political agendas behind the notion of *adat*. This is usually not the case, with some exceptions, such as the radical youth I mentioned in chapter 7 on the AMAN council in Sinjai. Expressing class in indigeneity can mean shifting the notion of *adat* itself to make it a project of emancipation. Rukka Sombolinggi's seemingly harmless take on *adat* as an identity of those who have always lost in history (and, one could add, of being dispossessed) can carry this notion of class and would make possible wider alliances based on the notion of being dispossessed by political-economic mechanisms. This is possible because class is sublated within indigeneity. Rather than simply conceptualizing indigeneity as an identity concerned with tradition that has to be preserved in contrast to class as a position within the process of production that is concerned with the change of the very system that it created, indigeneity has proven to have a more complex relation to class. On the one hand, it suspends class as it replaces it with a cultural identity. On the other hand, it is preserved in the notion of struggle against hegemony, which has been conceptualized as a struggle against a cultural-political-economic hegemony. Like class, indigeneity can aim to change the very condition of its own process of creation: Making Indonesia a nation of marginalized groups (or recall the idea of a nation that was originally intended to be of and for the marginalized and colonized), of those who have always lost in history, means universalizing the particular position of indigeneity and other marginalized groups, such as peasants or workers. The notion of what it essentially means to be Indonesian requires abolishing the idea of Indonesia as a society that is seemingly inclusive but, in practice, constantly privileges certain classes and groups over others. In the case of this latter consequence, this would also mean abolishing the economic mechanisms that reproduce classes and reinforce cultural marginalization.

The Task of Being Radical

Both Marxist and postcolonial approaches criticize the politics of recognition and, consequently, the ideology of indigeneity, which always has recognition as its foremost political aim. Marxist critiques concern economic structures, whereas criticism inspired by postcolonial theory suggests that the contemporary liberal politics of Indigenous recognition "promises to reproduce the very configurations of colonialist, racist, patriarchal state power that Indigenous peoples' demands for recognition have historically sought to transcend" (Coulthard 2014, 3). Many Marxists would agree but stress that state power is, in its racist, patriarchal, and colonialist mode, ultimately an expression of capitalism. Considering these critiques, indigeneity is more or less doomed to reproduce and be an integral part of what it criticizes, that is, the capitalist economy and the state.

Claim-making has to be done within the political and legal sphere of the state, a process that unfolds in the Indigenous dialectics. Running the political and bureaucratic (as well as juridical) treadmills has indeed become a task for Indigenous activists in Indonesia. But has it got them nowhere? So far, they have achieved some recognition and even some redistribution of land. Is that just a symbolic-political solution for a political-economic problem? Given the current state of the process, I would say yes. On the national level, the amount of land redistribution is rather symbolic and even Indigenous activists would not argue otherwise. Also, a broader legal framework is missing. Even with a broader legal framework and an accelerated process of land redistribution, it is not certain that Indigenous rights offer a political-economic solution. In Enrekang, the distribution of land to some Indigenous Duri communities has enabled them to legally use the resources from their territory. Along with the local government, they aim to extract more value from the land, whether by planting fruit trees, engaging in cooperation with a company extracting resin, establishing coffee cooperatives, or planning tourism sites in *adat* forest. Ideally, the communities make decisions and distribute the surplus as egalitarian communities. Research has shown that this is unlikely, even in iconic communities (Fisher and van der Muur 2019), and I have also argued that factions and thus struggles over participation within the Duri communities occur as well.

Indigenous activists in Enrekang, however, frequently stressed that their indigeneity is not a capitalist one. Because of political taboos, these activists did not describe their indigeneity as socialist, but their ideas are indeed socialist: Coffee production should be carried out on *adat* land as community land (which cannot be privately owned or sold), and the means of production such as roasting machines should be the property of the community. Decisions on production should be made collectively, although they have to be approved by the *adat* leaders. This approach establishes an outside of capitalism, but this outside is in itself part of a larger capitalist structure as the communities are nonetheless embedded in regional, national, and global capitalist markets. The establishment of an Indigenous space outside capitalism, I have argued, can actually be a means to increase the extraction of value from land poorly used when it was state forest. As such, Indigenous space is also an anchor for capital: Because Indigenous communities often lack capital, they rely on capital from outside. The cooperation between the Duri community of Orong and the resin company is but one example. The fact that in Uru many farmers have not thus far joined the economic cooperations of the *masyarakat adat*, because they feel more secure in their relationships with coffee buyers from outside and thus prefer to sell their coffee beans as individual farmers, indicates that even if land is redistributed, economic power relations might endure.

The question of exactly how far Indigenous spaces constitute realms outside capitalism is closely related to the question of autonomy and sovereignty. From the very beginning of AMAN's efforts, claims of autonomy and sovereignty were among its main claims. AMAN's motto *Berdaulat Secara Politik, Mandiri Secara Ekonomi, Bermartabat Secara Budaya* specifies the dimensions of sovereignty: political, economic, and cultural. This claim, however, does not pay much attention to the fact that Indigenous communities are part of a larger capitalist market and the state; without these structures, their indigeneity could not come into being. As in other countries, Indigenous peoples and activists occupy a paradoxical position: They must, on the one hand, count as legal entities in courts and thus subscribe to state sovereignty. When they demand legislation on Indigenous rights, they are in effect ruled by the state. On the other hand, they demand sovereignty in cultural, political, and economic terms. This constitutes the Indigenous paradox (Bens 2020). I have paid much attention to the way this paradox unfolds within the Indonesian context and have argued that the Indigenous movement in Indonesia has few reservations about being part of the nation. This is grounded in the history of *adat* in Indonesia, which is part of the original national culture and thus it is profoundly Indonesian. *Masyarakat adat* can be Indonesian patriots, but they demand autonomy *within* the state, not against it.

The relationship between the economic and political in this regard is not always clear. Michael Dove (2011), for instance, has argued that smallholders in Kalimantan need political empowerment to hold on to their land rather than to be uplifted economically. This is certainly true for the case of Sulawesi as well, but this political empowerment is above all an economic one as the main means of production is at stake. No clear divide exists between political and economic issues. Dove criticizes neo-Marxist approaches for "robbing local society of their history and agency" (Dove 2011, 248). He wants to save the local from being subordinated under the global through an analysis that emphasizes the transnational capitalist modes of production and perceives local people as passive victims of global capitalism. In my understanding, applying a dialectical approach and looking at social totality does not mean that only capitalism and global history matter. Rather, the state, the global, and the local are all facets of a social totality with all its inconsistencies and constitutive contradictions. When we talk about agency, we often assume that autonomous humans can effectively change society. By taking into account the notion of ideology as a representation of the people's relation to their political economy, agency can appear only within a certain ideological frame (figure C.1). NGOs and the state are not free from ideology but can operate and exist only through ideology. Political actors also have to occupy the state when they seek for agency and change.

That very state is itself no neutral ground when it comes to political economy. I have outlined how the state has taken possession of people's land, especially during the so-called New Order era. If we view the state as an arena for contradictions between capital and labor, struggles over access to natural resources can be carried out, just as the New Order state was almost exclusively in the hands of capital. This was ideologically justified with reference to

FIGURE C.1.   Political sovereignty, economic independence, cultural dignity: posters in the AMAN office in Makassar outlines the organization's claims

modernization and development, as outlined in chapter 1. Modernization and development as ideological tools were incorporated into a new ideology of indigeneity that was opposed to the state and its dispossession regimes. After democratization, the situation became less clear-cut. The state as an arena became porous; Indigenous activists entered this arena as institutional activists and Indigenous communities made claims in courts and to politicians. This democratization and political openness did not automatically change the political economy. Oligarchic interests are well as the nationalist notion of land in the hands of the state is still an influential ideological tool for prioritizing corporate interests. The other influential ideological formation is capitalist-entrepreneurial. This ideological formation benefits Indigenous interests insofar as Indigenous communities can emerge as entrepreneurs, extracting value from their land more efficiently than the state (or private companies) are able to. I have argued that some of AMAN's rhetoric applies this approach. When playing the entrepreneurial card, Indigenous activists can simultaneously emerge as capitalist and noncapitalist: They are players on capitalist markets and carry resources to these markets. Internally, however, they might not apply capitalist principles of private ownership of the means of production or the selling of individuals' labor with the aim of generating surplus value for capital owners.

This approach, it seems, does not challenge the foundation of Indonesia's political economy even though some land might be redistributed. It appears to strengthen the status quo by successfully incorporating dissident aspirations into the political-economic frame. At the same time, however, it demonstrates that this political-economic frame is not absolute, that there is an outside and thus alternatives, even though they might be small scale and the subject of internal struggles.

Another question is what alternatives the Indigenous activists have. Indigeneity might be an inherent transgression of the current political-economic order. This term of inherent transgression can help us to determine

> how "radical" different forms of resistance are: what may appear as a "radical critical stance" or as a subversive activity can in fact function as the system's "inherent transgression," so that, often, a minor legal reform which merely aims at bringing the system in accordance with its professed ideological goals can be more subversive than open questioning of the system's basic assumptions. These considerations enable us to define the art of a "politics of minimal difference": to be able to identify and then focus on a minimal (ideological, legislative, and so on) measure which, *prima facie*, not only does not question the system's premises, but even seems to merely apply its own principles to its actual functioning and thus render it more consistent with itself; however, a critic-ideological "parallax view" leads us to surmise that this minimal measure, while in no way disturbing the system's explicit mode of functioning, electively "moves underground," introduces cracks in its foundations. (Žižek 2008, 390–391)

When emerging as radical, that is, as anti-state, the Indigenous movement might transgress that very state and its economy only implicitly. AMAN's initial and oppositional threat from its founding congress in 1999 that it would not recognize the state if the state did not recognize Indigenous peoples is a case in point: As radical as it appears, AMAN is foremost concerned with recognition rather than the political economy the state represents. It also reinforces the state within the notion of indigeneity as it attaches indigeneity to the notion of the state (on this dialectical notion of Indigenous recognition in Indonesia, see Tamma and Duile 2020). The statement is thus pseudo-radical. In contrast, it might actually be the seemingly harmless reformist approaches that introduce "cracks in the foundation": Engaging with the state and its institutions while arguing that indigeneity is Indonesian by inserting it into nationalist discourses and the conformist notion of entrepreneurship might, paradoxically, actually provide spaces outside capitalism. Through small changes in legislation, the "politics of minimal difference," as (Žižek 2008, 390) puts it, is applied. In this sense, the

Indigenous movement has potential to lead to real change, rather than applying radical rhetoric that is from the very beginning incorporated into what is, on the surface, rejected. That is the kind of change Indigenous dialectics can bring.

Radical stances that do not bring actual change are not only an issue for the Indigenous movement. It is no less a problem in academic representation and the verdicts deriving from academic critique. The fundamental critique is voiced by scholars who provide a profound academic analysis but no actual alternatives, even implicitly suggesting that change is, at least for the time being, out of reach. It depicts indigeneity, embedded in ideological structures, governmentality, or political-economic regimes, more or less as a lost cause. In this way, radical critique becomes an inherent part of the social condition it aims at. This critique affirms existing social conditions because it does not offer a way out. It creates the consciousness of being outside these conditions through its critique. In practice, however, it does not change these conditions: The critique is in itself a part of the social conditions it criticizes. Critical scholars usually argue for political engagement, but this engagement is, in practice, often unlikely to happen. Tania Li (2007, 282), for instance, suggests a positively inflected *provokasi* (provocation) as a means to struggle for social justice. I too have thought that such a *provokasi* might be necessary to shake the very foundations of a political economy that reproduces social inequality. Because indigeneity as a political program often does not facilitate *provokasi* as a form of openly articulated indignation, I have often felt that the change the movement promises might be out of reach, that progress might be slow precisely because of the lack of *provokasi*.

A trend in cultural anthropology has been described Sherry Ortner (2016) as dark anthropology, that is, anthropology responding to the devastation of neoliberalism as capitalism's new and brutal form. This dark anthropology reflects the "harsh and brutal experience of human existence," as Ortner (2016, 49) puts it. In contrast, other anthropologists suggest an anthropology of the good (Robbins 2013) or a "positive anthropology" (Fischer 2014, 17). " 'Bright anthropology' is concerned with issues such as well-being, empathy, morality, care, hope, happiness, and change. It suggests that there must be better ways to live than the ones it [anthropology] documents" (Robbins 2013, 458; on dark and bright anthropology, see Haug 2020). Dark anthropology, at least in its better form, does not only describe life in the ruins of capitalism but also departs from a critical standpoint that was born out of the impulse to radically challenge. Critical anthropology needs this radical critique (as a rejection of current conditions) as it emerges in dark anthropology. If dark anthropology does not want to merely become an inherent part of the social conditions it is criticizing, it must also appreciate, for instance, Indigenous praxis and the small changes and critique it offers.

One way to achieve this might be academic acknowledgment of the potential of what I call the Indigenous politics of minimal difference. What counts as Indigenous politics of minimal difference? This politics refers to the "promising contradictions" of the Indigenous movement that Anna Tsing (2007, 33) has pointed out and that I described previously. These contradictions operate in and outside the state and its political economy: rejecting and reclaiming national development standards, demanding subsistence and wealth, embracing traditional knowledge and new technologies, seeking Indigenous autonomy and juridical acknowledgment. It is often easy to approach the state, its practices, and discourses through these contradictions, and critics might suggest that this pragmatic politics of minimal difference might do nothing but incorporate the Indigenous movement into the capitalist state. These promising contradictions never lie exclusively within the realm of capitalism. Maybe the most interesting way of looking at indigeneity is to retrace these contradictions, Indigenous political practices, and discourses in light of the question of how they move underground, introducing cracks in the foundations.

As I have argued, these challenges at the foundations might even start in inconspicuous places, such as the Duri highlands. The process of Indigenous recognition, I have shown, happened comparatively quickly in Enrekang. No major conflicts between the state, its apparatus, or large companies have occurred in the Duri highlands thus far. Critical anthropologists have often focused on rather conflict-laden sites and indeed many of these sites can be found in Indonesia (e.g., Robinson 1986, 2019; Potter 2009; Steinebach 2013; Haug 2014). This narrative of Indigenous communities or peasants struggling against powerful actors is also dominant in the Indigenous self-image. It indeed constitutes it, along with narratives of cultural and political marginalization. In many parts of the large archipelago, however, the state and resource-extracting corporations are rather absent. They might appear occasionally, but they operate on a small scale or leave after a short time. Decades-long conflicts carried out juridically or through violence arise often enough, but other Indigenous communities never experience them. Additionally, the focus on economic conditions and exploitation does not mean that other issues are not at stake. Cultural and religious discrimination, I have argued, are constitutive not only for the self-image of Indigenous people but also for their political struggle and their political agency. Indigenous activists also play along with hegemonic discourses to gain agency, as I have argued in regard to religious issues in the process of the Indigenous recognition of Duri communities and on the national scale.

I have shed light on a case that could be regarded, in many aspects, as a success for the Indigenous movement and as an example of cooperation between the state apparatus and the Indigenous movement. Is this an argument that the Indigenous movement becomes a part of the state and its capitalist political economy, rather than resisting it, seeking alliances with other progressive organizations, and vocally demanding alternatives for Indonesia? That might be the case, but a chance always exists that the ideology of indigeneity introduces cracks in the foundation of the political-economic system just by playing along.

I remember my discussion with the radical youths I was so surprised to find in Sinjai during the AMAN congress of South Sulawesi. Radical as they were (they discussed Marx as well as Indonesian thinkers such as Tan Malaka and Haji Misbach), they supported AMAN in its rather reformist approach. Although AMAN activists held ceremonies with state representatives during the day, these youths dreamt of a radically different Indonesia grounded in local peasant societies, not in the sense of returning to an imagined past but of embracing a future based on the everyday experiences and struggles of Indigenous communities. Alliances for profound change may come later. The first step, for them, was to prove that alternative economies work on the local level. Only in that way, they believed, could big issues such as the overall political economy, on the one hand, and the everyday concerns of ordinary people, on the other, be brought together. I do not suggest that this approach is dominant in Indonesia's Indigenous movement, but it is one possibility for the movement's future.

For scholars concerned with political economy, indigeneity is indeed a challenging subject. Should it be subject to criticism because it offers symbolic political solutions for problems deriving from the political economy, or because it offers a false consciousness (as ideology) that prevents people from demanding radical change? Should one support the Indigenous movement given that large-scale change within landownership structures (and those of other natural resources) will challenge the political economy? After my work on and with Indigenous activists in Jakarta, Makassar, and the Duri highlands, I hope to bring these approaches together dialectically. This approach represents what can be called a critique of ideology and a critique offered by the ideology: Indigeneity enables people to express their criticism of the state (or corporations) or, more generally, of the political-economic conditions in which they live. As such, indigeneity as an ideology also (and often foremost) expresses economic concerns. Therefore, the critique this ideology offers must be sublated in a critique of that ideology as a critique *against* the ideology of indigeneity. This is, I argue, a basic condition for critical scholarship on Indigenous peoples: When criticizing indigeneity as ideology, it is the task of critical scholars to sublate (i.e., preserve *and* transcend) the critique the ideology of indigeneity offers of economic dispossession, state control, and capitalist incorporation.

References

Acciaioli, Greg. 1985. "Culture as Art: From Practice to Spectacle in Indonesia." *Canberra Anthropology* 8(1/2): 161–69.

Acciaioli, Greg. 2004. "From Economic Actor to Moral Agent: Knowledge, Faith and Hierarchy Among the Bugis of Sulawesi." *Indonesia* 78: 147–80.

Acciaioli, Greg. 2007. "From Customary Law to Indigenous Sovereignty: Reconceptualizing *Masyarakat Adat* in Contemporary Indonesia." In *The Revival of Tradition in Indonesian Politics. The Deployment of Adat from Colonialism to Indigenism*, edited by Jamie Davidson and David Henley, 295–318. London: Routledge.

Affif, Suraya, and Celia Lowe. 2007. "Claiming Indigenous Community: Political Discourse and Natural Resource Rights in Indonesia." *Alternatives: Global, Local, Political* 32(1): 73–97.

Affif, Suraya, and Noer Fauzi Rachman. 2019. "Institutional Activism: Seeking Customary Forest Rights from Within the Indonesian State." *Asia Pacific Journal of Anthropology* 20(5): 453–70.

Alfred, Taiaiake. 1999. *Peace, Power, Righteousness: an Indigenous Manifesto*. Oxford: Oxford University Press.

Ali, Fachry. 1994. "Masses Without Citizenship: Islamic Protest Movements in Nineteenth-Century Java." In *The Late Colonial State in Indonesia. Political and economic foundations of the Netherlands Indies 1880–1942*, edited by Robert Cribb, 247–60. Leiden: KITLV.

Althusser, Louis. 2005. *For Marx*. London: Verso.

Althusser, Louis. 2014. *On the Reproduction of Capitalism. Ideology and Ideological State Apparatuses*. London: Verso.

AMAN. 2020a. "Abdon Nababan: RUU Masyarakat Adat Akan Menyelamatkan Bangsa." (Abdon Nababan: Indigenous Peoples Bill Will Save the Nation) *Aliansi Masyarakat Adat Nusantara*, September 13. https://www.aman.or.id/2020/09/abdon-nababan -ruu-masyarakat-adat-akan-menyelamatkan-bangsa.

AMAN. 2020b. "Komite Nasional Pembaruan Agraria (KNPA) keluarkan Manifesto Politik Agraria." (The National Committee for Agrarian Reform (KNPA) Issues a Manifesto on Agrarian Politics) *Aliansi Masyarakat Adat Nusantara*, September 26. https://www.aman.or.id/2020/09/komite-nasional-pembaruan-agraria-knpa -keluarkan-manifesto-politik-agraria.

AMAN. n.d. "Profil Aliansi Masyarakat Adat Nusantara (AMAN)." (Profile of the Indigenous Peoples Alliance of the Archipelago (AMAN)). *Aliansi Masyarakat Adat Nusantara*, accessed April 24, 2023. http://www.aman.or.id/profil-aliansi -masyarakat-adat-nusantara.

Ambarwati, Aprilia, Ricky Ardian Harahap, Isono Sadoko, and Ben White. 2016. "Land Tenure and Agrarian Structure in Regions of Small-Scale Food Production." In *Land and Development in Indonesia: Searching for the People's Sovereignty*, edited by John McCarthy and Kathryn Robinson, 265–94. Singapore: ISEAS.

Aminah, Andi Nur. 2016. "Adnan: Tak Ada Lagi Raja di Gowa." (Adnan: There is no King in Gowa Anymore) *Republika*, September 12. https://republika.co.id/berita /nasional/daerah/16/09/12/oddsgv384-adnan-tak-ada-lagi-raja-di-gowa.

L

Aminuddin, Katiman, and Syukri. 2019. "Sukarno's Thought About Marhaenism." *Budapest International Research and Crisis Institute Journal* 2(2): 420–26.

Anderson, Patrick. 2012. "Free, Prior, and Informed Consent? Indigenous Peoples and the Palm Oil Boom in Indonesia." In *The Palm Oil Controversy in Southeast Asia: A Transnational Perspective*, edited by Oliver Pye and Jayati Bhattacharya, 244–57. Singapore: ISEAS.

Andini, Batari Oja. 2017. "The Islamization in Bugis Society During the Darul Islam Era Under Kahar Muzakar in the 1960s." *DINIKA Academic Journal of Islamic Studies* 2(1): 23–34.

Antlöv, Hans. 2003. "Village Government and Rural Development in Indonesia: The New Democratic Framework." *Bulletin of Indonesian Economic Studies* 39(2): 80–114.

Antweiler, Christoph. 2000. *Urbane Rationalität. Eine stadtethnologische Studie zu Ujung Pandang (Makassar), Indonesien.*(Urban Rationality. An Urban Anthropological Study on Ujung Pandang (Makassar), Indonesia) Berlin: Dietrich Reimer Verlag.

Anugrah, Iqra. 2019. "Movements for Land Rights in Democratic Indonesia." In *Activists in Transition: Progressive Politics in Democratic Indonesia*, edited by Thishara Dibley and Michele Ford, 79–98. Ithaca, NY: Cornell University Press.

Aragon, Lorraine. 2000. *Fields of the Lord: Animism, Christian Minorities, and State Development in Indonesia*. Honolulu: University of Hawai'i Press.

Århem, Kaj. 2016. "Southeast-Asian Animism: A Dialogue with Amerindian Perspectivism." In *Animism in Southeast Asia*, edited by Kaj Århem and Guido Sprenger, 279–301. London: Routledge.

Ardhianto, Imam. 2022. *Hierarchies of Power: Evangelical Christianity and Adat Transformation in Indonesian Borneo*. Singapore: Palgrave Macmillan.

Arizona, Yance, and Erasmus Cahyadi. 2013. "The Revival of Indigenous Peoples: Contestations over a Special Legislation on *Masyarakat Adat*." In *Adat and Indigeneity in Indonesia. Culture and Entitlements Between Heteronomy and Self-Ascription*, edited by Britta Hauser-Schäublin, 43–62. Göttingen: Universitätsverlag Göttingen.

Arizona, Yance, Malik, and Irena Lucy Ishimora. 2017. "Outlook Epistema 2017: Pengakuan Hukum terhadap Masyarakat Adat: Tren Produk Hukum Daerah dan Nasional Pasca Putusan MK 35/PPU-X/2012." (Outlook Epistema 2017: Legal Recognition of Indigenous Communities: Trends in Regional and National Legal Outputs After the MK Decision 35/PPU-X/2012) *Epistema Institute*, accessed May 13, 2020. http://epistema.or.id/download/Outlook_Epistema_2017.pdf.

Arizona, Yance, Muki Trenggono Wicaksono, and Jaqueline Vel. 2019. "The Role of Indigeneity NGOs in the Legal Recognition of *Adat* Communities and Customary Forests in Indonesia." *Asia Pacific Journal of Anthropology* 20(5): 487–506.

Arnscheidt, Julia. 2009. *"Debating" Nature Conservation: Policy, Law and Practice in Indonesia: A Discourse Analysis of History and Present*. Leiden: Leiden University Press.

Arumingtyas, Luisa. 2019. "Penetapan Hutan Adat Hanya 1 percent dari Realisasi Perhutanan Sosial." (Customary Forest Determination is Only 1 Percent of Social Forestry Realization) *Mongabay*, March 17. https://www.mongabay.co.id/2019/03/27/penetapan-hutan-adat-hanya-1-dari-realisasi-perhutanan-sosial.

Aspinall, Edward, and Noor Rohman. 2017. "Village Head Elections in Java: Money Politics and Brokerage in the Remaking of Indonesia's Rural Elite." *Journal of Southeast Asian Studies* 48(1): 31–52.

Astuti, Rini, and Andrew McGregor. 2017. "Indigenous Land Claims or Green Grabs? Inclusions and Exclusions Within Forest Carbon Politics in Indonesia." *Journal of Peasant Studies* 44(2): 445–66.

Bakker, Laurens, and Sandra Moniaga. 2010. "The Space Between: Land Claims and the Law in Indonesia." *Asian Journal of Social Science* 38: 187–203.

Barnes, R. H. 1995 "Introduction." In *Indigenous Peoples of Asia*, edited by R. H. Barnes, Andrew Gray, and Benedict Kingsbury, 1–12. Ann Arbor, MI: Association for Asian Studies.

Bateman, Fiona, and Lionel Pilkington, eds. 2011. *Studies in Settler Colonialism: Politics, Identity and Culture.* New York: Norman Macmillan.

Bedner, Adriaan, and Yance Arizona. 2019. "*Adat* in Indonesian Land Law: A Promise for the Future or a Dead End?" *Asia Pacific Journal of Anthropology* 20(5): 416–34.

Bedner, Adriaan, and Stijn van Huis. 2008. "The Return of the Native in Indonesian Law: Indigenous Communities in Indonesian Legislation." *Bijdragen tot de Taal-, Land- en Volkenkunde* 164(2/3): 165–96.

Bens, Jonas. 2020. *The Indigenous Paradox. Rights, Sovereignty, and Culture in the Americas.* Philadelphia: University of Pennsylvania Press.

Bigalke, Terrance. 2005. *Tana Toraja: A Social History of an Indonesian People.* Singapore: University of Singapore Press.

Boomgard, Peter. 2007. *Southeast Asia: An Environmental History.* Santa Barbara, CA: ABC Clio.

Bourchier, David. 1998. "Indonesianising Indonesia: Conservative Indigenism in an Age of Globalisation." *Social Semiotics* 9(2/3): 203–14.

Bowen, John R. 2000. "Should We Have a Universal Concept of 'Indigenous Peoples' Rights'? Ethnicity and Essentialism in the Twenty-First Century." *Anthropology Today* 16(4): 12–16.

Bräuchler, Birgit. 2010a. "Integration and Exclusion: Islam *Adat* in Central Moluccas." *Indonesia and the Malay World* 38: 65–93.

Bräuchler, Birgit. 2010b. "The Revival Dilemma: Reflections on Human Rights, Self-Determination and Legal Pluralism in Eastern Indonesia." *Journal of Legal Pluralism and Unofficial Law* 42(63): 1–42.

Bräuchler, Birgit. 2018. "Diverging Ecologies on Bali." *Sojourn: Journal of Social Issues in Southeast Asia* 33(2): 362–96.

Breman, Jan. 1983. *Control of Land and Labour in Colonial Java.* Dordrecht: Forbis.

Bubandt, Nils. 2004. "Towards a New Politics of Tradition? Decentralisation, Conflict and *Adat* in Eastern Indonesia." Special volume, *Antropologi Indonesia* 2004: 11–30.

Budiman, Arief. 1988. "The Emergence of the Bureaucratic Capitalist State in Indonesia." In *Reflection of Development in Southeast Asia*, edited by Lim Teck Ghee, 110–29. Singapore: ISEAS.

Buehler, Michael. 2010. "Democratisation and Local Democracy in Indonesia: The Marginalisations of the Public Sphere." In *Problems of Democratisation in Indonesia. Elections, Institutions and Society*, edited by Edward Aspinall and Marcus Mietzner, 267–85. Singapore: ISEAS.

Burns, Peter. 1989. "The Myth of *Adat*." *Journal of Legal Pluralism and Unofficial Law* 21(28): 1–127.

Burns, Peter. 2004. *The Leiden Legacy: concepts of law in Indonesia.* Leiden: KITLV.

Burns, Peter. 2007. "Custom, That Is Before All Law." In *The Revival of Tradition in Indonesian Politics: The Deployment of Adat from Colonialism to Indigenism*, edited by Jamie Davidson and David Henley, 68–86. London: Routledge.

Butler, Rett. 2013. "In Landmark Ruling, Indonesia's Indigenous People Win Right to Millions of Hectares of Forest." *Mongabay*, May 17. https://news.mongabay.com /2013/05/in-landmark-ruling-indonesias-indigenous-people-win-right-to-millions -of-hectares-of-forest.

Choi, Nankyung. 2017. "Democracy and Patrimonial Politics in Local Indonesia." *Indonesia* (88): 131–64.

Chua, Liana, and Rusalina Idrus. 2022. "Introduction: Unpacking Indigeneity in Southeast Asia." *SOJOURN: Journal of Social Issues in Southeast Asia* 37(1): 1–26.

Colchester, Marcus, Aik Pang, Wee, Meng Chou, Wong, and Thomas Jalong. 2007. *Land Is Life: Land Rights and Palm Oil Development in Sarawak*. Bogor: Forest Peoples Program/Sawit Watch.

Corntassel, Jeff. 2018. *Everyday Acts of Resurgence: People, Places, Practices*. Olympia, WA: DayKeeper.

Coulthard, Glen. 2014. *Red Skin, White Masks: Rejecting the Colonial Politics of Recognition*. Minneapolis: University of Minnesota Press.

Cribb, Robert. 2003. "Environmentalism in Indonesian Politics." In *Towards Integrated Environmental Law in Indonesia*, edited by Adriaan Bedner and Nicole Niessen, 37–43. Leiden: Research School CNWS.

Cummings, William. 2002. *Making Blood White. Historical Transformations in Early Modern Makassar*. Honolulu: University of Hawai'i Press.

Davidson, Jamie S. 2007. "Culture and Rights in Ethnic Violence." In *The Revival of Tradition in Indonesian Politics. The Deployment of Adat from Colonialism to Indigenism*, edited by Jamie Davidson and David Henley, 224–46. London: Routledge.

de Jong, Edwin Bernardus Paulus. 2009. "Reshaping Tana Toraja: A Century of Decentralization and Power Politics in the Highlands of South Sulawesi." In *Decentralization and Regional Autonomy in Indonesia. Implementation and Challenges*, edited by Coen Holtzappel and Martin Ramstedt, 256–93. Singapore: ISEAS-Yusof Ishak Institute.

Djumena, Erlangga. 2016. "Soal Bupati Vs Raja Gowa, Ini Tanggapan Gubernur Sulsel." *Kompas*, September 13, https://regional.kompas.com/read/2016/09/13/05254921/soal.bupati.vs.raja.gowa.ini.tanggapan.gubernur.sulsel?page=2.

Dolar, Mladen. 2020. "What's the Matter? On Matter and Related Matters." In *Subject Lessons: Hegel, Lacan, and the Future of Materialism*, edited by Russell Sbriglia and Slavoj Žižek, 31–49. Evanston, IL: Northwestern University Press.

Dove, Michael R. 2011. *The Bana Tree at the Gate. A History of Marginal Peoples and Global Markets in Borneo*. New Haven, CT: Yale University Press.

Duile, Timo. 2021. "Paradoxes of Indigeneity: Identity, the State, and the Economy in Indonesia." *Dialectical Anthropology* 45: 357–81.

Duile, Timo, and Jonas Bens. 2017. "Indonesia and the 'Conflictual Consensus': A Discursive Perspective on Indonesian Democracy." *Critical Asian Studies* 49(2): 139–62.

Duncan, Christopher. 2004. "From Development to Empowerment. Changing Indonesian Government Policies Towards Indigenous Minorities." In *Civilizing the Margins. Southeast Asian Government Policies for the Development of Minorities*, edited by Christopher Duncan, 86–115. Ithaca, NY: Cornell University Press.

Duncan, Christopher. 2007. "Mixed Outcomes: The Impact of Regional Autonomy and Decentralization on Indigenous Ethnic Minorities in Indonesia." *Development and Change* 38(4): 711–33.

Dutch Colonial Heritage. n.d. "The Conquest of Makassar by the Dutch (1596–1800)." Accessed July 15, 2020. http://indonesia-dutchcolonialheritage.nl/KNIL1/ConquestMakassar.pdf.

Elson, Robert. 2008. *The Idea of Indonesia*. Cambridge: Cambridge University Press.

Erb, Maribeth. 2007. "*Adat* Revivalism in Western Flores: Culture, Religion, and Land." In *The Revival of Tradition in Indonesian Politics: The Deployment of Adat from Colonialism to Indigenism*, edited by Jamie Davidson and David Henley, 247–74. London: Routledge.

Eriksen, Thomas Hylland. 2002. *Ethnicity and Nationalism: Anthropological Perspectives*. London: Pluto.

Escárcega, Sylvia. 2010. "Authenticating Strategic Essentialisms: The Politics of Indigenousness at the United Nations." *Cultural Dynamics* 22(1): 3–28.

Fachrudin, Azis Anwar. 2017. "'Religion' and 'Belief' in Indonesia: What's the Difference?" *New Mandala*, December 20. www.newmandala.org/religion-belie f-indonesia -whats-difference.

Faiz, Ahmad. 2017. "MK Putuskan Aliran Kepercayaan Masuk Kolom Agama KTP." (Constitutional Court Decides Traditional Beliefs can be Included in Religion Column on Identity Card) *Tempo*, November 7. https://nasional.tempo.co/read /1031506/mk-putuskan-aliran-kepercayaan-masuk-kolom-agama-ktp /full&view=ok.

Fasseur, Cees. 2007. "Colonial Dilemma: Van Vollenhoven and the Struggle Between *Adat* Law and Western Law in Indonesia." In *The Revival of Tradition in Indonesian Politics: The Deployment of Adat from Colonialism to Indigenism*, edited by Jamie Davidson and David Henley, 50–67. London: Routledge.

Firmansyah, Teguh. 2017. "Saat Orang Rimba Bersyahadat dan Memilih Masuk Islam."(When the Rimba People Declared Their Muslim Faith and Chose to Convert to Islam.) *Republika*, November 21. https://www.republika.co.id/berita /dunia-islam/islam-nusantara/17/11/21/ozqmn8377-saat-orang-rimba-bersyahadat -dan-memilih-masuk-islam.

Fischer, Edward. 2014. *The Good Life: Aspiration, Dignity, and the Anthropology of Wellbeing*. Stanford, CA: Stanford University Press.

Fisher, Micah, and Willem van der Muur. 2019. "Misleading Icons of Communal Lands in Indonesia: Implications of *Adat* Forest Recognition from a Model Site in Kajang, Sulawesi." *Asian Pacific Journal of Anthropology* 21(1): 55–76.

Fitzpatrick, Daniel. 2007. "Land, Custom, and the State in Post-Suharto Indonesia." In *The Revival of Tradition in Indonesian Politics: The Deployment of Adat from Colonialism to Indigenism*, edited by Jamie Davidson, and David Henley, 130–48. London: Routledge.

Fynn-Paul, Jeffrey. 2009. "Empire, Monotheism and Slavery in the Greater Mediterranean Region from Antiquity to the Early Modern Era." *Past and Present* 205(1): 3–40.

Fynn-Paul, Jeffrey. 2018. "Introduction: Slaving Zones in Global History: The Evolution of a Concept." In *Slaving Zones: Cultural Identities, Ideologies, and Institutions in the Evolution of Global Slavery*, edited by Jeffrey Fynn-Paul and Damian Alan Pargas, 1–22. Leiden: Brill.

Gokkon, Basten. 2017. "Indonesian President Recognizes Land Rights of Nine More Indigenous Groups." *Mongabay*, November 21. https://asiancorrespondent.com /amp/2017/11/indonesian-president-recognises-land-rights-nine-indigenous -groups/#fXXdX5yl4th20mMx.99.

Goodale, Mark. 2016. "Dark Matter: Toward a Political Economy of Indigenous Rights and Aspirational Politics." *Critique of Anthropology* 36(4): 430–57.

Großmann, Kristina. 2019. "'Dayak, Wake Up': Land, Indigeneity, and Conflicting Ecologies in Central Kalimantan, Indonesia." *Bijdragen tot de Taal-, Land- en Volkenkunde* 175(1): 1–28.

Grumblies, Anna-Teresa. 2013. "Being Wana, Becoming an 'Indigenous People.' Experimenting with Indigeneity in Central Sulawesi." In *Adat and Indigeneity in Indonesia: Culture and Entitlements Between Heteronomy and Self-Isolation*, edited by Britta Hauser-Schäublin, 81–98. Göttingen: Universitätsverlag Göttingen.

Hadiz, Vedi. 2004. "Decentralization and Democracy in Indonesia: A Critique of Neo-Institutional Perspectives." *Development and Change* 35(4): 697–718.

Hadrayani, Ira, and Abd Karim. 2019. "Masa awal dan terbentuknya federasi Duri di abad XIV." (The Early Period and the Formation of the Duri Federation in the 14th Century) *Pangadereng: Jurnal Hasil Penelitian Ilmu Sosial dan Humanoria* 5(2): 275–90.

Hames, Raymond. 2007. "The Ecologically Noble Savage Debate." *Annual Review of Anthropology* 36: 177–190.

Harsono, Boedi. 1962. *Undang-Undang Pokok Agraria. Sedjarah penjusunan, isi dan pelaksanaannja hukum agraria Indonesia.* (The Basic Agrarian Law. History of the Formulation, the Content, and the Implementation of Indonesian Agrarian Law) Djakarta: Penerbit Djambatan.

Harsono, Boedi. 2003. *Hukum Agraria Indonesia.* (Indonesian Agrarian Law) Jakarta: Penerbit Djambatan.

Hartono, Sunarjati. 1979. *Dari Hukum Antar Golongan ke Hukum Antar Adat.* (From Inter-Group Law to Inter-Customary Law) Bandung: Penerbit Alumni.

Haug, Michaela. 2014. "Resistance, Ritual Purification and Mediation: Tracing a Dayak Community's Sixteen-Year Search for Justice in East Kalimantan." *Asia Pacific Journal of Anthropology* 15(4): 357–75.

Haug, Michaela. 2020. "Framing the Future Through the Lens of Hope: Environmental Change, Diverse Hopes and the Challenge of Engagement." *Zeitschrift für Ethnologie* 145(1): 71–92.

Henley, David. 2005. "Population and the Means of Subsistence: Explaining the Historical Demography of Island Southeast Asia, with Particular Reference to Sulawesi." *Journal of Southeast Asian Studies* 36(3): 337–72.

Henley, David. 2006. "From Low to High Fertility in Sulawesi (Indonesia) during the Colonial Period: Explaining the 'First Fertility Transition.'" *Population Studies* 60(3): 309–27.

Henley, David. 2007. "Custom and Koperasi. The Co-operative Ideal in Indonesia." In *The Revival of Tradition in Indonesian Politics: The Deployment of Adat from Colonialism to Indigenism*, edited by Jamie Davidson and David Henley, 87–112. London: Routledge.

Henley, David, and Ian Caldwell. 2019. "Precolonial Citizenship in South Sulawesi." *Citizenship Studies* 23(3): 240–55.

Henley, David, and Jamie Davidson. 2007. "Introduction: Radical Conservativism— The Protean Politics of *Adat.*" In *The Revival of Tradition in Indonesian Politics: The Deployment of Adat from Colonialism to Indigenism*, edited by Jamie Davidson and David Henley, 1–49. London: Routledge.

Henschke, Rebecca. 2017. "Orang Rimba masuk Islam demi KTP: 'Kini mereka mengenal Tuhan' kata Menteri Khofifah." (Rimba People Convert to Islam for ID cards: 'Now They Know God' Says Minister Khofifah) *BBC Indonesia*, November 17. https://www.bbc.com/indonesia/majalah-41937911.

Heryanto, Ariel. 1988. "The Development of 'Development.'" *Indonesia* 46: 1–24.

Hokowhitu, Brenda. 2021. Introduction to *Routledge Handbook of Critical Indigenous Studies*, edited by Brenda Hokowhitu, Aileen Moreton-Robinson, Linda Tuhiwai-Smith, Chris Andersen, and Steve Larkin, 1–6. London: Routledge.

Hollan, Douglas, and Jane C. Wellenkamp. 1996. *The Thread of Life: Torajan Reflections on the Life Cycle.* Honolulu: University of Hawaiʻi.

Hosen, Nadirsyah. 2016. "Islam Nusantara: A Local Islam with Global Ambitions?" *Indonesia at Melbourne*, February 26. https://indonesiaatmelbourne.unimelb.edu.au/islam-nusantara-a-local-islam-with-global-ambitions.

International Labour Office. 2013. *Understanding the Indigenous and Tribal Peoples Convention, 1989 (No. 169).* Geneva: ILO.

Jameson, Fredric. 2009. *The Valences of the Dialectic.* London: Verso.

Kadir, Hatib Abdul. 2019. "Hierarchical Reciprocities and Tensions Between Migrants and Native Moluccas Post-Reformation." *Journal of Southeast Asian Human Rights* 3(2): 344–59.

Kartodirdjo, Sartono. 1984. *Pemberontakan Petani Banten 1888*. Bandung: Dunia Pustaka Jaya.

Keagop, Paskalis. 2022. "Baru 105 Hutan Adat yang Diakui Negara." (So Far Only 105 Customary Forests Recognized by the State) *Suara Perempuan Papua*, October 27. https://suaraperempuanpapua.id/baru-105-hutan-adat-yang-diakui -negara.

Kenrick, Justin, and Jerome Lewis. 2004. "Indigenous Peoples' Rights and the Politics of the Term 'Indigenous.'" *Anthropology Today* 20(2): 4–9.

Khafi, Kharishar. 2019. "Indonesia Issues Map Acknowledging Lands of Indigenous Peoples." *Jakarta Post*, May 29. https://www.thejakartapost.com/news/2019/05/28 /indonesia-issues-map-acknowledging-lands-of-indigenous-peoples.html.

King, Dwight. 1982. "Indonesia's New Order as a Bureaucratic Polity, a Neopatrimonial Regime or a Bureaucratic Authoritarian Regime: What Difference Does It Make?" In *Interpreting Indonesian Politics: Thirteen Contributions to the Debate*, edited by Benedict Anderson and Audrey Kahin, 104–16. Ithaca, NY: Cornell Modern Indonesia Project.

Klenke, Karin. 2013. "Whose *Adat* Is It? *Adat*, Indigeneity and Social Stratification in Toraja." In *Adat and Indigeneity in Indonesia. Culture and Entitlements Between Heteronomy and Self-Ascription*, edited by Britta Hauser-Schäublin, 149–66. Göttingen: Universitätsverlag Göttingen.

van Klinken, Gerry. 2007. "Return of the Sultans: The Communitarian Turn in Local Politics." In *The Revival of Tradition in Indonesian Politics. The Deployment of Adat from Colonialism to Indigenism*, edited by Jamie Davidson and David Henley, 149–169. London: Routledge.

Koentjaraningrat. 1985. "Kebudayaan Bugis-Makassar." In *Manusia dan kebudayaan di Indonesia*, edited by Koentjaraningrat, 259–78. Jakarta: Djambatan.

Koentjaraningrat, ed. 1993. *Masyarakat terasing di Indonesia*. Jakarta: Granmedia.

Koesnoe, Mohammad. 1996. "Perkembangan Hukum Adat Setelah Perang Dunia Ke-II Dalam Rangka Pembaharuan Hukum Nasional." (The Development of Customary Law After World War II in the Framework of National Legal Reform.) In *Hukum Adat Dalam Alam Kemerdekaan Nasional dan Persoalan Menghadapi era Globalisasi: Kumpulan Lima Makalah Dari Prof. Dr. H. Moh Koesnoe, SH*, edited by Siti Soendari and Agni Udayanti, 1–35. Surabaya: Ubhara Press.

Kuper, Adam. 2003a. "The Return of the Native." *Current Anthropology* 44(3): 389–402.

Kuper, Adam. 2003b. "The Return of the Native." *New Humanist* 118 (3): 5–8.

Lane, Max. 2019a. "Indonesia's New Politics: Transaction Without Contestation." In *Continuity and Change After Indonesia's Reforms: Contributions to an Ongoing Assessment*, edited by Max Lane, 1–22. Singapore: ISEAS.

Lane, Max. 2019b. "Contending Rhetoric in Indonesia's Presidential Elections: An Analysis." *ISEAS Perspective* 2019(6). https://www.iseas.edu.sg/images/pdf/ISEAS _Perspective_2019_6.pdf.

Lane, Max. 2021. *Widodo's Employment Creation Law, 2020: What Its Journey Tells Us About Indonesian Politics*. Singapore: ISEAS–Yusof Ishak Institute.

Lev, Daniel. 1985. "Colonial Law and the Genesis of the Indonesian State." *Indonesia* 40: 57–74.

Li, Tania Murray. 1999a. "Compromising Power: Development, Culture, and Rule in Indonesia." *Cultural Anthropology* 14(3): 295–322.

Li, Tania Murray, ed. 1999b. *Transforming the Indonesian Uplands: Marginality, Power and Production*. London: Routledge.

Li, Tania Murray. 2000. "Indigenous Identity in Indonesia: Resource Politics and the Tribal Slot." *Comparative Studies in Society and History* 42(1): 149–79.

Li, Tania Murray. 2001. "*Masyarakat Adat*, Difference, and the Limits of Recognition in Indonesia's Forest Zone." *Modern Asian Studies* 35 (3): 645–76.

Li, Tania Murray. 2002. "Local Histories, Global Markets: Cocoa and Class in Upland Sulawesi." *Development and Change* 33(3): 415–37.

Li, Tania Murray. 2005. "Beyond 'the State' and Failed Schemes." *American Anthropologist* 107(3): 383–94.

Li, Tania Murray. 2007. *The Will to Improve. Governmentality, Development, and the Practice of Politics*. Durham, NC: Duke University Press.

Li, Tania Murray. 2010. "Indigeneity, Capitalism, and the Management of Dispossession." *Current Anthropology* 51(3): 385–414.

Li, Tania Murray. 2016. "Governing Rural Indonesia: Convergence on the Project System." *Critical Policy Studies* 10(1): 79–94.

Lim, Merlyna. 2017. "Freedom to Hate: Social Media, Algorithmic Enclaves, and the Rise of Tribal Nationalism in Indonesia. *Critical Asian Studies* 49(3): 411–27.

Lukito, Yulia Nurliani. 2016. *Exhibiting Modernity and Indonesian Vernacular Architecture. Hybrid Architecture at Pasar Gambir of Batavia, the 1931 Paris Colonial Exhibition and Taman Mini Indonesia Indah*. Wiesbaden: Springer VS.

Maarif, Samsul. 2012. "Dimensions of Religious Practice: The Ammatoans of Sulawesi, Indonesia." PhD diss., Arizona State University.

Maarif, Samsul. 2017. *Pasang Surut Rekognisi Agama Leluhur dalam Politik Agama di Indonesia*. (The Ebb and Flow of the Recognition of Ancestral Religion in the Politics of Religion in Indonesia) Yogyakarta: Center for Religious and Cross-Cultural Studies.

Martinez Cobo, Jose. 1986. *Study of the Problem of Discrimination Against Indigenous Population*. Document No. E/CN.4/Sub.2/1986/7/Add.4. Geneva: United Nations, Subcommission on Prevention of Discrimination and Protection of Minorities.

Marx, Karl. 1983. *Capital*. Vol. 1. London: Lawrence & Wishart.

Mattulada. 1975. *Latoa. Suatu lukisan analitis terhadap antropologi politik orang Bugis*. (Latoa. An analytical painting of the political anthropology of the Bugis.) Yogyakarta: Gadjah Mada University Press.

Mattulada. 1982. "South Sulawesi, Its Ethnicity and Way of Life." *Southeast Asian Studies* 20(1): 4–22.

Maulana, Reza. 2019. "Data HGU tidak boleh dibuka." (HGU data must not be used) *Tempo*, March 30. https://majalah.tempo.co/read/wawancara/157393/data-hgu-tidak-boleh-dibuka.

Maunati, Yekti. 2012. "Networking the Pan-Dayak." In *Questioning Modernity in Indonesia and Malaysia*, edited by Wendy Mee and Joel Kahn, 91–112. Singapore: NUS University Press.

Merlan, Francesca. 2009. "Indigeneity: Global and Local." *Current Anthropology* 50(3): 303–33.

Merlan, Francesca. 2013. "From a Comparative Perspective: Epilogue." In *Adat and Indigeneity in Indonesia. Culture and Entitlements Between Heteronomy and Self-Ascription*, edited by Britta Schäublin-Hauser, 185–200. Göttingen: Universitätsverlag Göttingen.

Merlan, Francesca 2020. "Indigeneity as a Relational Identity: The Construction of Australian Land Rights." In *Indigenous Experiences Today*, edited by Masrisol de la Cadena and Orin Starn, 125–50. London: Routledge.

Mikdashi, Maya. 2013. "What Is Settler Colonialism?" *American Indian Culture and Research Journal* 37(2): 23–34.

Moertopo, Ali. 2003. "The Floating Mass." In *Indonesian Politics and Society: A Reader*, edited by David Bourchier and Vedi Hadiz, 45–48. London: Routledge Curzon.

Moniaga, Sandra. 2007. "From *Bumiputra* to *Masyarakat Adat*: A Long and Confusing Journey." In *The Revival of Tradition in Indonesian Politics: The Deployment of Adat from Colonialism to Indigenism*, edited by Jamie Davidson and David Henley, 275–94. London: Routledge.

Moreton-Robinson, Aileen. 2013. "Toward an Australian Indigenous Women's Standpoint Theory: A Methodological Tool." *Australian Feminist Studies* 28(78): 331–42.

Muhaemin, Aisyah Suparman, and Khaerullah Ilyas. 2019. "Relation of Islam, Indigenous People, and Local Wisdom in Enrekang, South Sulawesi." In *ICONSS Proceeding Series*, 333–38. Palopo: Universitas Cokroaminoto Palopo https://proceeding.iconss.id/ips/article/view/55/63.

Nababan, Abdon. 2015. "Indigenous Peoples and the World Economic Forum." *Jakarta Post*, April 17. https://www.thejakartapost.com/news/2015/04/17/indigenous-peoples-and-world-economic-forum.html.

Nader, Laura. 1990. *Harmony Ideology: Justice and Control in a Zapotec Mountain Village*. Stanford, CA: Stanford University Press.

Neilson, Jeff. 2016. "Agrarian Transformation and Land Reform in Indonesia." In *Land and Development in Indonesia: Searching for the People's Sovereignty*, edited by John McCarthy and Kathryn Robinson, 245–64, Singapore: ISEAS.

Neumann, Birgit, and Ansgar Nünning. 2012. "Travelling Concepts as a Model for the Study of Culture." In *Travelling Concepts for the Study of Culture*, edited by Birgit Neumann and Ansgar Nünning, 1–22. Berlin: De Gruyter.

Niezen, Ronald. 2003. *The Origins of Indigenism: Human Rights and the Politics of Identity*. Berkley: University of California Press.

Nooy-Palm, Hetty. 1969. "Dress and Adornment of the Sa'dan Toraja." *Tropical Man* 2: 162–94.

Nooy-Palm, Hetty. 1986. *The Sa'dan-Toraja. A Study of Their Social Life and Religion*. Dordrecht: Foris.

Nordhold, Henk Schulte, Bambang Purwanto, and Ratna Saptari. 2013. "Memikir ulang historiografi Indonesia."(Rethinking Indonesian historiography) In *Perspektif Baru Penulisan Sejarah Indonesia*, edited by Henk Schulte Nordhold, Bambang Purwanto, and Ratna Saptari, 1–32. Jakarta: Yayasan Pustaka Obor Indonesia and KITLV-Jakarta.

Nugraha, Rizki. 2017. "Realita Getir di Balik Gelombang Islamisasi Suku Anak Dalam." (The Bitter Reality Behind the Wave of Islamization of the Anak Dalam Tribe) Deutsche *Welle Indonesia*, June 16. https://www.dw.com/id/realita-getir-di-balik-gelombang-islamisasi-suku-anak-dalam/g-39272878.

Ortner, Sherry. 2016. "Dark Anthropology and Its Others: Theory Since the Eighties." *Hau: Journal of Ethnographic Theory* 6(1): 47–73.

Palmer, Blair. 2004. "Memories of Migration: Butonese Migrants Returning to Buton After the Maluku Conflicts, 1999–2002." Special volume, *Antropologi Indonesia* 2004: 87–99.

Pelras, Christian. 1994. "Religion, Tradition and the Dynamics of Islamization in South-Sulawesi." *Indonesia* 57: 133–54.

Pelras, Christian. 1996. *The Bugis*. Oxford: Blackwell.

Pelras, Christian. 2000. "Patron-Client Ties Among the Bugis and Makassarese of South Sulawesi." *Bijdragen tot de Taal-, Land en Volkenkunde* 156(3): 393–432.

Peluso, Nancy Lee. 1995. "Whose Woods Are These? Counter-Mapping Forest Territories in Kalimanatan, Indonesia." *Antipode* 27(4): 383–406.

Peluso, Nancy Lee, and Peter Vandergeest. 2001. "Genealogies of the Political Forest and Customary Rights in Indonesia, Malaysia, and Thailand." *Journal of Asian Studies* 60(3): 761–812.

Peluso, Nancy, Suraya Afiff, and Noor Rachman. 2008. "Claiming the Grounds for Reform: Agrarian and Environmental Movements in Indonesia." *Journal of Agrarian Change* 8(2): 377–407.

Pemerintahan Kabupaten Jeneponto. 2000. "Peraturan Daerah Kabupaten Jeneponto Nomor 9 Tahun 2000 tentang Pemberdayaan, Pelestarian dan Pengembangan Adat Istiadat dan Lembarga Adat." (Jeneponto Regency Regional Regulation Number 9/2000 concerning Empowerment, Preservation and Development of Customs and Customary Institutions) Jeneponto: Pemeritahan Kabupaten Jeneponto.

Persoon, Gerard. 1998. "Isolated Groups or Indigenous Peoples: Indonesia and the International Discourse." *Bijdragen tot de Taal-, Land- en Volkenkunde* 154(2): 91–129.

Pichler, Melanie. 2014. *Umkämpfte Natur. Politische Ökonomie der Palmöl- und Agrartreibstoffproduktion in Südostasien.* (Contested Nature: Political Economy of Palm Oil and Agrofuel Production in Southeast Asia) Münster: Westfälisches Dampfboot.

Potter, Leslie. 2009. "Oil Palm and Resistance in West Kalimantan, Indonesia." In *Agrarian Angst and Rural Resistance in Contemporary Southeast Asia*, edited by Dominique Caouette and Sarah Turner, 105–34. London: Routledge.

Rachman, Noer Fauzi, and Mia Siscawati. 2016. "Forestry Law, *Masyarakat Adat* and Struggles for Inclusive Citizenship in Indonesia." In *Routledge Handbook of Asian Law*, edited by Antons, Christoph, 224–49. London: Routledge.

Reid, Anthony. 1983. "'Closed' and 'Open' Slave Systems in Pre-Colonial Southeast Asia." In *Slavery, Bondage and Dependency in Southeast Asia*, edited by Anthony Reid, Anthony, 156–181. St. Lucia: University of Queensland Press.

Robbins, Joel. 2013. "Beyond the Suffering Subject: Toward an Anthropology of the Good." *Journal of the Royal Anthropological Institute* 19(3): 447–62.

Robinson, Kathryn. 1983. "Living in the *Hutan*: Jungle Village Life Under the Darul Islam." *Review of Indonesian and Malaya Affairs* 17(1–2): 208–29.

Robinson, Kathryn. 1986. *Stepchildren of Progress. The Political Economy of Development in an Indonesian Mining Town.* Albany: SUNY Press.

Robinson, Kathryn. 2019. "Can Formalisation of *Adat* Land Regulation Protect Community Rights? The Case of the Orang Asli Sorowako and the Karongsi'e/Dongi." *Asia Pacific Journal of Anthropology* 20(1): 471–86.

Robison, Richard. 1982. "Culture, Politics, and Economy in the Political History of the New Order." In *Interpreting Indonesian Politics: Thirteen Contributions to the Debate*, edited by Benedict Anderson and Audrey Kahin, 131–48. Ithaca, NY: Cornell Modern Indonesia Project.

Robison, Richard. 1986. *Indonesia: The Rise of Capital.* Sidney: Allen and Unwin.

Rössler, Martin. 1990. "Striving for Modesty. Fundaments of the Religion and Social Organization of the Makassar Patuntung." *Bijdragen tot de Taal-, Land- en Volkenkunde* 146(1–3): 289–324.

Roth, Dik. 2005. "Lebensraum in Luwu: Emergent Identity, Migration and Access to land." *Bijdragen tot de Taal-, Land- en Volkenkunde* 61(4): 485–516.

Sastrawati, Nila. 2018. "Sombayya ri Gowa: Studi atas Peraturan Daerah tentang Lembaga Adat Daerah Kabupaten Gowa."(The King of Gowa: A Study of Regional Regulations on Regional Customary Institutions of Gowa Regency) *Jurnal UIN Alauddin Makassar* 7(2): 362–80.

Schefold, Reimar. 1998. "The Domestication of Culture. Nation-building and Ethnic Diversity in Indonesia." *Bijdragen tot de Taal-, Land- en Volkenkunde* 154 (2): 259–80.

Schrauwers, Albert. 1997. "Houses, Hierarchy, Headhunting and Exchange: Rethinking Political Relations in the Southeast Asian Realm of Luwu." *Bijdragen tot de Taal-, Land- en Volkenkunde* 153(3): 356–80.

Scott, James. 1976. *The Moral Economy of the Peasant: Rebellion and Subsistence in Southeast Asia*. New Haven, CT: Yale University Press.

Scott, James. 1998. *Seeing Like a State: How Certain Schemes to Improve the Human Condition Have Failed*. New Haven, CT: Yale University Press.

Simpson, Leanne Betasamosake. 2017. *As We Have Always Done: Indigenous Freedom Through Radical Resistance*. Minneapolis: University of Minnesota Press.

Sinn, Simone. 2014. *Religiöser Pluralismus im Werden. Religionspolitisvhe Kontroversen und theologische Perspektiven von Christen und Muslimen in Indonesien.*(Religious Pluralism in the Making: Religious-Political Controversies and Theological Perspectives of Christians and Muslims in Indonesia) Tübingen: Mohr Siebeck.

Sitonda, Natsir. 2012. *Sejarah Massenrempulu*. (The History of Massenrempulu) Makassar: Yayasan Pendidikan Mohammad Natsir.

Soepomo. 1947. *Kedukukan hukum adat di kemudian hari*. (The dominance of customary law in the future) Djakarta: Pustaka Rakyat.

Sombolinggi, Rukka. 2008. "Country Profile: Indonesia." In *The Concept of Indigenous Peoples in Asia: A Resource Book*, edited by Christian Ernie, 377–84. Copenhagen: International Work Group for Indigenous Affairs (IWGIA)/Asian Indigenous Peoples Pact Foundation (AIPP).

Sritimuryati. 2013. *Sejarah Enrekang*. Makassar: De La Macca.

Steinebach, Stefanie. 2013. "'Today We Occupy the Plantation: Tomorrow Jakarta': Indigeneity, Land and Oil Palm Plantations in Jambi." In *Adat and Indigeneity in Indonesia: Culture and Entitlement Between Heteronomy and Self-Ascription*, edited by Britta Hauser-Schäublin, 63–80. Göttingen: Universitätsverlag Göttingen.

Sudirman, Supriyadi. 2020. "Sekjend AMAN: Indonesia Sedang Menjagal Dirinya Sendiri Lewat Omnibus Law." (AMAN Secretary General: Indonesia Is Slaughtering Itself Through Omnibus Law) *Aliansi Masyarakat Adat Nusantara*, August 18. http://www.aman.or.id/2020/08/sekjend-aman-indonesia-sedang -menjagal-dirinya-sendiri-lewat-omnibus-law.

Sukri, Sukri. 2018. *The Toraja as an Ethnic Group and Indonesian Democratization Since the Reform Era*. PhD diss., Bonn University. https://bonndoc.ulb.uni-bonn .de/xmlui/handle/20.500.11811/7439.

Tamma, Sukri, and Timo Duile. 2020. "Indigeneity and the State in Indonesia: The Local Turn in the Dialectic of Recognition." *Journal of Current Southeast Asian Affairs* 39(2): 270–89.

Tanasaldy, Taufiq. 2012. *Regime Change and Ethnic Politics in Indonesia: Dayak Politics of West Kalimantan*. Leiden: KITLV.

Tempo. 2017. "Mentri Lingkungan Hidup dan Kehutanan Siti Nurbaya Bakar: Hutan Adat tak Bisa Dijual." (Minister of Environment and Forestry Siti Nurbaya Bakar: Customary Forests is Not For Sale) *Tempo*, February 6. https://majalah .tempo.co/read/lingkungan/152494/menteri-lingkungan-hidup-dan-kehutanan -siti-nurbaya-bakar-hutan-adat-tak-bisa-dijual?hidden=login.

Thee, Kian Wie. 2012. *Indonesia's Economy Since Independence*. Singapore: ISEAS.

Tsing, Anna. 2007. "Indigenous Voice." In *Indigenous Experience Today*, edited by Marisol de la Cadena and Orin Starn, 33–67. London: Bloomsbury.

Tyson, Adam. 2010. *Decentralization and Adat Revivalism in Indonesia: The Politics of Becoming Indigenous*. London: Routledge.

Tyson, Adam. 2011. "Being Special, Becoming Indigenous: Dilemmas of Special *Adat* Rights in Indonesia." *Asian Journal of Social Science* 39: 652–73.

van Bruinessen, Martin, ed. 2013. *Contemporary Developments in Indonesian Islam. Explaining the "Conservative Turn."* Singapore: ISEAS.

van der Muur, Willem. 2018. "Forest Conflicts and the Informal Nature of Realizing Indigenous Land Rights in Indonesia." *Citizenship Studies* 22(2): 160–74.

van der Muur, Wilhelm, Jaqueline Vel, Micah Fisher, and Kathryn Robinson. 2019. "Changing Indigeneity Politics in Indonesia: From Revival to Projects." *Asia Pacific Journal of Anthropology* 20(5): 379–96.

van Dijk, Cornelis. 1981. *Rebellion Under the Banner of Islam. The Darul Islam in Indonesia.* The Hague: Martinus Nijhoff.

van Vollenhoven, Cornelis. 1909. *Miskenningen van het Adatrecht: vier voordrachtenaan de Nederlandsche Bestuursacademie.* (Misrecognitions of the Adat Law: four lectures at the Netherlands Academy of Public Administration) Leiden: Brill.

Vel, Jacquline, and Stephanus Makambombu. 2019. "Strategic Framing of *Adat* in Land-Acquisition Politics in East Sumba." *Asian Pacific Journal of Anthropology* 20(5): 435–52.

Vel, Jaqueline, Yando Zakaria, and Adriaan Bedner. 2017. "Law-Making as a Strategy for Change: Indonesia's New Village Law." *Asian Journal of Law and Society* 4(2): 447–71.

Veracini, Lorenzo. 2010. *Settler Colonialism: A Theoretical Overview.* New York: Palgrave MacMillan.

Vink, Markus. 2003. "'The World's Oldest Trade': Dutch Slavery and Slave Trade in the Indian Ocean in the Seventeenth Century." *Journal of World History* 14(2): 131–77.

Volkman, Toby Alice. 1985. *Feasts of Honor: Ritual and Change in the Toraja Highlands.* Urbana: University of Illinois Press.

von Benda-Beckmann, Keebet. 2019. "Anachronism, Agency, and the Contextualisation of *Adat*: van Vollenhoven's Analysis in Light of Struggles over Resources." *Asia Pacific Journal of Anthropology* 20(5): 397–415.

von Benda-Beckmann, Franz, and Keebet von Benda-Beckmann. 2013. *Political and Legal Transformations of an Indonesian Polity: The Nagari from Colonisation to Decentralisation.* Cambridge: Cambridge University Press.

von Vacano, Mechthild. 2010. *ReiseReflexionen–SelbstBilder. Eine rassismuskritische Studie über Ethnotourismus in Tana Toraja, Indonesien.* (TravellingReflections–SelfImages. A Critical Race Study on Ethnotourism in Tana Toraja, Indonesia) Berlin: Regiospectra.

Warburton, Eve. 2017. "Jokowi and the New Developmentalism." *Bulletin of Indonesian Economic Studies* 52(3): 297–320.

Ward, Kerry. 2011. "Slavery in Southeast Asia, 1420–1804." In *The Cambridge World History of Slavery*, edited by David Eltis and Stanley L. Engerman, 163–85. Cambridge: Cambridge University Press.

Warren, Carol. 2007. "*Adat* in Balinese Discourse and Practice: Locating Citizenship and the Commonweal." In *The Revival of Tradition in Indonesian Politics: The Deployment of Adat from Colonialism to Indigenism*, edited by Jamie Davidson and David Henley, 170–202. London: Routledge.

Watson, James L. 1980. "Slavery as an Institution: Open and Closed Systems." In *Asian and African Systems of Slavery*, edited by James L. Watson, 1–15. Oxford: Basil Blackwell.

Wingyosoebroto, Soetandyo. 1994. *Dari Hukum Kolonial ke Hukum Nasional: satu kajian tentang dinamika sosial politik dalam perkembangan hukum selama satu setengah abad di Indonesia (1840–1990).* (From Colonial Law to National Law: a study of the socio-political dynamics in the development of law during one and a half centuries in Indonesia (1840–1990)) Jakarta: Raja Grafindo Persada.

Winters, Jeffrey. 2013. "Oligarchy and Democracy in Indonesia." Special issue, Wealth, Power, and Contemporary Indonesian Politics: *Indonesia* 96: 11–33.

Xin, Show Ying. 2018. "Exploring the Contemporaneity of Taman Siswa–Alternative Education in Indonesia." *Nusantara Archieve* 37, April 9. https://www.heath.tw /nml-article/explore-the-contemporaneity-of-taman-siswa-rethink-alternative -education-in-indonesia/?lang=en.

Yamashita, Shinji. 1994. "Manipulating Ethnic Tradition: The Funeral Ceremony, Tourism, and Television Among the Toraja of Sulawesi." *Indonesia* 58: 69–82.

Zakaria, Yando R. 2024. *Adat, Kelas, dan Indigenitas. Gerakan Masyarakat Adat di Indonesia.* (Adat, Class, and Indigeneity. The Adat Movement in Indonesia. Jakarta: Kepustakaan Populer Gramedia.

Žižek, Slavoj. 2000. "Class Struggle or Postmodernism? Yes, Please!" In *Contingency, Hegemony, Universality. Contemporary Dialogues on the Left*, edited by Judith Butler, Eresto Laclau, and Slavoj Žižek, 90–135. London: Verso.

Žižek, Slavoj. 2008. *In Defense of Lost Causes.* London: Verso.

Žižek, Slavoj. 2012. *Less Than Nothing: Hegel and the Shadow of Dialectical Materialism.* London: Verso.

Index

Acciaioli, Greg, 47
accumulation regimes, and struggle for
    Indigenous recognition, 186–87
Aceh War (1873–1914), 25
adat (custom, or customary law)
    analyses of, 5
    attempts at reconciliation between
        state and, 13
    challenging, 86–87
    conceptualization by state and its ideological
        apparatuses, 2
    as contested notion, 110
    as contested political resource, 88
    dialectical engagement between state and,
        176–77
    emergence of, as political force, 180, 183
    in Indonesian context, 7, 8
    intellectual activists' views on, 168
    and late colonialism, 20–28, 96
    as main marker of Indigenous identity, 136–37
    political application of, in South Sulawesi
        after Suharto, 90–97
    and political conflict in Gowa after Suharto,
        97–101
    and political processes and progressive
        outcomes, 9
    as political tool, 181
    and project system, 172–74
    seeing, as law, 87
    in South Sulawesi legislation after Suharto,
        88–90
    as strategic concept, 188
    as tool for violent conflict, 9
    youth activists on, 166
    See also indigeneity; Suharto, *adat* movement
        after
adat community
    internal conflicts in, 158
    recognition of Uru as, 140–43
adat forests. *See* customary forests (*hutan adat*)
adat forest scheme, 48, 54
adat institutions, 139–40
adat istiadat (custom and tradition), 89
adat law communities (*komunitas masyarakat
    adat*), 109, 124, 157

bond between, and their land under Basic
    Agrarian Law, 50
defined in Basic Agrarian Law, 49–50
in Enrekang regulation recognizing
    indigeneity, 134–36
adat movement
    class in, 60–64
    consolidation of, 46–48
    and project system, 173–74
    See also Suharto, *adat* movement after
adat rituals, 133, 141
adat values, 111–12
Adnan Purichta Ichsan Yasin Limpo, 98
Affif, Suraya, 52–53, 55
Agency for *Adat* Territory Registration (*Badan
    Registrasi Wilayah Adat*, BRWA), 51
agrarian reform, 59–61, 63
Aliansi Masyarakat Adat Nusantara (AMAN)
    activism strategies of, in South Sulawesi,
        110–11, 113
    and *adat* and political conflict in Gowa after
        Suharto, 100–101
    Agency for *Adat* Territory Registration
        established by, 51
    alliances with other progressive and
        democratic organizations, 60
    approach to indigeneity, 179
    autonomy and sovereignty of, 190–91
    Buntu Batu applies for membership in, 124
    and capitalist-entrepreneurial ideological
        formation, 192
    and conflicts in making of indigeneity in
        Duri highlands, 158, 159
    direct political engagement of, 186
    engagement with *kelompok ekonomi*, 153–54
    as engaging with state apparatuses, 171–72
    first congress of, 46–47, 50
    ideological conjunctures with politicians, 57–58
    and independence in economic issues, 168
    and indigenization of local economies, 111
    and Indigenous religions, 67
    and Law 8/2014, 51
    and Law on Indigenous Communities, 58, 64
    and local regulation on recognition of
        indigeneity in Enrekang, 136, 139

Aliansi Masyarakat Adat Nusantara (AMAN)
(*Continued*)
membership growth of, 48
and Mid-Term National Development Plan,
53–54
obstacles faced by, 54, 68–69
versus peasant movement, 62
and political application of *adat* and tradition
in Toraja, 93, 96–97
political manifesto on agrarian reform, 59–60
professionalization of maneuvering in
political system, 180
radical youths' support for, 196
recognition in post-Suharto Indonesia,
51–52
recognition of *adat* forests as concern of, 52
and recognition of Ammatoa Kajang in
Bulukumba regency, 101–5
and recognition of Uru as *adat* community,
141, 142, 143
resolution of, 169–70
second congress of, 47–48
sovereignty as advocated by, 47
strategy change in, 45, 51–52
struggle for economic independence, 150
success of, on national scale, 65
support for Jokowi, 45, 65, 109–10, 186
and sustainable use of *adat* forests, 151–52
and term *masyarakat adat*, 43
third congress of, 48
Aliansi Masyarakat Adat Nusantara (AMAN)
council (Sinjai, 2019), 161–68, 164*f*,
165*f*, 169
Alisjahbana, Sutan Takdir, 29
Alla, 124
Althusser, Louis, 12, 168, 171, 182, 183, 184
aluk tojolo religion, 120–21
Ammatoa Kajang, 101–5, 106–7
ancestry, and recognition as *adat* community, 141
Andi Idjo Karaeng Laolang, 98–99
Andi Kartini Ottong, 109
Andi Mapanyukki, 84
Angge Buntu, 141
animism, 121, 130, 133
anticommunism, 33–34, 46, 61
antithesis, 182
architecture, Duri, 120
Ardhianto, Imam, 182
Århem, Kaj, 121, 148
Arizona, Yance, 31, 51
Armed Forces of the Indonesian Republic, 82
Arung Palakka, 78
Astuti, Rini, 187
autonomy, 113, 190–91

Badan Usaha Milik Masyarakat Adat
(BUMMA), 111–13, 152, 153
bamboo / bamboo groves, 147–48
Bang Nur, 120, 142, 153, 168
Baringin, 148
baseline data
on Marena, 147–48
on Orong, 143, 144, 146–47
See also *etnografi*
Basic Agrarian Law (*Undang-Undang Pokok
Agraria*, 1960), 31–33, 38, 49–50, 103
Basic Forestry Law (*Undang Undang No. 5/1967
tentang Ketentuan-Ketentuan Pokok
Kehutanan*, 1967), 37–38, 49, 50
Batara Guru, 78
Bedner, Adriaan, 31, 38, 50
Benda-Beckmann, Keebet von, 27
Bens, Jonas, 5, 12, 68, 180
Berkeley mafia, 34
beschikkingsrecht (right of allocation), 24
Bhinekka Tunggal Ika ("unity in diversity"), 47
Bina Desa, 60
Bone, 70–71, 72, 78, 141
Bone Wars (1824–1906), 84
Boomgard, Peter, 20
Bourchier, David, 24, 29
bright anthology, 194
Budiman, Arief, 35–36
Buginese kingdom, 70–71
Bugis, 72, 74, 75, 77, 78, 79, 82, 116
Bulukumba regency, 101–5, 106–7, 108, 158
Bung Nur, 138–40, 141, 162
Buntu Batu, 124
bupati, 97–99, 104, 107
Burns, Peter, 21–22, 24, 27

capitalism
Indigenous spaces as constituting realms
outside, 190
liberal capitalism, 28, 59, 67
and struggle for Indigenous recognition,
186–87
capitalist-entrepreneurial ideological formation,
192–93
capital punishment, 147, 148
carbon economy, 187
Christianity, 77, 90–91
Chua, Liana, 7
class
class struggles, 9–10
and indigeneity, 188–89
in Indigenous movement's strategy, 60–64
clove trees, 83
coffee, 79, 153, 164–65

www.ingramcontent.com/pod-product-compliance
Lightning Source LLC
Chambersburg PA
CBHW030318270326
41926CB00010B/1415